Confessions of a Divemaster

Dedicated to

Mum, Roger, Beverly, Hannah, Max, and Suki

Copyright © 2020 by Kris Mears
All rights reserved. No part of this book may be reproduced or used in any manner without written permission of the copyright owner except for the use of quotations in a book review.

Acknowledgements to Mrs Julia Bodie at www.copy-proof.co.uk for her editing and proofreading services.

Cover image provided by Mr John Swind

CONFESSIONS OF A
DIVEMASTER

Kris Mears

Prologue

YOU NEVER FORGET seeing your first whale shark! It happened off Ningaloo Reef in Western Australia.

It was a rough day at sea with huge swells sending wedges of the Indian Ocean towards the shore. We sat on the boat's edge waiting for the signal to go. Eventually, our group slipped quietly into the deep, and sunbeams pierced the azure surroundings with laser-like precision. Our quest was to swim with the world's biggest fish.

Our leader swam at the front, her hand up in the air so we knew who to follow. After frantically swimming there were excited muffled screams underwater and a huge ten-metre dark shadow came closer to us; its spots came into full view as it gulped down the tiny plankton in the water column. The huge mouth looked as if it could swallow me in a second and its massive gills quivered as the filtered water gushed back into the ocean. With a couple of tail swipes, it was gone. I looked at the girl next to me and smiled, thinking we had just shared a perfect moment. We raised our arms triumphantly and pumped fists at our achievement.

She looked at me wide-eyed then took out her snorkel and vomited, the water turned a pale-yellow colour with the more substantial chunks sinking towards the bottom. Thrashing my arms wildly I tried to get away from the freshly delivered fish food and swam back to the boat, I glanced underwater hoping for a final look at a whale shark. Instead, a six-foot banded sea snake slithered towards me; its forked tongue flicked, tasting the scent in the water. It was my first encounter with the venomous snake that could kill in minutes. With that I shat my board shorts and rocketed out of the water, like a missile fired from a submarine, landing on the back deck with a slap that an elephant seal would have been proud of; I caught my breath and was so happy that I had survived.

During my year in Australia, it was these types of encounters that made me fall in love with the under-water world. It took me on a journey I never imagined in my wildest dreams.

IN THE LAST ten years, my travels have taken me to over fifty countries. I have become a scuba diving professional and have accumulated around 7,000 dives.

I want to share some of the crazy, beautiful, and sometimes tragic events that have happened above and below the surface. This book is a no shit assess-ment of life working in the dive industry. As a person my filter is very flimsy, so sorry if this book is a little rough around the edges for some of you.

Growing Up

I WAS BORN on the 26th of September 1978 in a small town called Aberdare in South Wales. It was a run-down area that was ravaged by coal mine closures in the eighties. We moved to Chepstow when I was ten years old. The famous Severn Bridge was visible from my window; it seemed like a nice enough place. Even though it was just an hour from my birthplace a lot of the kids ridiculed my strong Welsh accent, but after a while my accent faded and on returning to my roots for a visit, my old school friends accused me of being English, which was a terrible accusation.

My mother was about to start a career in public house management. It turned into a great move as it made me an expert drinker before my 13th birthday. It was a fun upbringing in the pub, and it was interest-ing hanging out with the daytime drunks like Stubbs, Phil and Billy. It was even more entertaining watching them play wall pinball as they stumbled home drunk through the exotic streets of Bulwark.

Chepstow Comprehensive School was a decent place and I mostly enjoyed my time there, but sadly, the subjects didn't interest me at all. As we came into our final year, my interest levels dropped to where I wasn't bothered. We all did our final exams, but didn't even bother checking my GCSE results because I never revised for them. The only thing on my mind in school was football; I couldn't wait to play at lunchtime and couldn't stop talking about it with my schoolmates, much to the disgust of my teachers. They put me in most of the lower-level classes with naughty children like Simon Clayton and Karl Kington.

My interest was fading rapidly. My music teacher went ballistic because I told her she had a mous-tache … being so young I didn't realise those kinds of comments to ladies caused such upset. My French teacher got so crazy she smashed my head against the wall. In history I just stuck my head in my school bag because it was so boring learning about the League of Nations and the teacher asked me to leave.

We got to our last day of school. Everybody was signing each other's school shirts with marker pens and on leaving the building I set fire to my school tie; it was a symbolic gesture that it was time to enter the big bad world.

Peeling Potatoes

AT FIFTEEN, I scored a gig peeling spuds at the local fish and chip shop. It wasn't the most glamorous of jobs getting soaked and covered in potato peelings. Getting free fish and chips was the only perk as the salary was only a few quid an hour.

After that started to work in a supermarket where my duty was to face up the shelves near closing time. It was nice being a working man and was offered a full-time job on leaving school.

It was quite ironic working in the store because just a few months before, our gang had been messing around outside and one of the young rogues had flicked lit matches through the letterbox. One of them had landed on some plastic packaging, and it started a fire. The fire wasn't massive. There was smoke billowing in the shop and soon enough a couple of fire engines and police had come onto the scene. We had legged it away and nobody ever found out it was us that had done it. Back then, there were no CCTV cameras; we were lucky because a lot of us would have ended up in prison if they had caught some of the mad stuff we used to do in our town.

WE WERE PART of Generation X. My love of electronic music started in 1991 and still love it today. My friends and I began nightclubbing while still under-age. We went to Gold Diggers near Bristol listening to DJ Dougal and ExtraT; it was the first time seeing my friends experimenting with soft drugs.

Soon enough we were all taking amphetamines and LSD, we never got any sleep on the weekends due to the drugs in our systems. You knew things were messed up when you were singing along to Barney the dinosaur on Channel 4 at 7 am.

We were young, stupid, and didn't care about anything. We travelled to watch Jim Carrey in the movie *The Mask* and we concluded it would be much better to drop acid to view it. We totally lost the plot in the cinema and screamed as this man with a massive green face came jumping out of the cinema screen at us.

Our group loved to go clubbing all over the UK. We went to Gatecrasher, Cream, God's Kitchen, and many of the great trance clubs of that era. There was a saying we were just like the computer game Pac-Man. We spent a lot of time in darkened rooms running around munching pills while listening to repetitive electronic music. People like Judge Jules, Lisa Lashes, and Pete Tong were our God like heroes.

We hit the big festivals like Glastonbury and the major trance and techno events. We made it over to the clubbers' Mecca of Ibiza a couple of times and we were popping pills like no tomorrow. We were having the time of our lives and we only cared about the weekend. Our lives were just like the cult movie *Human Traffic*. We hated Monday to Thursday, just praying Friday would come around as quickly as possible so we could get off our nut.

This went on until just after the Millennium then the fun had started to go out of it, the pills began to get crap, and it was taking until Wednesday to recover from the weekend's shenanigans.

Timeshares

LIFE WAS STAGNATING a little and a fresh challenge was needed.

Whilst looking in The Sun newspaper's job section, something caught my eye. A company was looking for young, stupid people to work in the timeshare industry in Gran Canaria. My mate Matt wanted to come with me and we managed to get a few hundred quid each and booked our flights to the Canaries.

We were pumped up about leaving, we had a farewell party in the pub, and departed on an adventure of a lifetime, or so we thought.

WE GOT PICKED up from the airport and dropped off at an apartment. This big black cockney fellow called Lloyd came to see if we were okay. He had a cracking lisp and told us some details about our job. We hit the bars that night to celebrate being in the new warm country and meeting new people.

We started working on the streets of Puerto Rico; it was our job to get holidaymakers to meet these sales guys at a timeshare resort. It was tricky because everyone avoided us like the plague. All tour opera-tors told their clients to stay away from the guys in yellow shirts promoting timeshares. They were informed it was a big scam, which could lose you thousands of pounds.

We were the new guys so were placed in the worst locations around Puerto Rico and sometimes we wouldn't see anyone for hours. Matt and I just stood on some street corners like a pair of ugly hookers that nobody wanted. We had these fake scratch cards to entice people to get involved. Every scratch card was a winner; the gullible person would scratch the card then you would put on an Oscar-winning perfor-mance saying, "Oh my God, I can't believe it, you are the first person that has ever won." Then a taxi would whisk the person away and the sales guys would try to get them to part with thousands of pounds. We would get a commission of £50 per person.

We were pretty much useless at our work and we lasted about three weeks in paradise before we got fired and sent back home.

WE WENT BACK home to Wales with shattered dreams and our tails between our legs. We slipped back into life and my old man, Roger, got me a pretty good job in the construction industry, so it was back to partying, football, and hangovers.

It was a hard time for our family though, because a supermarket company purchased the pub in which I had grown up and we watched the beautiful listed building being bulldozed. It was one of the saddest days of my life.

The money in my bank was growing and some close friends talked about going travelling to different places around the world. It was something that interested me, so started to look around for some ideas. The fire in my belly told me there was some-thing out there for me to grab... I just had to go and look for it.

Boyz n the Hood was one of my favourite movies, so Compton in LA was the first place on my list. Next, was Las Vegas because I wanted to count cards and 'drive slowly on the driveway' like Dustin Hoffman in *Rain Man*. Hawaii was the ultimate paradise destina-tion and that was due to be my third stop. New Zealand was a place of interest due to it having different sheep species than Wales. Australia was always on top of the list because of years watching Harold Bishop in *Neighbours*.

My application to get a year's working visa for Australia was successful; everything was good to go. It was time for another farewell party; this time a massive weekend in Cardiff. I still have a picture of all my friends at my mate's house in Cardiff. We went out in style and had a great weekend of debauchery.

My folks dropped me off at Heathrow with a few tears, my flight to Los Angeles was on time, and the big adventure was finally underway.

First Turtles

MY FIRST TASTE of tropical waters was in Hawaii, where the hostel on the north shore of Oahu rented me some masks and fins.

There were some small coves that were protected from the huge waves on the surfing beaches and I watched in awe at the colossal size of the waves; it had me thinking my life would be over in seconds if one hit me. From the first moment I put the mask onto my face, it felt like my life changed … it was as if someone had injected seawater into my heart, and I was now hopelessly addicted.

Four sea turtles came swimming past me; they seemed to be all around me and didn't have a care in the world. They munched on the algae growing on the volcanic rock. Parrotfish and Moorish idols added splashes of vivid colour to the reef. I took my first images of the underwater world with a cheap underwater camera with no flash, the best picture was of a turtle's arse, they were complete garbage, but it was the start of something.

ON ARRIVING AT the airport for my next flight, there was nobody from Air New Zealand and nobody else was queuing to check-in. After showing my ticket to another airline worker, he looked at me strangely.

"Sir, you are very late for this flight."

Being three hours early for my midnight flight I was a tad confused. "What do you mean? It's 9 pm."

He looked at me with a raised eyebrow. "Sir, your plane departed at midnight, so you are nearly a whole day late for your flight."

A feeling of dumbness spread over me as my mis-take became apparent. It took the next hour to rebook my trip – the flexible ticket was handy – there was only a small admin charge to fix the issue. They told me the next flight was not for another three days, so I went back to Waikiki to re-join my new friends who chuckled at my inability to tell the time or use a calendar.

This German guy Stefan was still at the hostel and he invited me to join him driving around the island in his rented Mustang car. This car was the biggest pussy magnet ever seen. We cruised around the island with the top down … it was a beautiful day and we checked out stunning viewpoints like Diamond Head and Waimea Bay. We saw pineapples growing as far as the eye could see and we enjoyed drinks on Sunset Beach with Julia and some bush pilot from Canada; everything was right in the world.

There was another treat for me there, as I met my first real-life crack head. Jimmy was a guy from Austin, Texas, a land full of steers and queers apparently. A banker by trade, he sadly got caught up in crack addiction and lost his wife, job and house. He was now living on welfare hanging out on Waikiki beach and eating 99c Jack in the Box cheeseburgers.

He seemed quite happy out there playing his guitar in beautiful surroundings.

After being out of Wales for a few weeks, the feel-ing of new adventures was spine tingling and it was exciting to have so many adventures ahead.

New Sheep

THERE WERE NO issues on getting the flight three days after that.

New Zealand is a beautiful country and is very similar to Wales in population and climate. It has a love of rugby and a reputation for carnal relations with a sheep or two. After a few days in Auckland, I jumped on the Kiwi Experience bus. It was well known as a party bus, so it was right up my street and it was full of young people on gap years from college or university. People were asking me what university I went to and I told them I came from the 'University of Life'. The bus was full of interesting people and we visited the significant tourist places during the day; and spent the nights exploring the bars wherever we stopped. Things like skydiving and bungee jumping were top of my bucket list.

The skydiving was the biggest rush I've ever experienced in my life; falling for forty-five seconds from 12,000 feet while doing somersaults was such a thrill and it felt like my heart was in my mouth and my eggs in my throat.

The Heli Hike up the Franz Josef Glacier was su-preme; it was amazing to explore the ice tunnels and crevices. It was my first time in a helicopter so I hummed the theme tune from *Air Wolf* as we took off. The views flying up to the glacier were out of this world. We were dropped off on the ice and they gave us these shoes with spikes – they would have been perfect to wear at a Cardiff v Swansea football match. As the helicopter took off, it looked like a tiny model against the backdrop of the immense snow-capped mountains.

The snowboarding experience in Wanaka with the kiddie from Derry was shockingly bad. Being frozen on my ass all day with a stinking hangover was no fun. When a six-year-old kid skied past me with a look of contempt, I knew the game was over, so we retreated to the bar for some après-ski.

We also explored an underwater cave system on a rubber ring whilst looking for glow-worms; the worms on the cave roof lit up like tiny stars. We rafted down a grade 5 river in an area where they filmed *Lord of the Rings*. The rapids were furious and a couple of times the raft flipped over dunking us into the icy water.

The adventures were non-stop; the Kiwis were amiable people, it felt like the UK but maybe twenty or thirty years ago. After getting around the North and South Islands in six weeks, my time there was coming to an end. Despite the fantastic scenery, it was wintertime and my main reason to leave the UK was because of the cold weather, so I said my goodbyes to New Zealand and G' day to Australia, the Land Down Under.

THE FLIGHT FROM Auckland to Melbourne had the

worse turbulence I had ever experienced. Promises were discussed with the man upstairs; he would have a loyal servant as long as we all got off the plane alive.

Melbourne is a beautiful city, but the weather was just like the UK, the sun was calling me, so I flew up to Cairns in Queensland. The tropical heat smashed into me on arrival, it felt so lovely. I found out the famous bar The Woolshed was the place to be. It was party central with loads of travellers going mental most nights; they served meals for a dollar so it was always busy.

The hostel employed me as a night security guard in exchange for a free room; the job wasn't suited to me as I used to sneak off to party until the early hours at The Woolshed.

It was great to see Brummie Matt from our time in New Zealand and there was this other funny looking guy called Stephen who was at the hostel. He was the perfect son of Hitler with beautiful blue eyes and wispy blond hair. I knew he was a bullshitter when he told me that he had snorkelled the whole of the Great Barrier Reef ... this would be the start of a great friendship and he would play a big part in my life over the coming years.

The Great Barrier Reef is the most well-known reef system on the planet. It has been on TV many times with David Attenborough talking about it in his soothing voice. Walking around Cairns you could see many trips advertised by the dive companies and one guy offered me a free tour to the reef with a Discover Scuba dive experience, in exchange for me giving out flyers for a couple of evenings.

I gave out the flyers for the gentleman, he booked

me on a dive boat, and it was off to see the world's biggest coral reef, which is so big it's visible from space.

The weather was a bit rough and a bunch of Japa-nese tourists were getting greener by the minute as the boat rocked in the waves. The water was still choppy when we got to the dive site. My dive instructor was an older gentleman, who gave his briefing, mostly about equalizing my ears and kitted me up in dive gear. The smell of the diesel fumes was also turning me queasy, so it was great to get in the water. The instructor took me down the ladder and I took my first breaths underwater.

My mind was racing with thoughts … what was this horrible plastic thing stuck in my mouth? It didn't feel great, it was weird, it didn't sound right, and it just wasn't natural. Bubbles were flying up over my face making this horrendous racket as they escaped to the surface. All of the red flags in my brain started flapping furiously, but after a while I got used to sounding like Darth Vader. The instructor could see my eyes were not bulging out of my head, they darted around our surroundings, and I slowly got used to being comfortable underwater. The instructor asked me to clear some water from my mask and remove and replace my regulator and after that we went off to see the reef.

The rest of the dive was a blur, because staying alive was my main concern and I held the instructor's hand so tightly I'm sure the blood circulation was cut off. An impressive Napoleon wrasse came swimming close to us, the turquoise body and massive forehead looked magnificent as he swam back and forth.

We got back on the boat alive and well and the relief was intense. I took a moment to let it sink in; we didn't die or get eaten by a shark. The instructor looked at his watch, and he told me we had been underwater for thirty-five minutes. It seemed like we were down there for only seconds.

A videographer was on the dive so I handed over my money for the VHS video of the experience. It was a little weird paying money to see me holding hands with another guy. Sadly, VHS tapes would be pretty much extinct in a few years, so I only got a chance to watch the video once. That $75 was not well spent.

MY TIME IN Cairns was coming to an end; they fired me from my job as the night security for the aban-donment of post; it was time to hit the road again. The red centre of the Australian Outback was next up.

Uluru or Ayers Rock had a very spiritual feel to it. We camped as close as we could and it was amazing to watch the sunset and sunrise. The rock and the desert around it changed to different shades of orange during these times. It looked like the landscape of Mars minus the little green men. Out of respect for the Aboriginal people's culture, people didn't climb the rock; those people who know me who are thinking I was probably too fat to climb the rock, can go to hell.

We checked out some other canyons and sights around Alice Springs. It was nice to meet some Aboriginal people in the red centre. My only other interaction had been seeing some passed out drunk in the streets of Cairns by mid-afternoon. It was nice to get a feel for life in the Outback. Alice Springs felt like the hottest place on earth and the sweat was pouring out of me like never before. As my friend Dan would say we were sweating like Zambian bus drivers.

A couple of guys from Israel were looking for someone to share travel costs in their car, so we drove back to Queensland through the fantastic Outback. It was a true wilderness and it was amazing to see the landscape change from dark orange sands to almost African-like savannas. We didn't kill any kangaroos driving at night, although we saw a poor cow that had been mangled by a truck. The size of the trucks was impressive; they looked more like trains with three trailers each due to the long distances they travelled.

It was nice to learn some Israeli culture from the guys; they had just got out of national service and had some interesting stories. They taught me how to make hummus, and I showed them that drinking one beer only, was worthless.

After driving for four days and passing through the mining town of Mount Isa, we made it back to the Queensland coast; we said our goodbyes and my journey continued south.

AIRLIE BEACH IS the jump-off point for sailing trips out to the Whitsunday Islands. My yacht's name was Broomstick; it was used in the Sydney to Hobart race a few years back. The sailing trip lasted for four days and most of my shipmates were irritated because of my snoring. I didn't hear anything, but that's what they told me.

Our yacht had a small compressor and an English scuba diving instructor from Oldham told me we could dive, even though we were still not properly certified. So, another three dives were added around the Whitsunday Islands ... there were no holding hands with the instructor this time.

The beautiful corals were in pristine condition and the sun burst colour over the sea fans and soft corals. Carpet anemones swayed in the current and there were patches of cabbage corals, which were home to feisty damselfish. The reefs around the Whitsundays were much better than Cairns. It looked more like the beautiful place Mr. Attenborough had been talking about with such enthusiasm.

The instructor stayed close by and even though I was not adequately trained; he let me figure out my buoyancy. It was a blast to swim next to the exotic coral species and schools of reef fish. Once our dives had finished, he told me I was a natural in the water and should get myself certified.

We made a stop at Whitehaven Beach, which had lush soft white sand that was fine enough to polish silver jewellery. It was a truly magnificent area lined with green mangrove trees.

One of the boat crew got mad at me and called me a fat Pommie bastard after I ripped out his middle stump while playing beach cricket; the Aussies always were poor losers when it came to sports.

On our return to Airlie Beach our group had some farewell drinks and after a few rums the dunny was calling. As I sat down on the seat my head started to spin out, a bout of land sickness had struck. There was no choice but to put both hands on either side of the wall to stop the spinning, while thoughts of Goose and Maverick flashed through my mind after they flew into a jet wash. After a while, things settled down, the spinning stopped, and I managed to get back to the bar for more Bundy rums.

THE TRAVELS CONTINUED down the East Coast and we made a stop at Noosa Heads for some surfing lessons … I was pretty shitty at them.

I spent my birthday on Great Keppel Island where I met this mental Sheila called Kathryn. As a true Queenslander she was mad as cut snakes and after a heavy night drinking, I ended up lost on the small airport runway. The security guards helped me find my hotel once they stopped me from trying to get into one of the Cessna planes.

Next up was Brisbane for a city break and I stayed at the homely Banana Bender hostel. I spent a few days watching the Ashes cricket with the Barmy Army at the Gabba Stadium. Shane Warne had a chat with us which was pretty awesome. Later in life he would get to see Liz Hurley's boobs, which I would imagine to be a real privilege.

The Open Water Course

WE SPENT THREE days at Fraser Island as we wanted to see the famous wild sandy dingo's that are known to eat babies. If you don't like sand then you should give this place a miss. We cruised around in a 4x4 and got stuck a bunch of times.

Byron Bay had magical sunsets and space cakes to help enhance the surroundings and after all this fun, my mind started to think about getting to Sydney.

The journey was a long one, so we planned a stop at Coffs Harbour for a night. This town is famous for its giant bananas and is the birthplace of Gladiator Russell Crowe. There was a place called Jetty Dive, the sign outside said, *'The Cheapest Price for your Open Water Dive Course in Australia.'* I saw the chance for a bargain. Mike, the owner, sold me the course; it was going to start the next day.

After passing the dive medical and physiological exam, we began with the classroom work. My brain cells are not great after listening to too much electronic over the years, so I can't remember much of the knowledge development part. After that, it was into the swimming pool for confined skills. Something I had not really considered before signing up for the course was the water temperature. My mind assumed it would be the same as the Great Barrier Reef as it's just up the coast a little bit. So, a 3 mm shorty wetsuit would do the trick right? Wrong, and I was way off by quite a few degrees.

They gave me a 5 mm wetsuit, gloves, and a thick hood to wear. Putting this stuff on was not easy, it felt so constricted, and was hard to breathe. Just before we entered the water, our instructor mentioned to us that we might see some big sharks on the dive and not to be scared if they came close to us. After what seemed like an eternity in rough seas, we finally got into the water and we made our descent.

The conditions were much more challenging than Cairns and The Whitsunday Islands. The water was cold; the surge threw us back and forth and it wasn't much fun. I had now worked out why this was the cheapest price for the 'Open Water Course in Austral-ia'.

My mind was expecting to see the same corals and fish as the Whitsunday Islands. It took me a while to figure out that the Great Barrier Reef ended a few hundred miles north of me. The topography of the sites on the Solitary Islands was interesting, but nowhere like the beauty of the Great Barrier Reef. The reef was covered in green algae with some anemones dotted around, but there was no rainbow of colours like on the Great Barrier Reef.

In life, you can make some bad decisions, and for me, one of these happened during our last training dive. It was chilly, so I thought that peeing in my wetsuit would bring some warm comfort against the cold. It was a nice warm feeling for a few moments as the warm liquid battled against the cold twenty-degree water. But, once back on the boat, the wetsuit came off, and this steamy piss smell engulfed my nostrils. Glancing around at my classmates, I checked to see if they had had a whiff of the contents of my bladder, nobody said they did, but it was a horrifying moment.

It would be the last time that would happen to me. There's a famous saying known among the diving community, "There are two types of people in this world, those who pee in wetsuits, and those who lie about it."

The next day we passed our final exam and were certified divers. It was such a happy moment as the course was more robust than expected; I still have the certificate; and the photo with me shaking my instructor's hand at home.

It would be interesting to dive in the area again. Even though we didn't see any big sharks during our dives, there is footage of grey nurse sharks, schools of manta rays, and hammerheads in large numbers. It would be nice to return someday to relive the moment.

Sydney Living

IT WAS CITY living in Sydney for the next few months. Steve showed up from Cairns and we stayed in Bondi Junction inside an old Korean restaurant. We lived with a bunch of Korean students who were learning English and we enjoyed teaching them bad English words like twat and wanker. We sat down one evening and one of the Korean guys turned to Steve, keen to practise his skills. "Steve, I think you are shallow and timid." It was pretty impressive that he worked Steve out in such a short space of time.

It was unique, living in the old restaurant. We had two beds that were mixed in with the old tables and chairs. The kitchen was a bit of a disaster; the army of cockroaches could have declared war on Sydney; there were that many. Steve set up a tent in the back garden so he could shag this Dutch bird. Sometimes, people just walked in off the street thinking that the restau-rant was still open. Our landlady lived across the street and owned a small convenience store and our rent was $50 a month. It was the best deal around and as we lived next door to an off-licence, profits from sales of VB beer and boxes of wine went through the roof during our stay.

CHRISTMAS TIME ON Bondi Beach was excellent; it was so strange being in twenty-seven-degree heat. We ended the year witnessing the fireworks display on the Sydney Harbour Bridge and while we drank from a $10 box of wine, we watched thousands of dollars go up in smoke. The value of fireworks didn't impress me especially as we were living on peanut butter sandwiches and two-minute noodles.

Steve scored me a job working part-time washing dishes in the Pavilion Restaurant on Bondi Beach. It was always a nice walk to work looking at the bikini babes on the beach. The Bondi area is so beautiful and is rightfully one of the world's best beaches; the coastal walks either side of the beach are stunning. Often dolphins would come by the bay splashing around and the shark siren would sound if the coastguard had spotted any close to the beach.

We explored other areas around Sydney like the Blue Mountains and we made a trip up to Palm Beach, where they filmed the Aussie soap opera *Home and Away*.

Things didn't turn out well while swimming off the beach one day. We didn't realise it but we got stuck in a rip current. After kicking away and realising we were going nowhere, the other guys close to me started to panic. My legs began to get tired, then, all of a sudden, a lifeguard on a surfboard came skimming through the surf towards us. The five of us grabbed on, and he took us back to shore. If we had been out there for a few minutes longer, I'm not sure this book would have been written. The lifeguard gave us a little lesson on what to do if we ever got stuck in a rip current again, and ever since that day, I have had a fear of swimming in large waves.

MY OLD MATE Remy from Wales was also in Australia and we had some cracking nights out around Kings Cross, both falling in love with a cross-eyed table dancer, who was looking at both of us during her performance.

He had a camper van, so we went south to Jervis Bay to try some fishing. We hired a small tin boat and went out around the river trying to catch some flatheads. The guy who sold us bait told us to watch the tide level. We were fishing, but didn't catch anything and things turned to shit soon after as the tide went out and we were stuck on the riverbed. The propeller got all clogged up with grass from the bed and just as we thought things couldn't get any worse, we noticed thick smoke from a bush fire had started nearby. The sky began to turn orange with a mixture of smoke and fire. We cleared everything from the prop and managed to get away quickly. That was the last time I ever went fishing with Remy.

Credit Card Fraud

AFTER FIVE MONTHS on the East Coast of Australia, it was time to move on.

The train journey from Sydney to Perth was some-thing that really interested me and with money being tight, my friend offered me the use of his Nomad backpacker card to get a discount on the ticket. I used his name to book the ticket and used my credit card to pay the lady on the counter. That's when everything went horribly wrong!

The lady asked me to show her the backpacker discount card; I didn't have it because it was my friend's. Coming clean, I told her that it was not my discount card. She picked up the phone and dialled a number.

"Who are you calling?" I asked her.

She gave me a cold stare. "I'm calling the police sir as I believe you are committing credit card fraud."

A cold sweat came over me, "No, no, you have got it wrong; the credit card belongs to me, I'm using my friend's discount card to save some money."

The dragon lady looked at me with an evil smile and said: "Well, sir, due to your dishonesty, I regret to inform you that you will not be travelling with us today."

I pleaded poverty with her to try and change her mind as the trains didn't run every day, but she loved the fact she had busted me and wouldn't budge an inch.

Realising the game was up I called her a heartless bitch and left the ticket office with my tail between my legs. Stephen cracked up when he heard the news. I had had enough of Sydney, so with a sour taste in my mouth I decided to jump on the next flight to Perth.

It was one of the biggest regrets of my time in Australia of not doing the train journey from Sydney to Perth as it's supposed to be beautiful … maybe next time.

Western Australia

THE WEST COAST of Australia was a different world compared to the east. Perth was a small, relaxed city, time flew by, and a month passed quickly.

There were great people at the Witches' Hat hostel, including a mad group from Essex and we drank a lot most nights. After one heavy night, I woke up around lunchtime and went to get a drink of water. I saw a couple of the others that had been drinking with us; they were smiling and laughing at me. I was wonder-ing what was going on.

Later that day, my roommate showed up and he pissed himself laughing at me. He told me what had happened, and it was not good. He said I got home around 2 am and climbed into the top bunk; after a while, he heard a massive thud on the ground. He turned the light on and I was stark bollock-naked on the floor. Once he turned the light on, I jumped up on my feet and said, "I'm OK, I'm OK" and then pro-ceeded to walk out of the door naked and walked around the hostel dazed and confused. After a while, I came back to the room and passed out. Luckily no ribs were broken but I did have nice bruises.

The manager of the hostel spoke to me the next evening; he looked at me with raised eyebrows as if to say pull that shit again and you are out of here.

I HAD NOT been diving since my Open Water Course, but met a couple of divers at the hostel and we decided to go to Rottnest Island, which was supposed to have great diving.

We turned up at the dive shop on a Sunday morn-ing; the dive shop guys seemed to be still drunk from the Saturday. They got our diving gear and off we went on the boat. As it had been five months since completing my course, there was a level of nervous-ness, but they didn't seem to care. They said they would be supervising us from the boat with no divemaster in the water with us.

When we got to the dive site, the dive team briefed us, giving us compass headings for the site, so we dropped into the water and got lost within minutes. We spent the whole dive swimming over seagrass beds; there was not one fish or any coral worth talking about. They didn't want to put a divemaster with us for a second dive, so we didn't bother going again. It didn't feel great that my first dives by myself turned to shit. It knocked my confidence and I wasn't even sure that I would ever bother to dive again at this stage.

AFTER A MONTH in Perth, my funds were nearly in the red; I had burned through £10,000 in eight months. It was time to work, so I moved to a small town called Dongara, where I worked in a lobster factory.

As a lover of marine life, it broke my heart to kill

thousands of rock lobsters each day. It was a seasonal job so you could do long hours and save money quite quickly because there was absolutely nothing else to do apart from work.

Massive containers full of live lobsters would come into the factory. The prized catch was dropped into freezing cold water to stun them, or they were boiled, and then they were sawed in half with the use of a saw machine. The lobsters were shipped off to Korea and Japan for sushi and sashimi.

It was hard work for 15 hours a day, the lobsters are very sharp, and there were cuts all over my hands and arms even though I was wearing gloves and a long-sleeved shirt. When working the saw machine, I was caked in lobster shit and guts. It was tough but a good laugh working with a bunch of backpackers from all over the world.

After earning about $2,000, it was time to hit the road again; my next stop would be one of my favourite places in Australia. On the way out of Dongara, I asked for forgiveness for the rock lobster mass murder I had taken part in and ever since the experience, the thought of eating lobster still makes me feel queasy.

Ningaloo Reef

CORAL BAY IS a quaint little town near Exmouth; it's about halfway up the West Coast of Australia and I spent a beautiful month enjoying extended time with the Indian Ocean. It is home to the UNESCO listed Ningaloo Reef, the largest fringing reef in Australia.

Turquoise Bay has such natural beauty and has been rightfully voted as one of Western Australia's best beaches. The squeaky soft sand and bluest shallow water make it a true haven; it took an hour to drive there so it was never really overcrowded.

A couple of girls from Germany took me under their wing as we explored paradise. The snorkelling was out of this world and it was the first time I experienced sharks in the water.

On one occasion, we were snorkelling around the coral gardens with huge bommies and brain corals all around us. My mask kept fogging up, so took it off to clean it. In an instant, one of the young German girls started to scream out loud; she had a secure grip on my arm that stopped the blood from flowing. Quickly replacing my mask, my head dropped down into the water, and there was a two-metre shark swimming about five metres in front of us. Goosebumps ap-peared on my arms and we watched in awe as the sleek beast swam by us; my eyes couldn't leave the beautiful shark. It darted around for a while, making sharp turns before swimming out to the deep.

After peeling the lady off my arm, we went back to the beach and looked at our waterproof fish ID chart that we had purchased from town. We had seen a blacktip reef shark; it turned out they were relatively common and didn't eat people very often. It was the first shark encounter in my life and the reaction of the German girl made it more exciting; she was still shaking like a shitting dog once we got back to the beach.

There were many white and blacktip sharks in Turquoise Bay, and we spent hours and hours in the water each day … my list of shark species grew with sightings of leopard and grey reef sharks.

Exmouth is world-famous for whale sharks with an estimated population of 300-500. They would send up a small spotter plane that would radio in the coordinates to the boats below. The world's biggest fish was something I had to see, so I booked a few day trips to the outer reef to try and find them. The first time we went, we had no sightings but were very lucky to see an Orca, which jumped out of the water; about 50 metres from the boat.

The first paragraph of the book is about my first sighting of a whale shark. If you have forgotten, you can go back to the first page and reread it. It was awesome.

One of the dive staff talked about a whale shark experience that didn't go to plan. The spotter plane thought they had seen one, so the boat went over, dropping the people near the shark. It turned out to be a massive tiger shark instead of a whale shark. The guy said he had never seen people get back on the boat so fast in his life.

Ningaloo Reef had plenty of manta rays; the same plane would spot them before sending the boats in. Even though it was great to see the manta rays, there wasn't the same affection for them as for the whale sharks. The boat always dropped us behind the mantas, as they swam fast and we couldn't get to see them well. We did have an enjoyable experience seeing one jump out of the water before splashing back down. The guide was excited, saying she had never seen that happen before that day.

Later in life, I would spend much more time with manta rays and they would cement themselves in my heart forever.

After watching the airplane circle above us, the thought crossed my mind that it might be possible to see the giants from up above. The next day the pilot asked for a massive fee of $40 and took me up in his small Cessna for a two-hour flight looking down on the manta rays… they looked like little black dots from above. However, looking down at the scenery below and watching the waves crash from the Indian Ocean onto Ningaloo Reef was terrific.

Advanced Open Water Course

AFTER A FEW weeks playing around in Turquoise Bay, it was time to do some scuba diving.

The dive shop in Coral Bay talked me into doing my Advanced Open Water Course. My instructor was this Aussie guy; he wasn't a barrel of laughs, to be honest, and had the personality of a piece of sandpa-per. My luck was in with my choice of dive shop though, as they were the only ones to have a permit to dive on the navy pier.

The navy pier was a disused US naval base but still under protection, so only a limited number of divers could visit each year. The pier's pillars made the perfect hiding place for many species of fish; there had never been so many in one place. Huge moray eels, schools of bannerfish, whitetip sharks, giant frogfish, and Queensland groupers, which were bigger than I was. The wobbegong sharks were so well camouflaged I had no idea what they were. It was a fascinating dive and with my confidence restored, I was looking forward to my advanced course.

The Muiron Islands were a few hours sailing time from Exmouth. My course began with a deep dive, the water was so clear, and the reef was full of vibrant colours. The sea floor was plastered in fluffy soft mushroom corals with multicoloured parrotfish and butterfly fish darting around.

Being so spellbound by the beauty, it was hard for me to tell that I was down at thirty metres. The only difference was that I had to suck on my regulator a little harder as the air was denser at depth. My instructor tested me for nitrogen narcosis with a simple maths test. I'm terrible with numbers, so the chance of failure was high at the surface let alone down at thirty metres' depth. After a few moments of staring at the white slate and scratching my head, my instructor gave up so we carried on with the dive.

Next up was the navigation dive; it was impossi-ble to concentrate on the compass while surrounded by so many schools of fish. The water was so clear, as we made our descent. The instructor told me to slow down after ripping through my navigation of a square. Next up was a bit of natural navigation, learning to retrace my path through the coral reef.

My course was completed on the navy pier; my first ever night dive was unforgettable. It was nervy being down in the dark depths, especially after hearing about tiger sharks coming by at night. At the end of the dive, my buoyancy control deserted me and
I ended up busting my three-minute safety stop. My inexperience got the better of me, as my tank was getting low, so I drifted towards the surface without realising it in the dark. As I did, a massive 300 lbs Queensland grouper with enormous lips shocked the shit out of me as it swam into my light beam.

The last task was an underwater photography dive; this time, it was no shitty disposable camera. It was my first time using a high-quality digital version and it was possible to take more than twenty-four images. At the end of the dive, the instructor looked through the photos with a pained look on his face and speaking through gritted teeth he told me it was a job well done.

The next part of my diving journey was complete, and it was nice to be an Advanced Open Water Diver, but truthfully, you can't call yourself advanced with only twelve dives to your name.

Some friends from Perth turned up in the bar unexpectedly as I was contemplating my next move and luckily Keith had space in his 4x4 truck for a great adventure through the Aussie Outback. At the same time, Steve came up from Sydney; it was good to see ole blue eyes again.

This epic adventure would take us up to Broome then across the famous Gibb River Road up into the Northern Territory of Australia. We spent weeks climbing gorges and swimming in freshwater pools; there were crocodiles, monitor lizards, and many birds of prey, the wildlife was everywhere. We embraced the wilderness of the rugged Kimberley region. It was simply amazing to see the raw Outback of Australia and the dark orange desert was all around us.

It was a fantastic journey and I will always be thankful to have met Keith and the others again. That's the beauty of travel; this part of the journey could have been missed by us not meeting in the bar at that moment … fate helped us to connect again.

We arrived in Darwin and spent about four hours in the shower; there seemed to be more orange sand in our bags than in the Outback. We spent a few nights drinking together before most people went their separate ways. It was just me and my pal Stephen left, and we were staying at a shitty YMCA hostel that was full of drunks and junkies, we fitted in well and were on first-name terms with everybody in a few hours.

MY LAST FEW weeks in Australia were spent cleaning campervans, trying to save enough money to help me travel through South East Asia on the way home. Steve and I left Australia on the very last day of my one-year work visa. If there had been a chance to stay longer, I probably would have taken it, as it was the best year of my life and was happy to have travelled around one of the most exciting and beautiful countries in the world.

South East Asia

WE FLEW FROM Darwin to Indonesia for the next adventure. Bali is a delightful place; we relaxed on the beach in Lovina. enjoying the delicious fruits and banana pancakes.

It was my first experience of Asian culture, and it was so refreshing. The locals were very friendly and would do anything for you. Steve decided to rent a motorbike for a couple of days. I had no experience of riding so he thought he'd teach me how.

"It's not that hard, just pull back on the throttle, and steer it."

So, I jumped on and he got on the back. I pulled the throttle right back and lost control immediately, we both came off the bike, which was about a metre from going down the side of a steep cliff. We had a couple of cuts and bruises but survived.

Later that day, we went to visit a temple and we had to drive up a steep hill. Steve dropped the bike into first gear, but it caught me by surprise and I landed on my arse in the middle of the road. We tried to enjoy the peace and tranquillity of the temple but we were in pain from the accidents.

AFTER A COUPLE of weeks in the sun we were the same colour as the locals and we decided to head to Java.

We ended up missing the last bus, so managed to hitch a ride in a massive truck, but we got stuck in traffic due to an accident. The last bus, which we should have taken, had had a head-on crash, the front of the bus was a twisted mess, and we heard four people had died. We looked on in disbelief that we could have been on it.

Our hotel in Java was terrible. It was great being in Asia, but the toilet situation took some getting used to. There was never any toilet seat, just a hole in the ground and a place for your feet, so you had to squat down and hope for the best.

We stopped off for a few days to climb a massive volcano at Mount Bromo. Some locals took us hiking in the early hours so we could see the sun rising over the volcano. There was thick ash everywhere and a lot of seismic rumblings. The sky started to turn that beautiful dark blue colour as daybreak approached, we got to the top of the crater, and the shape of local horses made elegant silhouettes against the skyline. Luckily, she didn't blow up on us, and we made it back down safely after the most fantastic sunrise. The tip of the day would be not to wear flip-flops for this kind of activity.

We had the shit scared out of us when we arrived on an overnight train into Jakarta. It was still dark on the platform as we arrived. There had been a bomb that had killed three people at the Marriott Hotel the day before, so were already a bit nervous. This tall man with long hair and a beard started to talk to us, asking us our names and what we were doing in Jakarta. We tried to be polite to him, but he began to get aggressive, saying how we were killing his brothers in Afghanistan and Iraq. I tried to say it was nothing to do with us; we were travelling through his country, but he didn't care and just kept chattering on about infidels.

We tried to get away from him, but he followed us outside the station. We had initially planned to spend a few days in Jakarta, but now we were shitting ourselves. We jumped into a cab and headed to the port to get the next boat to Sumatra. As we started to drive away, I looked out of the window, and the fundamentalist was now following us on a motorbike. My heart was thumping and we expected him to pull a gun out and start shooting us. All kinds of bad thoughts were going through my mind; maybe we will be beheaded and put on YouTube. We yelled at the driver to speed up to get us away.

Eventually, we arrived at the port and tried des-perately to find a boat to Sumatra. We were constantly looking over our shoulder expecting that guy to show up, but we couldn't see him. We ran inside the terminal, but it turned out that no boats were travel-ling that day. In the end, we got a taxi to the airport and got on the next flight to the capital of Sumatra, Medan.

It was pitch black when we got to our hostel; we were exhausted after a fucked-up scary day of travelling and we passed out for the night. Just before the sun came up, we were awoken by the call to prayer. I looked out of the window and saw that we were about a hundred metres away from the spectacu-lar Grand Mosque of Medan.

We looked at each other praying that there wasn't going to be another loony waiting for us outside.

Orangutans

THINGS GOT A lot better in Medan, the locals were friendly, and we felt safe again.

We relaxed for a while and one day, got chatting to some local girls at a restaurant. They asked us if we'd like to see some orangutans in the wild. We found out there were only two places in the world where orangutans still lived in the wild; the other place was in Borneo, Malaysia.

The girls picked us up the next morning, and we went deeper and deeper into the jungle and as we did, we saw many palm oil plantations that had devastated the habitat for the orangutans. We arrived at the WWF station and paid at the entrance to the protected park. Steve thought he was going to meet Hulk Hogan, but he was a bit thick like that.

We hiked through the jungle for what seemed like hours. It was a proper workout, and we sweated buckets. When we arrived at the location, we were told to wait and not make any noise. After a while, we could see movement in the trees, and then a family of orangutans came and sat on a wooden platform. It was a special moment to spend a couple of hours watching them playing around and there were a couple of young ones that were just a year old. We got some excellent images before heading back to Medan after a great day and we thanked our guides for giving us a fantastic experience.

It's all about meeting the right people at the right time. If we hadn't stopped at the restaurant, we would never have met the girls and would never have even known that the orangutans existed in that area.

OUR NEXT STOP was Georgetown in Malaysia, the British colonial buildings were impressive, but we were most impressed with the Indian food … it had been a while since we had seen an onion bhaji and a chicken korma. After that we wanted to get to Thailand for the famous full moon party.

We had a quick stop at Koh Phi Phi Le Island, visiting Maya Bay, the beach where Leonardo Di Caprio stole some French dude's girlfriend and caused a shark to kill a couple of backpackers.

A few more dives were added to my logbook after I explored the reefs of Phi Phi; the leopard sharks were so relaxed resting on the bottom, but the corals were nothing compared to Australia. Safety was a bit of an afterthought as our boat captain dropped his anchor about ten feet from where we were diving.

A local told me about a place called Shark Point, saying it was best to go there at first light, so, I grabbed my mask and fins the next morning. Within seconds of entering the water, hordes of blacktip sharks were all around me. The cello from *Jaws* was playing continuously in my head, but it was exhilarat-ing seeing so many sharks in one place. I was the only person around so early, so if they ate me nobody would ever have known. Later that day we took a hike to a beautiful viewpoint, my legs were wobbly, and my heart was bursting out of my chest as we got to the top. However, the exercise was worth it as the panoramic view took your breath away. There was a tiny yellow slither of a sandbar that joined the island and tall palm trees were each side of the emerald coloured ocean.

Just six months after we left Koh Phi Phi, the is-land was profoundly affected by the massive tsunami that cost the lives of around 4,000 people.

WE CROSSED TO the east coast of Thailand by bus then made the boat crossing from hell to Ko Pha Ngan. There were about thirty people all sleeping on thin mattresses, the sea picked up at night, and there were so many sick people the smell was terrible. There was nowhere to move, so people were lying in their own sick and the night seemed to last forever with people crying to get off the boat.

On arrival, we soon forgot about the ordeal be-cause we had made it on time to the most famous party in Asia.

Full Moon Party

EVEN TO THIS day, flashbacks and vivid memories of the full moon party flash through my mind. Thou-sands travelled each month to Hat Rin beach.

You didn't have to ask us twice to get into the party spirit by trying the famous mushroom milkshakes, which certainly enhanced the situation. Various sound systems from the bars churned my brain, the light shows and lasers had me looking up at the sky open-mouthed. I'm not sure how many buckets of Samsong and Redbull we consumed, but we managed to keep going until eleven the next morning.

As the sun came up, the scene on the beach was one of total carnage. There were people in the clutches of passion in the sea, next to them a person was urinating. There were plenty of white guys passed out with lady boys clinging onto them like koala bears; it would have been a picture to see their faces when they woke up. We were in a right state, we had spent all of our money, our room keys were on the beach some-where, and we couldn't even remember where we were staying. We wasted another hour trying to figure it out until somebody helped us on our way.

With our frazzled brains, we decided we wanted

to get away from the full moon party people, and made our way to another island called Koh Tao, where we found some chilled little cabins, and spent a week repairing our brain cells by eating some great Thai food, snorkelling in the beautiful bays, and seeing impressive reefs full of staghorn coral gardens. Steve got stoned most days and was talking about designing some non-drip pans or some bollocks to another chef he met.

WITH MY CASH about to run out, we hit Bangkok for a few days before heading home.

We stayed on the Khao San Road with the rest of the great unwashed. There was so much great food on offer, but the burger urge got to me, so a double whopper with bacon and cheese won the day. We watched a couple of ladies in a ping-pong tournament on my last night; it was the first-time seeing table tennis played without any paddles.

My funds had run dry; the bank of mother helped me find my way home via Hong Kong. Saying goodbye to my pal Steve wasn't that emotional, we had had a wild ride together, but there was a feeling our adventures would continue somehow. It had been a fantastic year and a half travelling around the world; people said I had done more things in one year than they might do in a lifetime.

THE TIRES OF the plane screeched on landing at Heathrow. Being in flip-flops and with a rucksack full of shitty clothes, I was a prime candidate to get the rubber glove treatment and was amazed when they allowed me to pass.

Totally broke, jobless but with thousands of great memories, I returned to Wales as a certified scuba diver … it was something worth pursuing, but it would take me a few years to get there.

St Anton

BACK HOME, I found a short-term contract working in a warehouse and just after this contract finished, Steve gave me a call. He was working as a head chef in a ski resort, St Anton, in Austria and asked if I fancied working as a pizzeria chef. I had no experience of being a chef and tried to explain that to my mate.

He just said, "Never mind just get your ass to Austria."

With nothing better to do, I booked a flight to Zurich before taking a beautiful train journey into St Anton.

AUSTRIA AND THE Alps were mind-blowing; the challenge was to pretend to be a chef and learn how to snowboard. The restaurant was bustling, serving around 200 pizzas a night. The duties included everything from rolling pizza bases to making the starters on the menu. I had an earpiece and intercom system for the orders coming downstairs; panic set in as it was hard to hear the orders over the noise of a busy kitchen. I felt out of my depth and was sinking fast. Luckily, the guys come to my aid when I was getting behind.

AFTER A FEW weeks, I started to enjoy working in the kitchen; it was a great feeling after a busy service and all the chefs looked forward to a few beers. Work began at 11 am, so there was plenty of time to get over any hangovers. There were some great guys in the kitchen like Olly the nacho king and Meaty the kitchen porter. Sadly, there was one Scottish bell end who tried to steal my tips because I dropped the last calzone on the floor one night.

We enjoyed awesome nights in the bars around St Anton, but one night the shots got the better of me, and I passed out on a bench somewhere outside. Steve found me and dragged me home; calling me a stupid Welsh prick as I could have caught hypothermia. It was funny working with Steve and he had a couple of Gordon Ramsey moments and went ballistic at his chefs.

On one occasion, he found an open can of tomato puree in the fridge, stormed into the middle of the kitchen, and yelled, "Who the fuck has left this open in the fridge?" He launched the can across the chefs' heads before it smashed into the wall, smearing the red paste all over the place. It looked like someone had blown out his or her brains. After the outburst all the chefs kept their heads down and carried on with work, I was sniggering to myself around the corner.

Being a fake chef was fun when I was working with the other guys. One day though, Steve dropped me in the shit, making me do the breakfast service on my own. He told me he would come in and help but did he hell? It was just the dishwasher boy and me. Everything went tits up; the bacon was over crispy in the oven; the fried eggs looked like dog shit. Someone asked for a soft-boiled egg, and it took me three times to get it right. I didn't know that due to the altitude, the cooking time was different. The guests were complaining like hell and it was the longest morning of my life.

Steve strolled in about five minutes before the end of service, "Everything okay, Kris?"

I looked at him. "You should go and ask the guests how their breakfast was, and then you'll find out."

Thank God that was the only time I had to do the breakfast shift.

There were many ways to die in the Alps; it was a daily occurrence seeing the rescue helicopter bringing somebody down from the slopes.

My mate tried to teach me the basics of snow-boarding on the easy runs. It was hard to enjoy it too much being on my ass most of the time. Even though my level was novice, I used to go on the difficult blue and black runs with the guys. They would all bomb ahead of me, and I would meet them about half an hour later after finally making it down the slope.

Slowly, my confidence grew, I got to grips with everything, and by the end of the season I started to feel comfortable on a snowboard.

Hitchhiking

THE CONTRACT RAN out at the end of the ski season and we made a plan about how to get to the UK. We decided to hitchhike home and not spend any money on accommodation along the way.

We slept in Geneva Airport to start the trip and then managed to hitch a lift down to Méribel in the French Alps. We were lucky to know some people that were working in a chalet for the season and we stayed there for a free week … another bonus was that they were not checking lift passes, so we got to snowboard for free too.

The next stop was a few days in Val-d'Isère before blagging a lift to Paris with a lovely family. We crashed in Charles De Gaulle Airport and spent some time exploring Paris and the Eiffel Tower.

Our travels continued and we headed north to-wards Belgium; we got stuck for a place to stay near Lille; we couldn't get anybody to pick us up, so, we crashed in a field next to a service station – a couple of funny things happened during the night. We could see a car was driving around all the parked trucks in the service station. Every so often the car would flash its headlights and then stop alongside one of the trucks, then, this older lady would get out of the car and jump into the cabin of the truck. She would reappear sometime later; it turned out it was some old hooker noshing off the truck drivers.

We cracked up once we realised what was going on; I had to hold back Steve as he was shouting, "Me next, me next."

Later that night, there was a flashlight on my face; it was a policeman trying to talk to us in French; he was probably thinking we were two illegal immi-grants trying to get somewhere. He wanted to move us on, but we told him we were okay and he finally left us alone. We woke up at first light and were happy to see that we hadn't managed to sleep in the cow shit that was a few feet away from us. We had a quick wash in the service station and started to hitchhike again.

We made it to Lille, which was a lovely small city full of cobblestone streets and after a few hours looking around we managed to find a lift towards Belgium. We decided we had to visit Leuven, where the famous Stella Artois beer is brewed before being consumed around the world – with wives everywhere ending up with black eyes!

We crashed in Brussels Airport before exploring the city; we didn't stay too long though as there were too many dodgy Moroccan guys with knives running around. We contacted a good friend of ours, Michal, from Rotterdam who we had met in Cairns. He is a great guy, loves to party hard, and is a schoolteacher. Michal and I have met on four different continents over the years; he is a quirky guy that doesn't believe in washing dishes, so he uses paper plates with plastic knives and forks for every meal.

We arrived in Holland for Queen's Day; it was perfect timing as everybody was in the mood to party. We hit a load of places over a few days, and it was brilliant. We ended up in Amsterdam, where we met some other friends and continued to enjoy the Dutch way of life.

After partying for five days straight, we had a head full of broken biscuits and it was time to go home. We were so happy that we didn't pay for any accommodation along the way, although we did have to pay for the ferry ticket to the UK.

ONCE BACK ON UK soil, I went back home to Wales skint as a dog, but armed with another bunch of great stories to tell the grandchildren.

At home again, it was the same shit different day. I got a soul-destroying job working in a wine ware-house. It was freezing cold in January and while loading trucks with wine I promised myself to move to a warm country and never come back. Even though it was my home, my mind was always pushing me; there was something different out there for me. The savings were building up nicely; so, it was just a matter of time.

UK Diving

THE SCUBA DIVING started up again and I joined the local BSAC club with my good friend Chris. We went on a few diving trips down to Cornwall and Devon and I purchased my first set of dive gear at this time, including a dry suit and a Buddy Commando BCD. There was a fella down in Swansea that sold dive gear for a good price, so I bought a new mask and fins from him.

They say if you can dive in the UK, then you can dive anywhere; it can make or break you. We headed down to Torquay and there got a quick lesson on how not to dive in the UK. I decided not to wear a hood in early March and the water was so cold that it felt like my brain turned into an ice cube. The dive was held up as I went back to get my hood and some of the older club members were not impressed as the water was only fourteen degrees. To make it worse during the dive, the only thing we saw was a bloody hermit crab.

It was a struggle with the dry suit so I replaced it with a 7 mm wetsuit. It was cheaper to buy the wetsuit than replace seals on the dry suit.

The dives down in Cornwall were pretty good; we saw cuttlefish among the kelp forests and lobsters hiding under ledges. However, the UK shore diving just seemed such hard work after all the warm water diving in Australia and Thailand. Getting ready on the beach then lugging all the weight with thick hoods and gloves was not so easy, also getting back out of the water was also a challenge in itself.

It was an excellent experience to see a basking shark though. They come around in the summertime and have to be the ugliest sharks around, looking like the Emperor from *Star Wars*. Even though they have a large mouth, they only feed on plankton and are the world's second-largest fish after the whale shark.

MY GIRLFRIEND AND I had been together for just over a year and we decided to go travelling together. We planned to travel on the Trans-Siberian railway from St Petersburg to Beijing before exploring more of South East Asia and this time we planned to spend a short time in Australia before starting a two-year work visa in New Zealand.

We went to Sharm El-Sheikh in Egypt for a cheap holiday. The Red Sea is the closest warm water to the UK and has some of the best diving in the world. My girlfriend wasn't interested in diving and looked at me with disbelief as I did three dives in one day. There were already doubts deep down that it wouldn't last as I believed my future was in diving.

We saved up decent money and even started ap-plying for travel visas. Then all of a sudden it was over between us, and the travel plans went out of the window.

Life carried on as usual for the next couple of weeks then out of the blue, my mate Steve called me again.

Deal or no Deal

HE WAS WELL excited on the phone, because he had been chosen to play on the TV game show 'Deal or no Deal' hosted by Noel Edmunds, which was very popular in the UK at the time.

The show was recorded at a studio in Bristol, which was thirty minutes away from my house and he asked me to be his friend in the audience. My boss couldn't give me any holiday leave from my mundane job in the wine warehouse, so I took a sickie for a week and decided I would deal with the consequences later if they saw me on Channel 4.

The TV production company put us up in a decent hotel with free meals included; it was a sweet deal to be fair. They filmed three shows a day and we watched people win life-changing amounts of money. At the other end though, some people came away with just a penny, so there were mixed emotions throughout the filming. It was fun every night as they had an open bar and we took full advantage of the big winners' generosity staying out partying until the early hours.

On the day that it was Steve's turn to play, the production team called me asking me to get to the studio. The make-up artist put some slap on my face, and the game started. Steve did a cracking job and got himself up to £25,000. The presenter Noel Edmunds asked if we would take the deal or play on, we both agreed to take the money. As it turned out if he had played until the end, he would have won £100,000. He was a little bit sore after that, but still, he had £25,000 in his pocket, so it was a pretty fantastic day for him. We celebrated long into the night visiting many bars around the Bristol docks.

The next day we sat in a bar having a hair of the dog Stella Artois, and a couple of my mates who had met Steve in Australia came over and we talked about what we would do next. We both had money in the bank and dead-end jobs, so the world was our oyster again. After a few more Stella's we decided our next travel destination was going to be South and Central America with the first stop being Rio de Janeiro in Brazil.

WE ARRANGED THE flights to Brazil while we were still working in the shitty warehouse. There was a problem in the company; they had somehow managed to lose a whole truck full of wine. The company put a mole into work with us, pretending he was an agency worker. He worked with us for a few weeks secretly gathering information and then the company called us all in at the same time.

We were all suspended on full pay after this guy tried to pin a bunch of offences on us – there was everything from the destruction of company property to drug use in the workplace. We had a series of meetings with the company and the union while they tried to get us all fired. They didn't have anything on me and after a few weeks reinstated most of the staff.

They still never found out who took the whole trailer of wine from the warehouse, but my money was on Wayne. This entire situation had left a bad taste in my mouth, because I was leaving the country soon, I called in sick blaming the stress of being accused of things I didn't do.

THE TIME HAD come to leave Chepstow again, I didn't know it, but it would probably be the last time ever living in Wales again.

My flight departed while still on the sick from my job, I wanted some payback from those pricks trying to set me up. We were in South America for a whole two months while getting paid and even sent the company a postcard from Copacabana Beach. It was nice to get my final pay check and some unused holiday pay from them while in Brazil.

South America

IT WAS A real buzz being in Brazil; the country has such an electric vibe to it. I met up with Steve at Ipanema Beach and we spent a couple of weeks around Rio enjoying the beaches and the buzz of the city.

We visited the Christ the Redeemer statue, which must be one of the best viewpoints in the world and we also visited one of the world's most famous stadiums, The Maracanã. As a stadium trainspotter this was a dream of mine and we watched Botafogo v Flamengo with about 60,000 people in the stadium.

The electric atmosphere pulsed through my body, the chanting echoed around the stands, fans bounced around setting off flares and firecrackers, and beer was thrown up in the air when a goal was scored. Outside the stadium, there was a hall of fame, famous Brazilian players like Pele and Ronaldo had concrete casts of their feet, so off came my flip-flops, and I stood in the place of greatness.

We had a mega super Saturday drinking session. It was the Euro 2008 qualifiers back at home and with the time difference, games began at 10 am. The day sticks in my mind as Wales got stuffed 5-1 at home against Slovakia. Steve ripped the piss out of me all day saying Wales was a third-world country and we all shagged sheep.

We decided to head to Lapa and the famous sam-ba clubs. Some random guy from the hostel joined us ... he was keen to get some supplements to liven us up after a long day drinking. He started talking to the taxi driver, who was getting agitated and the driver said it was hazardous to go into the favelas late at night. However, we had been drinking all day, so the alcohol dampened the danger element. The guy bribed the driver and he took us up some narrow streets and pulled up at some gates. Some guy lifted a barrier, and we drove into a compound.

The driver got out with the guy and went inside one of the buildings. Steve and I sat in the car and suddenly, there was a metallic tapping on the window. I couldn't see what was outside so I opened the taxi window. Looking out, my heart nearly exploded with fear, because there was a massive man with a M60 machine gun pointing in the window.

The M60 machine gun was used in the Rambo film *First Blood*. Sly Stallone goes mental in the end and shoots up the whole place with this type of machine gun.

This guy was looking inside the taxi to see who we were; the danger element came back in a flash, we froze and shrank as deep into our seats as possible. After a couple of seconds, which seemed like a lifetime, the guy walked away from the car and I closed the window quickly, wondering what the hell we were doing there. Soon after, the driver returned and we were off to Lapa to party.

The night carried on until 10 am the next morning. We visited some of the samba clubs and some of the local ladies tried to show us the moves, but after a ten-hour drinking sesh, our co-ordination wasn't going to rival John Travolta's.

As the sun was coming up on Ipanema Beach things got a little hairy. It turned out the bar owner was charging everyone's drinks to our bill. We ended up legging it away with some of the locals chasing us down the street. We made it back to the hostel in one piece and slept for nearly a whole day. When I woke up, there was somebody's boxer shorts on the end of my bunk, which made me want to vomit.

We enjoyed a great time in Rio, but started to make some rough travel plans for South America. We did things in a relaxed, disorganised way that often got us into difficult situations.

We decided on a very short thirty-six hours bus journey taking us into Argentina to visit one of the most famous waterfalls in the world, *FOZ DO IGUAÇU*. We got off the hell bus on the Brazilian border with Argentina and then got on another bus thinking it would stop at the border crossing so we could get our Argentina stamp.

The local bus just went straight through the border without stopping, so now we were officially illegal aliens in Argentina. We tried to explain the situation to the bus driver, but as we spoke about ten words of Spanish and two in Portuguese, he didn't quite understand us. He let us off the bus, and we had to take a taxi back to the border crossing to get our visa situation solved. We just played the dumb tourists and smiled at the immigration officers, who looked a bit angry at us.

We stayed in a hostel in Puerto Iguazú and spent a couple of days visiting the waterfalls. They were an astonishing sight and went on for as far as the eye could see, bordering both Argentina and Brazil. We got a ride on a speedboat that took us very close to the bottom of the waterfalls and the noise of millions of tons of water crashing down was furious; the spray made beautiful rainbows right in front of us. Once we got back to the shore, we explored the walking trails through the park.

WITH A LITTLE regret, we decided to leave Argentina and make our way back to Brazil.

However, we soon wished that we had spent a bit more time exploring Argentina. The country was so much cheaper than Brazil, and it seemed like a lot of fun.

With our arses still numb from the nightmare bus journey, we decided to fly into Fortaleza, which is close to a beautiful place called Jericoacoara. We had a great time playing around on the sand dunes and watching locals who were doing capoeira dancing. If you have never seen this before think of a karate fighter doing roundhouse kicks while dancing along to a nice bongo drumbeat. The drumbeat with people acrobatically flying through the air was an astounding experience. The performance happened as the sun set against the silhouettes of the dunes. This place was one of our favourite spots in Brazil; it was so chilled and relaxed.

We spent a few more days, sandboarding and off-roading in 4x4 vehicles, before leaving. To the north of us was the Amazon rainforest and we were looking forward to seeing some of it.

The Amazon

WE TRAVELLED NORTH to Belém, a hundred miles from the Atlantic Ocean and the gateway to the River Amazon. This typical port city was rough around the edges with plenty of dodgy fellas walking around. Luckily, we still hadn't learned any Portuguese, so we had no idea what people were saying to us.

We bought some tickets that would take us up the Amazon River to the City of Manaus. As we were on a budget, we bought the cheapest tickets we could find and our chariot for the trip was a hundred feet longboat, which slept 130 people. We had to buy hammocks, so there were 130 hammocks all tied up on the deck. You were in close quarters with many strangers for five days. I tied up my hammock and jumped in, the knot gave way, and I smashed into the deck much to the locals' delight. On a side note, there were only two bathrooms for everybody, and the food choice wasn't exactly like a Las Vegas buffet either, no sign of any king crab legs but plenty of rice and beans.

As the ropes went off, we were excited to explore the most famous river and rainforest in the world. It was great being in a small area with many local people. They were very poor, but still offered to share food; the children were always smiling and playing with us.

I didn't get much sleep in the hammock on the first night; we went upstairs to the top deck and managed to get some beers. The boat only had one CD for the whole trip, so we got to remember the songs off by heart.

We woke up just before sunrise the next morning. All of a sudden, the whole rainforest sprang to life and we were witnessing the morning call of the birds and monkeys that were either side of the riverbanks. It was spectacular to hear the Howler monkeys and thousands of other creatures making a beautiful chorus to kick off a new day.

Travelling slowly west we caught glimpses of what life is like on the Amazon. As we went past small villages the tribes would jump into the dugout canoes paddling as fast as they could to catch up with the boat. Once close enough, they would throw a line and hook themselves onto our vessel, and then they sold fruits and sweets to the people on board the boat. Once they made enough money, they unhooked the canoe and went back home.

Even though the tribes lead a primitive life, it was also possible to see the industrial side of the Amazon. Sometimes it resembled the M25 motorway around London with massive barges carrying many trucks heading to Manaus. Sadly, we lost count of the number of barges that were full of logs that had recently been torn down from the rainforest.

We saw the meeting of the two waters, where the River Negra meets the *SOLIMÕES RIVER*. The water in the River Negra is black, and the River SolimÕes is a light brown colour. They run side by side without their respective waters mixing for nearly four miles due to confluence. This unusual activity only happens in a few places around the world.

We had a break from the boat for half a day in a place called Alter do Chão. You have to rub your eyes in amazement at this place. There were beautiful white sand beaches that rivalled the best we had seen on our worldwide travels. We had a few relaxing hours on the sand thinking we were in Ibiza not on the Amazon River in Northern Brazil. We didn't go into the water though; there were stories about parasites that swim up your penis and lay eggs, they then climb out of your mouth or something along those lines.

Our Amazon trip reached its climax as we ap-proached Manaus. On the last morning, we had the pleasure of watching some endemic pink river dolphins. It was surreal seeing the endangered strawberry milkshake coloured dolphins splashing around in the water next to the huge barges. They looked to be around two metres long and had melon like heads. It was a perfect end to our trip to the Amazon River. We unhooked our hammocks and said goodbye to our shipmates.

WE ARRIVED IN Manaus the capital of the Amazonas state; sadly, I had caught some virus during the boat trip and was leaking like a rusty radiator for weeks afterward. Every cloud has a silver lining though, as I lost some bodyweight, so I wasn't such a fat twat in the eyes of my pal Steve.

He did one of the nicest things ever while I was in

bed with stomach problems … he bought me a McDonald's quarter pounder and I was over the moon. It didn't stay in my system long though, but the thought was great from one of the shallowest people around.

Interrogation

WE HEADED NORTH to the city of Boa Vista then planned to cross into Venezuela. Arriving at the border, I realised I had lost my Brazilian entry visa card. If you didn't have it you would be fined $50 and being a tight backpacker, I didn't want to pay the fine. So, I decided to create a story to get away with it.

We approached the border control; Steve went through okay as he still had his entrance card and the smug bastard smiled at me as he went through. The immigration officer looked at me stony-faced after I told him that my wallet with the card was stolen in Rio. The guy didn't speak much English and he asked me to wait for a while. Then two other guys arrived, asking me to follow them. They took me into an interview room locking the door behind them; my ass started to twitch, thinking I was in trouble. The guy spoke excellent English and started to ask me ques-tions.

He didn't believe my story about the stolen wallet and he kept asking me for the police report and crime number. I told him I didn't get a report as there was nothing worthwhile inside.

They left the room, locking the door behind them and leaving me alone with my thoughts for thirty minutes. My mind was racing with the worst thoughts before finally they returned, telling me I was free to leave Brazil. The officer gave me a stern warning to keep my papers in order if I ever returned to Brazil.

I got across the border with a massive smile be-cause I had saved $50, but the look on Steve's face was a picture as he had been waiting for me in the blazing Brazilian heat as I was questioned in an air-conditioned room. He mouthed some obscenities at me as we posed for some pictures at the border crossing.

ON ARRIVAL IN Venezuela, I was prepared to use my extensive knowledge of around thirty Spanish words that I had learned in classes a few years back. Back in the pill munching days, I thought about moving to Ibiza to give out flyers for the nightclubs and in return I would see my favourite DJs for free. That didn't quite work out but anyway that experience of learning thirty words would be helpful in Venezuela.

We talked about going to Angel Falls, the highest waterfall in the world. We made it to the small town where the trips departed from, but I was still feeling weak after being ill from the Amazon trip. It was going to be a two-day hiking trip, so we decided not to do it.

We carried on further north towards the Caribbe-an coast where we hoped to see some beautiful islands with excellent snorkelling and diving. We met this old French guy there, who owned a small dive shop, so we arranged a trip with him to go and check out the coastline. It was a waste of time because the beaches were covered in rubbish and it looked like nobody gave a shit about the place.

Even though we were only in Venezuela for around a week, I never really enjoyed my time there, so we decided to haul ass and make our way to Colombia.

Colombia

WE LOOKED AT the Lonely Planet guide and decided to head to the beautiful city of Cartagena. The book recommends not arriving in the border town of Maicao after dark as the place is dangerous and there is a history of muggings, kidnappings, and stories of young white backpackers getting their kidneys removed with no anaesthetic!

I made the last bit up, but you get the idea. We screwed up somewhere and got on the wrong bus, and yes you guessed it we ended up in the dodgy border town after dark with nowhere to stay. We got off the bus, and it wasn't looking good. People were coming towards us, asking us many questions that we could not understand. We just smiled politely and walked off at a fast pace looking for the nearest hotel.

We found one that looked more like a maximum-security prison with bars on all the windows, the security guard had a pump-action shotgun, but we didn't care. We checked into the shitty room and even though we were starving we didn't risk going out for dinner. We were happy to have both our kidneys and money as we went to sleep.

COLOMBIA HAD A nicer feel to it than Venezuela; the people seemed to be a lot happier and were always smiling at us. We took the bus to Cartagena and during the ride we had some experience of the drug wars that were going on in the country.

We drove along the road and saw lot of soldiers hiding in the tree line with machine guns. There were so many checkpoints, it was unbelievable. Each time, around ten soldiers would come aboard and search every person and their luggage; they never searched our bags, just asked to see our passports. They took all the bags from under the bus and their sniffer dogs checked for cocaine and weapons. It was a surreal experience to see this first-hand. I thought I would tell the army that Steve had an ounce of coke shoved up his ass, but I bottled it at the last second. It wasn't until later, that I learned more about Pablo Escobar and the drug wars that had occurred in the previous decades.

We were happy to get off the bus in Cartagena, which was one of our top cities of the trip. I saw a huge billboard poster of the singer Shakira, who was doing a concert in her town of Barranquilla just down the coast. Little did I know that this concert was going to have an effect on our travels down the line.

The UNESCO world heritage site of Cartagena was outstanding; we explored the fort area, enjoyed some fantastic colonial architecture, and tight streets. The city had a great atmosphere and was buzzing with people. We ate in great restaurants smashing our backpacker food allowance each day.

We visited the El Totumo mud volcano where you can climb up wooden steps to the top of the thirty-metre cone. Inside, there is this thick mud that stinks of sulphur and if you slip into the thick mud and relax, they say that it is good for your skin. But I don't believe that as thousands of people are pissing and farting and leaving dead skin in it each year.

You can also get a massage from the locals if you wish. Once you have finished, you can go to the lakeside and get a wash from one of the local ladies. They are not shy at all, and my lady had my shorts off in seconds. Even though she said she had finished, I still found mud about a month later in every orifice of my body.

We had a few more nights in the city before we were starting to get itchy feet again. We considered exploring some other parts of Colombia, but we couldn't be bothered to get searched every couple of miles. We looked at the notice board in the hostel, and our next move was staring us in the face … we were going to sail to Panama via the San Blas Islands.

We made our way to this posh yacht club in Car-tagena. Steve and I were in our cheap clothes and flip-flops, mixing with all these snobby guys with their private yachts and Henry Lloyd windbreakers. I'm sure the waiter thought we were homeless bums when we sat at a table and ordered a club sandwich.

We had been asked to meet a boat captain who arranged trips from there to Panama. It took a couple of days to get everybody ready for the journey; we were with a couple of guys from Quebec and a girl from California. There was one other guy who made us wait for another day while he went to the Shakira concert. The guy from Austria turned out to be a first-class bell end and the spawn of Adolf Hitler.

The captain briefed us that we needed food and water for four days, so we went to the store and bought some stuff; substituting most of the food for alcohol while spending our last Colombian pesos at the store. When we got back to the boat, we realised we had about half as many provisions as everyone else – little did we know that later this would turn out to be a problem for us.

We said goodbye to South America, and the last memory was a sad one, because someone stole my camera at the hostel and I lost so many great images.

We got on board and the captain, who spoke hard-ly any English until the last day of the trip, told us very clearly that no drugs were allowed. He had long salt-crusted hair and one of his legs had been affected by polio when he was a kid, so he dragged it around with him. He reminded me a bit of Tom Hanks when he was stuck on *The Island* for a couple of years. I looked around the boat, but there was no volleyball in sight.

He took all of our passports and got the exit clear-ance from the local immigration office and we set off towards the horizon; the San Blas Islands were 241 miles away. Even though we were in a 42 ft sailboat, there wasn't a breath of wind for the entire trip, which I'm sure pissed off the captain as he was on engine power for the duration.

One day, we had a surprise as the Colombian coastguard boarded us. They were mean-looking guys, who were armed to the teeth and they went through all of our bags. I noticed that they had a 50 Cal machine gun aimed at our boat, which made me kind of uneasy, but after a while, they gave us the all clear, and we motored through the night.

The Austrian guy was getting on my tits, but the other people were nice. We had fun having a few beers each night and eating way too much food. The captain warned us that we were going to run out if we were not careful.

One of the Quebec guys looked at him and said, "Niggers got to eat right?" and started to boil up some pasta.

Steve and I were down to our last supplies al-ready, but luckily the guys were generous sharing with us. The girl from California had picked up something from the Amazon jungle; her leg had a parasite that was growing inside and it was not looking good.

San Blas Islands

AS WE CROSSED the Caribbean Sea, we had the pleasure of seeing a massive pod of Spinners dolphins that splashed around the bow for a while. After two days, we finally made it to the San Blas Islands.

These islands are some of the most beautiful ever seen; there were deserted sand bars and tiny little islands with just a single coconut tree just like the Bounty advert. The coral reefs were magnificent and we spent time snorkelling, trying, badly, to catch some lobsters that were hiding in the reef.

We swam at night and I saw the magical bioluminescence in the water for the first time. It was amazing to see the tiny plankton lighting up as we moved our arms and legs in the water. We were in the middle of nowhere, there was no light apart from the stars and the anchor light on the boat, and it was as if we were covered in millions of tiny blue lights as we splashed in the water.

The next day the captain arranged for us to go onto an island for lunch. It was great to see local tribes living off the land and they prepared a great meal of fresh fish and lobster cooked in coconut milk. Even though we were on a speck of land the local tranny pranced around the place smiling at us with his hot pants on. It was apparent Steve was getting horny, but I told him to cool down in the sea as there was a bulge in his board shorts. As we were enjoying our visit to the beautiful island, we didn't know everything was going to turn to shit, in a few hours' time.

We got back on the boat in the evening and the captain told us a hurricane was approaching. We would have to get to the Island of El Porvenir as quickly as possible so we were not on the boat when the hurricane arrived. We arrived at the island after a couple of hours of travel; it was tiny, but it had an airstrip and one small hotel. The captain dropped us off at the pier and went back out to sea to try and find safe anchorage. That idea didn't work out very well.

As usual, we had no plans in place for our arrival in Panama and we had planned to go to immigration to get our entrance visa, assuming we would get a bus from the east coast to Panama City. At the moment though, we were stuck on another island and our only mode of transport was by plane to Panama City.

We tried to get tickets for the flight, and they kept telling us the aircraft was coming, but all we could see were grey storm clouds gathering. After a few more hours we realised we weren't going anywhere anytime soon and we were told to check into the hotel, which was very basic. It had open sides on the roof so the mosquitoes could have unlimited access to us juicy white folk that stayed in the rooms.

The big problem was we had no money left, there was no ATM on the island, and it was impossible for us to pay with Visa as the machine was out of order. The others had a few dollars between them, so it covered the hotel for the night. We thought the storm would pass by quickly and we would be able to leave the next day. That didn't happen. As night fell, the wind and rain smashed into the hotel and you could hear the massive waves crashing onto the beach not far from us. At times I thought the roof would come off.

When we woke up the next morning, we found out from the hotel staff that our boat had had severe problems during the night. It had been dragging its anchor and had got stuck on the reef causing damage to the hull. We felt sorry for the salty captain that his boat and livelihood had taken a hit. He had got us off just in time, so we respected him so much for that.

The weather was still nasty the next day and the staff said there was no chance of us getting off the island. The rest of the group had also run out of money. We had to beg and borrow some money from other tourists who had shown up also trying their best to get on the next plane to leave the island. The other issue was that the parasite in the girl's leg was getting much worse and she needed to be evacuated ASAP. The hotel let us stay for free for the last night as they had no other option.

The next day the seas had calmed down and we knew the plane should be able to take us to Panama City. We made our way to the airport, but as we didn't have any money, they let us pay for the tickets in Panama City, which was pretty good of them. There was quite a crowd of people desperately trying to catch international flights out of Panama. The small plane landed, but it could only fit around fifteen passengers. Once it had taxied and opened its door all hell broke loose. The crew were giving out boarding passes, but there were not enough for everyone, so a massive argument began. There were a couple of French guys that were getting aggressive because they didn't get a boarding pass and they started to argue with the Austrian guy, and then there was a scuffle with some punches thrown.

The Californian girl was panicking and was plead-ing with the pilot, "I need to get on this fucking plane as I have a parasite growing in my leg."

We all managed to get a boarding pass and then, thank God, we took off and headed to Panama City. As the plane flew over the landmass of Panama, I was happy we were flying over it and not travelling by bus. It was just thick jungle; you could hardly see any roads, so I'm guessing we missed out on a tough bus ride.

By this time, we were at our wits end with the Austrian guy. All of this shit was his fault anyway. If he hadn't made us wait an extra day because he went to watch Shakira in concert, then none of this would have happened and we would have left the island before the storm arrived.

As we stowed away our tray tables and put our seats in an upright position, we had a first glimpse of the Panama Canal and the huge container ships. We touched down and made plans to stay at a hostel in the city. The Austrian guy made his last fatal mistake by insulting our taxi driver over the fare. The driver took out our bags and dumped them on the floor. That was the last time we spoke to him.

We got to the ATM; it was great to have cash in our hands again. The girl went to the doctor to get the parasite treated and we had a last night together in

Panama reliving our adventures.

It was quite funny the next morning as we saw the Austrian guy at reception.

He said, "What happened to you guys; I thought we were having dinner together last night?"

So, we all said, "You are a bit of prick, so we de-cided to ditch you."

Goodbye my Friend

STEVE DECIDED TO return to the UK, because when he was on the Deal or no Deal TV show, he had met a nice lady called Hannah, who was another contestant. They had got together during the show, and Steve, the soft cock, was beginning to miss his bird. He booked his flight back to London, and we said our goodbyes.

A tribute needs to be made to my great travelling friend; I have never had as much fun as I did during our time together, from meeting in Australia and travelling through South East Asia and Europe together. We got into so much trouble and it was simply outstanding. We have stayed in touch over the years; he is living in the UK with his wife and two daughters. In my eyes, though he will always be a fat, suit wearing blue-eyed German looking twat.

There was only one thing on my mind now and that was to get to Honduras quickly to become a divemaster. The only problem was getting through Panama, Costa Rica, and Nicaragua by bus first.

The first part of the journey was Panama City to San Jose in Costa Rica, which took twenty hours, then from San Jose to Managua by Tica bus before spend-ing the night at the hotel in the bus terminal. They advised us not to go walking around at night because of the banditos. Next morning, it was back on the bus for the journey through Nicaragua into San Pedro Sula, Honduras.

Altogether I travelled 2,000 miles in four days; it was exhausting. I never wanted to see another bus again in my life. On arrival in the murder capital of the world, San Pedro Sula, I crashed out for the night. It felt like my buttocks had already been murdered anyway. There would be a final three-hour bus journey to get to the Caribbean coast.

The Bay Islands

LA CEIBA IS the entry port for the Bay Islands of Roatán, Guanaja, and the smallest island of Útila. It's about twenty miles from the mainland.

I planned on going to Roatán for my dive course but made a last-minute decision that changed my life. According to the Lonely Planet book it was the biggest and best island to visit, but before buying my ticket, I got talking to a girl who had been to Útila. She told me to change my plans and head there instead. We spoke for a while and she changed my mind and the whole path of my life … the funny thing was I didn't even catch her name.

As the ferry pulled into Útila harbour it really wasn't much of a paradise and I muttered under my breath, "Where the hell am I, that girl has stitched me right up."

There were a bunch of run-down buildings, half of which looked abandoned and there was no real beach; it was far away from what I had in mind. Thoughts flashed about getting back on the ferry and heading to Roatán, but after sitting down I decided to give it a couple of nights.

The island is around seven miles long and two miles wide. The reason many divers head here, is it's located at the southern end of the Mesoamerica Barrier Reef, which is the second-largest in the world and backpackers come for the low-price dive courses. There were a mix of tourists and great local people. The locals are a mixture of black Garifuna, Hispanics from the mainland, and some European settlers. The island was small, and you could walk the most populated areas in around twenty minutes.

The ferry had people who worked for the dive shops and they tried to sign me up for a dive course before setting foot on the island. Getting off the boat, I witnessed the 'Ferry Wars' for the first time. Most of the local dive shops sent down staff to get business right off the ferry. It was competitive and pushy; over the years, workers would fight over people coming to the island.

Ignoring the mass of people with flyers, I decided to walk around the island myself, checking out all the dive shops and noticing where they made me feel most welcome. Captains Morgan's dive shop let you leave your bags with them as you explored, so I set off on foot checking each dive shop for rescue and divemaster packages.

After already visiting five shops nothing felt right for me, but then this vast light blue wooden house came into view. It was the biggest and most impres-sive home on the road and it had a small dive shop downstairs. A huge laugh boomed out from the building, so I decided to have a chat with them.

It was one of the best decisions I ever made. The staff made me feel so welcome, it felt a great place to hang out, and the facilities looked outstanding. There were a few Brits around, so that made it easier to make a decision. I signed up for the courses after about five minutes there. They put me up in a basic hotel next to the shop and we celebrated with a few sunset beers and checked a few bars on the island.

It was a rum-induced paradise; a great feeling washed over me. I was in the right place and couldn't wait to start my diving courses. The next morning, manager Remi checked my logbook, thirty-seven dives to my name so far. I needed sixty dives to complete my Divemaster Course, so I spent the first week diving every day to raise my rookie numbers.

The majority of people lived on the south coast of the island and even though the island had beautiful reefs on the south shore, the spectacular diving was on the north side. It took an hour to get there and was a beautiful scenic boat ride. If the sea was calm you could go around the east coast passing the Iron Shore and the highest point, Pumpkin Hill. If you headed west, you would pass the Cays. They were home to local fishermen and some stunning small islands with palm trees just like those in Panama, a real taste of the Caribbean.

The island attracted backpackers from all over the world and it was amazing to meet people from all corners. It was effortless to slip into the chilled-out island lifestyle with hazy days turning into weeks very quickly. People only planned to stop for a few days and then stayed for weeks, some stayed for years, and others I met would be there for life.

The primary benefit of taking your Divemaster Course is you can dive loads to gain experience. My instructors and dive shop managers Remi and Kirsty told me to dive every day, which was fine by me and I got up early to load the boat with tanks and safety equipment. The travel to the dive sites gave me a chance to get to know the staff. The core staff were Rob and Lizzie from Devon, mad Sasha from South-port, multilingual, beautiful Maya from Denmark, Kate from the US and Martijn from Belgium. Every-body was great; it felt like a tight happy family and over the coming months, we would become firm friends.

TURTLE HARBOR IS the famous marine park on the north side. It had the deepest walls on the island down to six thousand feet with some spectacular swim throughs. Duppy Waters was the most famous dive; you swam out of the L-shaped sand patch through a narrow cut in the reef, the brilliant deep blue hitting you, making you gasp at the beauty. Schools of purplish-blue creole wrasse filled the water, along with grunts and yellowtail snappers. The deep wall was covered in massive barrel sponges and seahorses clung onto orange rope sponges dangling on the edge of infinity. Hawksbill turtles with barnacle-encrusted shells cruised around, and nurse sharks hung out in the shallow gullies.

Diver, Diver are you OK?

WE STARTED THE Emergency First Responder and Rescue Diver Course and Danish Tomas showed up ... we would do our Divemaster Course training together. He seemed all right, but got highly strung out when he was off his nut drunk.

The Rescue Course was intense but very reward-ing; learning how to save someone's life underwater was serious stuff and a game-changer as a diver. Kirsty was our instructor and got mad as one of the trainee divemaster's showed up drunk, as she was supposed to play a victim in the course. She drilled us with the rescue breaths until we were competent. We practised search patterns for missing divers and brought up unconscious divers to the surface.

Our last scenario was a fun dive where a couple of the trainee DMs were under instruction to break all the diving rules, leaving us to solve the problems they created.

We had everything chucked at us in quick succes-sion from Rob wearing sunglasses instead of his mask to people wearing fins on their hands. People pre-tended to run out of air, some decided to split from the group; there were a lot of problems for us to fix. It was a great way to complete the course.

A new confidence was instilled in me and I was pumped for the DM training to start. My instructors and mentors had gained my utmost respect; I watched in awe as they were treated like gods by their stu-dents. They commanded authority, and people listened to every word they said. My mind was already set on being like them one day.

Island Food

ISLAND LIFE WAS perfect, with diving in the morning and hammock time in the afternoon. There were small beaches close by and the place grew on me fast. Sunset drinks at Tranquila Bar became a tradition with Monica, Brooks, and Dani being great owners. The food on the small island was surprisingly good; the guys introduced the Honduran delicacy the baleda. Martha, a thickset lady with strong arms from making millions of tortillas, was the owner of the Seven Seas Restaurant across the street. The basic baleda consists of a thick soft tortilla, refried or reused beans are spread inside with cheese and pickled onions. You could add chicken or ground beef if you liked, there were plenty of variations for your taste.

We often had baledas for lunch as it didn't take long to prepare. Martha also made arroz con pollo every week, which was the bee's knees and one of my favourite meals. She also made these things called pastelitos, which were a deep-fried pastry filled with potatoes and meat; it looks a bit like a mini Cornish pasty and the nearest thing to eating from the UK bakery Gregg's that was on the island. The fried chicken was pretty good from Mermaids, and the Spanish omelette from El Pancho was also famous.

We visited Camilla in the morning, she owned a small bakery that had cracking bagels with peanut butter or cream cheese. These hit the spot and soaked up a lot of rum in our system before the morning dives. Posher night dining took place at Kate's La Picolla Italian restaurant and awesome pizzas were available at The Mango Inn.

Some of the best meals though, were at Rob and Lizzie's place; they used to make great roast dinners just like home, and they had a stash of products from the UK such as curry pastes and Marmite. Rob impressed the hell out me when he demolished a whole pack of Pringles with an improvised dip of mayo and hot sauce in a couple of minutes.

THERE WERE SOME events on the island where you really could enjoy the culture and the carnival was one. We made a float at the dive shop and joined the procession through the town, with our boss and sons riding some beautiful horses. All the locals lined the main street and we tossed Mardi Gras necklaces to everyone.

They would bring over reggae stars like Eric Donaldson for concerts, which were great nights. September 15th was always another wild time, as it is Independence Day for Honduras and the date of Lizzie's birthday, so we always had a mad one celebrating with the locals. They tried to climb a greasy pole to collect the cash that was on top, there was a boxing ring where locals scrapped it out if they had some beef with each other, locals cooked chicharrons on the side of the road, and it was just one big party.

The islanders' tastes in music was always interest-ing, there was a lot of reggae; the mainlanders enjoyed reggaeton with Daddy Yankee being popular. You could often hear soca and a little bit of calypso drifting through the air. The older Utilians enjoyed country music, crying into their Salva Vida beer over broken hearts.

Divemaster Training

IT WAS TIME to start the DM training and we had an orientation with Remi. There was a board at the dive shop which listed the requirements we had to complete; we ticked off each item after completion. The last achievement was the equipment exchange or stress test. There were four of us doing the course together; Tomas, Denise, who was a feisty blond Kiwi, her man-mountain boyfriend Ben, and me.

First up were the swim tests and I excelled at the fifteen-minute float, as my man boobs acted like great floatation devices. The rescue assessment was a breeze as we had done the course the week before. The exams were going to be the hardest part for me, reading the physics chapter my brain just turned to mush. It was a real struggle, and no matter how many times I went over it, it just didn't sink in.

The dives were clocking up nicely; I wore a bikini on my hundredth dive, which was hardly flattering. Our instructors taught us the enriched air, wreck, and deep specialties as part of the deal, which meant we had a load of cert cards coming from our training organisation.

The Haliburton Wreck was purposely sunk as an artificial reef near the Lighthouse; it was where our wreck training took place. We learned how to use the guide lines while penetrating and how to map the wreck. I looked at the sketch on my dive slate; a four-year-old could probably draw a better shipwreck than I could.

The deep specialty was my favourite. We trained at the Pinnacle in Turtle Harbor. This dive had a fantastic swim through which came out at forty metres and we did some deeper decompression stops and out of air drills at the end of the dive. We also became nitrox divers at the same time. I always wondered why some tanks had green caps and others black and this course taught me the difference, and that you could have convulsions at depth if you weren't careful on nitrox.

We returned to the Pinnacle for a fun dive. We decided to break our depth record planning a bounce dive down to sixty metres. This time we went down the wall to the ocean depths, hung around for a few minutes then headed back up into the swim through, before staying in the shallows for an extra-long deco stop for thirty minutes. The dive wasn't the smartest thing to do with my level of experience, but it still ranks as one of my favourite dives.

Once we got down to sixty metres, it felt like being on the moon. The sandy ridges made the perfect moonscape against the dark blue of the deep water. The nitrogen narcosis kicked in and the drunk, wobbly feeling washed through my mind. My vision began to narrow and my dive computer showed we had only four minutes of deco time. Rob was narked out of his brain; his booming laugh echoed through the water and my chest. It was loud enough on the surface, but down at sixty metres, it sounded like a ghost laughing underwater.

A few days earlier, Rob had taken us for a practise run of the scuba skills circuit; my execution of the buoyancy skill of hovering was pathetic. Rob thought it was a good idea to practise this skill and not wanting to disappoint my mentor; we practised hovering on the face of the moon down at sixty metres. My depth record was set and still stands today. Once older and wiser, getting really deep didn't appeal to me, but that dive will always be one of my best.

The DM training continued with me assisting on courses with Kirsty, Rob, and Martijn. It was my turn to act the goat while helping on a rescue course. It was great to see the instructors in action and I learned so much. It was great to learn techniques on how they helped students develop into competent divers. From watching students flapping around in confined water sessions to becoming confident in open water dive four was so rewarding and it felt great to be part of the students' experience. It's a special moment to open up the underwater world to people.

Next up, I completed the dive site-mapping pro-ject; Remi assigned me the dive site Ted's Point, which was one of my favourite places on the south shore. There was a small wreck on the sand and often, you could see spotted eagle rays cruising by and find stargazers buried in the sand. Sometimes there were seahorses on the reef. Art was never one of my strong points, but the effort counted and it was another box ticked in the quest to become a divemaster.

AFTER NEARLY THREE weeks of training, I was finally getting close to the finish line; the scuba skill circuit test was complete after finally getting my hover sorted out. I passed the boat supervisor part as well as the leading certified divers' element. There was just the equipment exchange or stress test to do.

They paired me up with Ben, who was a lot taller than I was, and we started to exchange the equipment. Remi kept throwing handfuls of sand into the water, so we were down to zero visibility. Our air was turned off at regular intervals, my BCD was off so I clung onto Ben's arm while we buddy breathed, we swapped jackets finally, and the rest was a piece of cake. Once we finished, we got back to the surface and it was hugs and high fives all around.

That was the final hurdle for the course; we were now certified DMs. It made me so proud to achieve something worthwhile and after flunking school this felt really good. As a traditional welcome to the world of professional diving, we then had to tackle the famous snorkel test in Tranquila Bar.

Snorkel Test

WE SAT ON the bar with a mask and snorkel that was attached to a funnel. Remi got everybody cheering us on before pouring a litre of alcohol into the funnel. You have to drink it without spilling any or throwing it back up. The amount of alcohol is chosen by your instructor and with me being a good drinker they put me to the test with rum, tequila, and sambuca mixed with coke.

I downed the lot, despite them adding a beer chas-er for good measure and the celebrations lasted until sunrise. I woke up around lunchtime with a massive hangover but still had the new divemaster glow about me.

THERE IS A time as a scuba diver when everything clicks into place, you become competent, and start to feel so relaxed while swimming along. You have your breathing technique down and your buoyancy control is so perfect. You get in close to tiny creatures like the cryptic tear drop crab without causing any damage to the reef.

It's funny as you are told never to hold your breath as a diver, but once you become comfortable, you realise it's not entirely true. Yes, it is hazardous to hold your breath while ascending quickly, but during dives, the less you breathe, the longer the dive. So, it's essential to get your breathing technique sorted early in your training. Once this is all worked out, you will feel a massive change in your mindset as a diver.

It took me around sixty dives to get into the zone; and you realise diving is genuinely one of the most relaxing activities you can do. There are no traffic jams down there, you can't hear your wife or girlfriend complaining about something, and there is no politician talking garbage, it is just you and the sound of your bubbles, looking at the beautiful marine life.

IT WAS TIME to gather my thoughts on the next move, my flight tickets from Chile to New Zealand plus a two-year work visa were still in my bag. The issue was life on Útila was tremendous, and already there was a sense of belonging. It was so much fun with my new friends, so a big decision was on the horizon.

After hanging around the shop for a few days, Remi asked if I wanted to start working as a DM for him. My mind took a millisecond to say yes, and now I was working in the dive industry. Part of my deal included accommodation; there was a shed-like room at the hotel; it had a bed, desk, fan, and a mosquito net. It had a shared bathroom and kitchen and there were a couple of resident rats that used to check on me at night. I was offered the room for free if I kept an eye on the accommodation at night.

To get a new job and a free garden shed on the same day was great. We discussed my salary for working at the dive shop; I would get paid a massive $10 for two morning dives, another $10 for afternoon dives, and night dives were $20. Apart from when I planted Christmas trees in Wales, this was the lowest-paid job ever, but there wasn't a care in the world as I was in paradise.

One time, there was a German couple staying with us and Remi told me I would be their divemaster; it was just us on the boat, so no back up from the experienced dive staff. I tried to look calm, but inside, I was shitting bricks! All kinds of thoughts were going through my head: What if I got lost? What happened if the dive was boring? What if I couldn't find anything?

The boat was loaded with tanks and safety equip-ment and we left the lagoon and headed under the bridge to the open water. Our dive site was Ron's wreck; I did the dive briefing, trying to sound like a true professional. We did our buddy checks and then descended and I said a silent prayer, "Please let me find some good stuff to make them happy."

Within a couple of minutes, a big green moray eel poked his head out of a hole, his mouth opened and closed with the needle-like teeth in full view. It felt like the pressure lifted from my shoulders in an instant. Confidence flowed from there and we crossed over the sand patch directly to a small wreck, where a couple of lobsters hid in the hull. On the way back along the reef, a turtle swam past much to the delight of my divers. The dive was coming to an end and we got up to safety stop level.

I looked for the dark shadow of the boat on the surface, where was it? I couldn't see it for what seemed like a lifetime, then, the dark shadow swung into view. Elation ripped through me; I had just completed my first guided dive; the divers had enjoyed it and they thanked me. It was the best $10 ever earned.

My confidence grew as I became more familiar with the sites and the fish, and the coral ID books by Paul Humann and Ned Deloach were so helpful. I studied them to sound as knowledgeable as possible. It wasn't just the fish identification it was about learning the habitat of where the fish and creatures lived.

AT A DEMA dive show a few years ago, I was lucky enough to meet Paul Humann, it was great talking to him, and I thanked him for the great work he had done over the years. I stopped short of asking for an autograph but was a massive fan.

The books quickly became my bible to the under-water world. It was so enjoyable spending time with my divers and going over our discoveries while filling out logbooks and signing them Kris Mears DM # 644115.

ONE DAY STUCK in my mind as a young DM; it was when someone gave me a nice tip for taking them diving.

Most guests were broke-ass backpackers who were too busy spending money on rum to give anything. I had been diving with a Honduran guy for a while and once we completed the dives, he shook my hand.

"Kris, it was great diving with you, thanks so much." He then put $50 in my hand. I hadn't even thought about getting tips, so was over the moon to get this extra money to add to my $10 salary.

THE NEXT COUPLE of months flew by; my logbook had just passed five hundred dives. The final validity day of my flight from Chile to New Zealand had arrived and it would be worthless in 24 hours. It was time to the make the final decision about my future. I had the paper ticket in my hand as the boat passed the Airport Caves dive site and I ripped the tickets up into small pieces. It was a symbolic gesture that cemented my decision to stay around for a while.

Seasick

MY TOURIST VISA was due to run out, so I had to pay the immigration officer to extend it. You slipped $50 inside your passport for his services. There were a couple of hundred people working on the island, so the little Spanish fellow was doing all right for himself. You could usually get a few extensions, but after a year you had to exit the country for at least a day before re-entering.

WHEN YOU'RE LIVING in a small space, sometimes the dreaded island fever hits you. Every little problem seems magnified and when it hits, you have to get off the rock for a few days to recover mentally. People escaped to La Ceiba and the rule was if you went you had to bring Pizza Hut pizzas back for everyone in the dive shop.

On one visit, I gorged myself on so much fast food that I probably smashed over 4,000 calories in a few hours. I got the last boat back, feeling like a stuffed pig. A group of girls were keen to dive with us and I was chatting with them, giving the sales pitch that we were the best shop with the best boats, and the best part was getting to dive with a handsome Welshman.

The girls were hooked and were coming with me.

The sea got a little rough on the journey home and beads of sweat formed on my forehead. All of a sudden, without notice, I projectile vomited 4,000 calories of junk food all over the floor in front of me; you could see chunks of KFC and a mountain of soggy fried rice on the floor. I wished the sea could have swallowed me up, a hundred eyes stared at me, and there were some sniggers of laughter. One of the boat crew helped me to clean up the mess; a shovel would have been useful for the mountain of rice. I didn't know where to look as we got to the dock and I tried to play it cool with the four girls. Luckily none of my vomit had touched them, and they still decided to dive with us.

I did not realise it, but I was about to become good friends with another guy called Steve, who was working with a conservation group on the island. They had some great projects such as a conch farm and tried to help the locals with sustainable fishing practices. The seagrass expert Sharon was nice and always used a dive flag while studying the seagrass and the motorboat captain, Heather, was one of the most helpful, and caring people I had ever met. One-night Steve was at the bar, so I introduced myself to him.

He said: "Yeah, I know you, I saw you puke all over the ferry a few days ago."

IT WAS STRAIGHTFORWARD getting into the massive drinking culture on the island. The dive shop always had a fridge full of cold beer, which we emptied frequently. There was always an occasion to go out and party – it was someone's last night, someone's birthday, someone's snorkel test, or Wednesday or Friday night at Bar in the Bush. It was never-ending but so much fun. I wondered how many bottles of Flor de Caña rum we drank and how many bottles of Salva Vida or Port Royal beer we got through during my time on the rock.

It got to the stage where if we were sober in the morning, then something was seriously wrong. Sometimes, we only got a couple of hours' sleep before going to load the boat. Places like Bar in Bush regularly carried on until the early hours and then it was back to someone's house. The best parties there were on a Wednesday and whenever Coco Loco did an all-nighter.

Johnny was the owner of Bar Bush and played good techno music; it was just like 1999 again. There were always plenty of supplements flying around and they had nitrous oxide balloons or laughing gas. Quite often you would see people rolling around on the floor after a nitrous hit.

Coco Loco bar was right on the waterfront; the toilets weren't the best so people used to pee in the sea. One night, I needed the little boy's room, so walked to the edge of the dock and not realising, as it was dark, that they had removed some of the wooden flooring planks, I walked straight off the edge into the water. My body was submerged in diluted backpacker urine and my phone was destroyed in my pocket. I scrambled out of the water and climbed back onto the dock.

This guy looked at me, "Dude that was one of the

funniest things I have ever seen in my life."

"Well I'm glad you enjoyed it," I replied. I should have called it a night, but went back to my place had a quick shower and returned to the party.

ANOTHER NIGHT AT Coco Loco was quality; they had a couple of DJs playing and some fire dancers added to the atmosphere. It was already past 3 am and it was getting wobbly. One of the fire dancers had just finished performing and I was thirsty, so I picked up a water bottle from the table. I took a massive gulp, but it wasn't water. It was the kerosene the fire dancers use to light up their equipment. I swallowed some of the disgusting fluid but managed to spit the rest of it out. It was time to call it a night and head back home. I was tempted to see if I could breathe fire, but I thought it would only end in tears and the removal of my eyebrows.

Sun Jam

THE BIGGEST PARTY in Útila happened once a year. Sun Jam was a spectacular event held on the small Cays during the first weekend in August. Thousands of people travelled from all over to enjoy some pure party pleasure. Alfred was the main organiser and he brought in some top DJs from across the globe.

The party started in the early afternoon and went on until sunrise and beyond ... into the next day. After that it was straight back to Coco Loco for an after-party that finished up at dawn the next day. It was absolute bedlam but such a great event.

Most of the dive shops closed for two days as everybody wanted to party. A flotilla of boats transported the ravers to the island and not long after, everybody was dancing on the sand, and the techno beats filled the air. As the sun went down the lasers fired up, the party got better and better, we danced on the sand and I got deeper and deeper as the music took hold. People were having the time of their lives; the fishermen on the Cays got no sleep during the night for sure. As the sun came up, plenty of people looked a little worse for wear and there was a queue trying to get a boat off the island to recover. Others, still off their faces splashed around in the sea, dancing to the music in their heads.

The first Sun Jam was tip-top, because my old travel buddy Michiel showed up for the party. He reminds me of a Dutch version of Zed from the movie Police Academy, the one who had a meltdown over a broken Mickey Mouse watch. He was already a certified diver so it was great to dive with him.

After one dive, we were discussing some of the fish we had seen. He said, "Kris what was the small flat bluefish all swimming together?"

After having a quick look in the fish book, I said, "Those were surgeonfish mate."

He looked back at me and replied, "Surgeonfish ... they look more like fucking moron fish to me; the way they swim is not natural." He had a way with words that could stop you in your tracks.

The morning after the Coco Loco after-party, we returned to work. Everyone was in such a mess as we crawled into the dive shop. People wanted to do scuba refresher courses and some fun dives and I had to gather all of my strength after not sleeping for a few days. It was the longest working day of my life.

I wanted to keep it simple, so I chose Moon Hole to dive as it's easy to navigate. At the end of the dive I signalled we had to do the safety stop. As we hit the surface, I did a quick headcount and realised my Chinese guest had disappeared; he was already getting low on air, so I was very concerned about him. Looking all over the reef below, we couldn't see any trace of the guy. After two days without any sleep, my mind started to get paranoid the guy was already dead, and it was my fault.

The other divers helped me look for him on the

surface and after a few minutes of frantic searching he came back to the surface. Losing my cool I ripped into him and told him that he should never go back down once we have surfaced. He was so apologetic and didn't realise he had done wrong. After calming down, I was so happy he wasn't dead. We got back to the dive shop on our last legs; we had all just about survived the comedown day after the Sun Jam weekend.

THERE WERE CHANGES at the dive shop, because Kirsty and Remi had decided to move on. It was a sad time to see them go; they will always have a massive place in my heart, because they were the ones who got everything started for me.

Kate took over the management of the shop; she was a great girl, very tall and softly spoken but could party harder than most. She lived in a beautiful house on the waterfront owned by an English guy call Rob and his dog, Tosspot. He had a liking for skulls and had both dolphin and pilot whales in his collection. Martijn, Tomas, Courtney and Megan, and other trainee DMs stayed there and we spent many nights on the deck enjoying the breeze and a few Flor De Cana's.

ONE DAY, KATE told me a couple of girls wanted to do the Open Water Course. They were in contact via email, but the communication stopped suddenly. We thought they had changed their mind, but later they turned up out of the blue.

We asked what happened to the emails and their answer left everybody in the shop speechless. The girls had planned to confirm everything with us once they arrived in La Ceiba, unfortunately when they arrived at a cheap hotel the situation had changed dramatically. They had walked into the hotel and seen two dead guys on the floor, full of bullet holes with blood splattered on the walls. The police were clearing up an attempted armed robbery at the hotel.

The girls were in total shock at what happened, but incredibly the hotel staff were calm and said to the girls, "Don't worry this mess will be cleaned up in no time, your room is ready to check-in."

If this had been me, I would have left within sec-onds, but because the girls were in total shock, they took the room. They checked in as the blood was mopped up from the floor and they hid in the room for the night and didn't leave. They found out the two dead guys had tried to rob the place. The hotel staff had refused to give them any money, so one guy got shot in the shoulder. What the bandits didn't know was an off-duty policeman was upstairs in one of the rooms. He had heard the gunshot and went to investigate and once he saw the situation, he killed the two robbers.

As the day went on the girls said the policeman was still in his room getting drunk and celebrating the fact he had pumped two criminals full of lead. The final twist was later that evening, when some family members of the deceased came to the hotel to see what had happened. There was a confrontation between the policeman and them.

The poor girls had had a day from hell and didn't

get a chance to confirm their visit with us. Once they arrived, they told us this incredible story. They were still shaking and we listened with our jaws dangling. Once the girls had got over the trauma, they both passed the Open Water Course and had a great time with us. I'm pretty sure they didn't stay in La Ceiba on their return to the mainland.

I WAS APPROACHING one thousand dives and my first Christmas on the island. Martin and Helen were some of my best friends from my schooldays and they came to visit.

Before leaving the UK, I had been seeing a nice girl for a while and she also arrived; we had decided to keep in touch and have an open mind about the future. The problem was now I had no plans to return home, it put us in an awkward position. The writing was on the wall when she came on the dive boat with Martin and Helen. They were getting their Open Water Certificate, and I got to assist on the course. She had no real interest in diving, so the rest of the vacation was strained. When they left the island to go back to Wales, we quickly realised it wasn't going to happen for us. We have remained friends to this day and she has a great life out in Australia.

Pelagic Action

ÚTILA IS PART of the migration route for whale sharks. The world's biggest fish travel from Honduras past Belize and up to the Gulf of Mexico. There were no spotter planes searching as there were in Western Australia, it was up to the boat captain's eyes to find them.

The boat would take us a couple of miles offshore looking for signs of activity. The search area was massive and sometimes we looked for a few hours not seeing anything. When the stars aligned and they showed up, it was very exciting for all onboard. The search began off Turtle Harbor then either headed west towards the Cays or east to Black Hills Sea-mount.

The captain scanned the sky for seabirds; once spotted they could lead to schools of tuna. The tuna pushed the food towards the surface which created a boiling effect, the birds would then dive-bomb into the sea and feed, with the tuna, on small fish and plank-ton. This created a feeding frenzy and underneath all of this action, the whale sharks waited for the right time. They headed for the surface with their mouths wide open and gulped down the tiny creatures. They fed horizontally or vertically depending on the situation and sometimes they would stay for a long time, depending on how many people were around them.

Rules were put in place to help protect the sharks, with only ten people max per group. They had to stay at least three metres away from the sharks and were not allowed to swim in front of them. Once the group had a few minutes with the sharks, then the next boat would drop in. Some of the boat captains didn't care, dropping people right on top of the sharks. This action was infuriating as it usually scared the sharks away.

In four years on Útila, I was lucky enough to swim maybe two hundred times with whale sharks. It was something that never grew old. You saw the same whale shark on occasion; Old Tom was around eighteen metres in size and probably the most famous. One of the dive centres even named a boat after him.

Being out in the deep blue looking for pelagic species was great. I would stand on the bow of the boat bouncing with the waves, looking for the giants. Fishermen would also take advantage as tuna were an easy catch. Boats would see the water boiling and drop lines; and they caught handfuls of fish in seconds.

We did not just see whale sharks on surface inter-vals; often there were vast schools of Spinner dolphins, and they usually allowed us to swim with them. Sometimes the pods numbered around two hundred dolphins; the sleek grey bodies sliced through the water, making small white caps. These graceful mammals leapt out of the water spinning through the air before crashing onto the surface. If you could score them you would give them ten every time.

They were a little shyer if they had babies, we could observe them from the boat, but they didn't come close enough for us to swim with them.

On a few occasions, we encountered pilot whales and one spectacular day we hit the trifecta. We saw a couple of whale sharks off Black Hills; we were the only boat out so watched endless jumps. The whale sharks didn't care because there were just a few of us in the water so the interactions were immense. We thought the day couldn't get any better, but then a pod of pilot whales showed up. They were around five metres long and a slick charcoal colour.

The boat approached slowly; they seemed relaxed, so we slipped into the water. I couldn't believe my eyes as five pilot whales swam around me. There were a couple of calves about a metre long and one of the adults came within metres of me. I will never forget looking into the giant's eye with its soft wrinkles underneath. What a buzz! I watched him slowly swim past me, we shared a moment, and it was awesome. We spent another hour with the pilot whales and it was turning into one of the best days of my life. On the way back to base, we saw a pod of dolphins thrown in for good measure. The experience was fantastic and never happened again. Our guests were over the moon and felt lucky to experience a day like that.

Later, I watched a video of a pilot whale grabbing a swimmer by her leg before taking her down to a hundred feet and then releasing her. They managed to save her life by doing CPR on the boat; she was fortunate to survive. When I had that eye contact with the whale, I wonder if he was thinking: shall I grab this fat little man and drag him to the bottom?

On another search, we had already spent hours seeing nothing and there were no sharks around, but then I spotted something floating on the surface. Captain Kerry wanted to check it out; we thought it might be cocaine or cash from the Cali cartel. As we got closer, we realised it was a fridge that had been floating around for some time as it was covered in barnacles. The sea was so clear and we saw some dolphin fish swimming in circles below it. A few of us jumped in the water watching them for a while and then we noticed a silky shark was below them. It wasn't massive, probably close to three metres, but we weren't too familiar with silky sharks so got a little worried about what else lurked around us. My heart skipped a beat, because when I looked again, there was a much larger shark with a rounded dorsal fin splashed with white. It was an oceanic whitetip.

Paul Humann's book considers it dangerous to humans so we all quickly returned to the boat. I already had eyes on a diver that would be sacrificed if the shark got aggressive! It was another great adven-ture in the deep blue; there wasn't a better place in the world to spend surface intervals.

Level Up

SOME PEOPLE STARTED their Instructor Course straight after becoming a divemaster. For me it felt better to gain experience as a DM first. I had a thousand dives under my belt before I even considered the Instructor Development Course. There were plenty of people that went from zero to hero in a short space of time; it irritated me sometimes that dive agencies could call someone an instructor with just a hundred dives to their name.

There were more shop departures, so a door opened and I was offered a position as an instructor if I passed the course. A couple of the bigger dive shops held large classes every month with as many as twenty students. That class size didn't feel comforta-ble to me, so I signed up with Phil at Deep Blue. Phil is a proper Aussie from Melbourne, no messing around and straight to the point. We had got to know each other at Trancs … spending many a sunset together. The course cost $2,000 in total, so the $10 salary wasn't going to cut it. I had to bash the credit card for the rest and pay for it over time.

Mike from San Francisco would be my classmate. He was a lanky guy who ran like a Welshman, he was a good laugh to be around and also did some tech diving and we ended up working together later on. We had ten preparation days for the Instructor Examinations (IE); we also completed the Emergency First Responder Instructor Course, which cost a few more dollars. I put another dollar in and hoped it would be worth it. Everything was going well with the training; Phil was a great educator and drilled us the entire time. The open water and confined training went swimmingly and we were looking ready for the big day. Towards the end of our training, we spent extra time on the exams. The work was worth it and we passed all the mock exams.

On the last day, Phil told us we'd have an easy day, so we should go and have a few beers! After being sober for ten days, I did have a few beers, the dreaded flavour hit me, and before I knew it was 5 am and I was well and truly off the wagon.

I crawled in at midday and tried to hide the fact I was hungover as shit. I took the exams quickly and failed all of them. Phil was deeply concerned as he had a 100% exam success rate and didn't want a drunken dick messing that up. He called me a 'fucken idiot', which was fair enough and made me come in the next day to re-sit them. Because I was sober, I passed them with flying colours. Phil called me an idiot again but said we were ready for the IE the next day.

My nerves were still jangling as I went in for the written exams. Even though I had spent hours and hours practising, I didn't want to fail. I worked harder for the Instructor Course than my school exams. They took place in a classroom at The Mango Inn Resort. We spent the whole afternoon up there and there were around twenty people in different groups. The problem was if you failed the written exams, you couldn't pass the course and would have to come back again at the next IE.

While I worked through the questions, I had a nagging feeling I had screwed up. Once the time was up, they began to mark the papers. Sitting there for what felt like a lifetime was nail-biting stuff. They called people up individually and you could see them shake the candidate's hand, although you couldn't hear what they were saying. My palms were sweating badly, and I thought: "Hurry up and put me out of my misery you shit."

Then finally, the examiner called me forward. "Congratulations Kristian we will see you for the open water session tomorrow."

I let it sink in for a few moments. "Are you sure?" I mumbled.

"Yes, you passed. We'll see you tomorrow." Walking out of the classroom, I jumped up and
punched the air. I was buzzing and hadn't felt this good since Scott Young scored for Cardiff V Leeds in 2002. Mike also passed the theory, so Phil was pleased with us. We just had to pass the open water session tomorrow, and we would be dive instructors. We went to Trancs for a beer, this time only having the one before going home like good boys.

The next day, we headed out to the Jack Neil dive site to complete the open water examination. Every-thing went well, and we passed with flying colours. It was a massive relief and I thought I had achieved something worthwhile in my life. The adrenalin pumped around my body. Out of the twenty or so candidates, three didn't pass and would have to come back next time.

After posing for group photos, it was time to cele-brate. We went back to see Phil; he was happy his 100% pass rate was still intact. I was on cloud nine and celebrated for three days straight. There was a party at Treetanic and the event was made even better by Rob who was working behind the bar wearing a bikini … he didn't even bother to shave his bikini line. The rum flowed for the next few days, and it all got hazy, but I grinned because I was now Kristian Mears #644115 OWSI.

A Legend Departs

THE TIME HAD come for one of the legends of Útila to leave the island. My good friend Rob had decided to take a job in Turks and Caicos.

We were all gutted to see him go because he was the life of the party. Rob's family were regulars to the island, Lizzie had been around for over a year already, and their parents, Elly and David, came over a few times a year. It was awesome when they came as they brought suitcases full of food from the UK, things like Marmite, Branston Pickle, and items we had no chance of getting in Honduras. Lizzie was also a dive instructor and mum and dad did their DM course with us. They are some of the nicest people I have ever met and they always made me feel like part of the family when we were together.

There were a few reasons why Rob had legendary status on Útila. The first reason was that he managed to break his back while jumping off the roof, drunk, in Coco Loco. This was before my time, but many people told me about it. The full story was told by the most famous doctor on Útila, Dr. John, who did my DM medical. He asked me to cough while holding my eggs and he told me his first-hand account of what happened that night.

Rob is about six feet tall with long curly hair, he is a mixture of the honey monster and Chewbacca, and his booming laugh can be heard a mile away. He literally knew everybody on the island and walking down the street took a long time as everyone would say hello to him. He was a great dive instructor and helped me immensely and I helped him to become extra famous, with our antics one night.

We were already pretty wasted when we bumped into these older ladies at the bar, some might call them cougars. They were staying at one of the higher-end resorts and we started to drink with them, and things got out of hand. It was apparent the ladies wanted to know us better and after a few more rums they were turning into supermodels. They were quite old supermodels though with a combined age of a hundred. Being so wasted we didn't care anymore and our friends were egging us on and sniggering.

We got to the resort, and one of the ladies was shy about us all staying in the same room. Rob wanted to toss a coin to see who would stay; I didn't fancy going back to the shed, so he kindly agreed to go back to his place. I can't really remember much of what hap-pened, but on waking up there was an empty bottle of hair conditioner next to the bed. I don't remember washing my hair.

Gossip travels very fast on a small island. On mak-ing the walk of shame back home, I got to the crossroads and some of the local boat captains saw me. They all burst out laughing and started calling me a granny shagger. They gave me tons of abuse as I quickened my walk home. It was the same on getting to the dive shop, everybody gave it the big one, laughing and cheering at us. Lizzie cracked up, telling me how she found Rob in the shower with the other old bird and she was washing his feet. We never lived down that night and were ribbed by the whole island for the next couple of months. We had joined the 100 club, and were very proud of it. Even the boss got wind of the story and congratulated us on our success.

After Rob moved away, Lizzie asked me to move in with her. It was emotional saying goodbye to my shed as I was on first-name terms with the crabs and rats, but it was time to move on. It was great living with Lizzie and we got on really well. The house was next door to work and was owned by a local couple called Fred and Betty. Fred was a well-known spearfisherman and a diving icon on the island.

Lizzie managed the Treetanic bar, which is one of the wackiest bars in the world. It's a treetop bar with handmade mosaic features all around the place. If you took a bunch of mushrooms and walked around, then you would have a blast. We spent many a night drinking in that bar and there was a great group of people.

Annie, Nat and Sasha worked with Lizzie. These guys partied so hard I don't know how they survived. Annie and Lizzie soon got the nicknames Annie Winehouse and Lizzie Lohan. It was wild up there and some nights it felt like the treehouse was going to fall down it was rocking so much.

The other main characters at that time were Rich, Adam, Sarah, Gypsy Jenn, Kate the Great and Grey Chris. They ran another dive shop in town. Adam was amazing with his knowledge of marine life and he taught me a lot during his fish talks. Grey Chris was a real genuine guy and was still proud he got an allowance from his parents even though he was in his forties. Our paths would cross in both Indonesia and Thailand after we left Útila. He sadly passed away a few years ago while starting a new dive venture in Sulawesi and his death hit all of our friends really hard. He was a top fella and even to this day, when I see his picture pop up, I get a lump in my throat, but I always remember the good times we had around the world.

My favourite memory of Grey Chris happened while we were doing some freelance work. We were at Little Bight dive site and we had a couple of Discover Scuba students, two girls from Scandinavia. They were terrified and had real trouble doing the skills near the beach. The east wind picked up, the waves were getting bigger, and after an hour they still were struggling in the waves. All of a sudden, a big wave hit them and washed them up on the beach, and they landed on the sand with their fins up in the air. It was getting comical and I chuckled to myself while watching from the boat. Grey Chris never gave up though and finished the course.

When he got them back on the boat, I said, "Fair play mate, you had your hands full there."
He looked at me. "They tried to quit a couple of times but if you think I'm coming out and not getting paid you're wrong."
His attitude was terrific.

Scuba Poo Explained

THAT SAME DAY also sticks in my mind for another reason.

I was diving with two girls who were a bit less problematic than Chris's divers were. After our first dive, we were enjoying our surface interval, when all of a sudden, my stomach cramped up. There was no holding back from this; I needed to use the little boy's room very soon. We were on a speedboat, so there was no head and there was only one option left. It was time to take a scuba poo. If you find this subject not to your taste, then kindly skip to the next page.

There is a technique to the scuba poo that should be explained. I made an excuse to my divers that something had dropped out of my BCD pocket. My stomach growled at me again, so I jumped into the water, dropping down to twelve-metres deep. While diving, I only wear board shorts and a rash guard, so wearing this type of exposure protection makes it easier to complete the task. I had a quick look around, making sure no other divers were heading my way, and it was all clear. Now here is the technical part; it's essential to test the water, because the softer it is, the messier it can be. If you had a curry the night before you could be in grave danger, so don't push too hard at the start is my top tip. If you push too hard and it's a runny one, then you can be heading for disaster. It's essential to check which way the current is moving as you might get it all blown back over you.

After testing the water, it was luckily a hard one. Now here is my second tip, once you have snapped off a section, it is vital to move forward quickly. You do this because if it's a floater, there's a chance it could drift up under the back of your BCD. Just imagine if you got back on the boat, and the section dropped on the floor from under your BCD. You would want the sea to swallow you up right? I was over the moon to see it fall onto the sand and not up into my BCD. After dodging that bullet, I was happy with a job well executed.

After pulling up my board shorts, I noticed a sea-horse just a few feet away from my business. He was a beautiful seahorse and I thought to myself that my divers would love it, so I cleaned my hands in the sand and made my way back to the boat. I made a visual reference of the area so I could return to the same spot. After getting back, I told the girls about my find and I asked them if they wanted to see a seahorse and they got very excited.

We changed tanks and back rolled into the water. Using my excellent natural navigation skills, we got to the area. I could see my impressive log resting on the sand, and there was a surgeonfish taking a nibble. Next to my business was the beautiful seahorse. I brought the two divers closer to have a look at the seahorse and I was hoping and praying they wouldn't put their hands in the wrong place. After a few moments of admiring the hippocampus, it was time to move on. The girls were so happy to see a seahorse for the first time, and I was delighted to use my textbook visual reference navigation skills to find it.

I hope you found this section helpful ... if you ever have to take a scuba poo; you have the knowledge to do it successfully.

IT TOOK A few days for my instructor's teaching status to come through. Things were looking up; I was living in a real house and earning more money now as an instructor. While waiting for students to show up I still worked as a divemaster, and there was an added income for filling nitrox tanks for my boss's resort. That was good money getting paid a dollar for each tank and if the resort was busy, I would fill up to seventy-five tanks a day. It was long hours but really worth it.

My teaching status was confirmed and I had a nice easy start as an instructor with one female student. I decided it was best not to mention that she was my first, as I didn't want her to feel any extra nerves. The course went like a dream and it felt terrific to teach somebody a new skill. When you have your student's attention, and they listen to everything you say, it makes you feel so proud. It made me appreciate what great jobs schoolteachers do and it also made me think of my terrible and disruptive behaviour while in school.

Mrs. Ashton, Mrs. Trott, and Mrs. Keenan, I'm sorry for making your life difficult. As an educator, I truly understand you need to be listened to ... it was a valuable lesson to learn.

The course with the young lady went well, it was great to see her progress into a diver, and each day she improved and nailed the skills. On open water 4, she looked like a pro underwater, she breezed the final exam, and was delighted to become a diver. She gave me the biggest hug at the end and I was like a hero in her eyes. It was a nice feeling to get off the mark as a dive instructor.

IT'S A LOT of fun teaching the Advanced Open Water Course. The deep training dive included skills which showed how the colour red disappeared at depth and the narcosis tests gave the chance to mess around with your students' heads.

Before the dive, there was a quick visit to Bushes supermarket, where I would purchase one small tomato and another larger one. During the briefing we would talk about pressure at depth and the effect it has on you. At this time, I would show the students the larger tomato, keeping a straight face.

"Take a look at this tomato; you will not believe what the pressure at thirty metres does to it."

I would place the tomato in the students' hands so they had a good feel of the size, and once we were at thirty metres, we would look at the colour chart and see how the red had faded away. We would do some simple timed maths test to see if the brain worked slower down there. Then it would be time for my party trick. I would write on my dive slate: 'Do you remember the size of the tomato?'

The students would nod at me, so I'd reach into my pocket and take out the much smaller tomato and place it in their hands. Acting astonished underwater, I would write again on the slate: 'Can you believe the tomato is nearly 50% smaller at depth?'

Ninety per cent of the time the students would nod back at me with much excitement in their eyes. Once I knew they had become my latest victims, I would pull out the larger tomato from my other BCD pocket and place it in their hands. They would look puzzled for a while before they finally worked out what had happened. We would have a good laugh underwater about it but I always made sure that the note: 'I really thought a tomato changed shape underwater at depth' was written in the logbook.

THE COURSES CAME thick and fast over the coming months and I reached fifty certs in no time. The money I had earned had already paid back the cost of the course, so it was an excellent investment. The shop was busy, we had new trainee divemaster's, and some people made a return to the island.

Al was a nice guy from the UK, and butter wouldn't melt in his mouth. We would end up working together for a couple of years. Another Welsh nutter showed up ... Dan was from Porthcawl so not far from me and it was nice talking about home. He used to be in the army, so he was used to doing crazy shit. Once intoxicated with rum and lemon drops, he would show us his party piece, introducing every-body to his close friend Brian the snail. Dan would somehow turn his dick inside out and twist it around, so it resembled a snail. He was happy to show everybody in the bar who was interested in seeing it.

Jeff, the Canadian hockey hooligan rocked up along with a guy called Rimas who has an interesting nickname of Rim job. Jon and Chiara also came from Canada. Ohad and Roi came from Israel. Ohad told me the only reason he wanted to become a DM was also to be a muff master. Roi had an obsession with the English word twat, he was annoyed that he couldn't pronounce as well as me. Good times were ahead and now it was my turn to help them become divemaster's.

Bluebirds

MY OTHER PASSION outside of travelling and diving is football. I had watched Cardiff City since my early teens and apart from spending time with friends and family, it was the only thing I missed from home.

Cardiff had been a mediocre team for decades, spending most of the time in the lower divisions with minimal crowds at the games. Things changed when Sam Hamman pumped millions of pounds into the club and they slowly started to rise up the divisions. When in Australia I missed the league one play-off final. The final was held in the Millennium Stadium in Cardiff as they were rebuilding Wembley Stadium. All my friends went to the game while I was stuck in the Australian Outback with hardly any Internet. Cardiff won the game 1-0 against QPR, and I was gutted to miss the occasion.

In 2008, Cardiff went on a run in the FA Cup, which is the oldest and most famous cup competition in the world. It gives the smaller teams a chance to play against the big guns like Man Utd, Chelsea, and Liverpool. It is not very often that teams from lower leagues got far in the competition. It is the luck of the draw and Cardiff had a couple of easy games in the early rounds that year. They beat Wolves at home, and suddenly they were in the quarter-final, and had to play Middlesboro, which was a Premier League team at the time.

I couldn't believe my luck as they showed the game on TV in Honduras. I watched it at my friend's house, and Cardiff upset the odds winning 0-2 with Peter Whittingham scoring a peach. It was one of the biggest upsets in the cup that year and meant that Cardiff was going to play at Wembley Stadium in the semi-final. It was the first time Cardiff had played there since they won the FA Cup in 1927.

It's every fan's dream to see their team play at Wembley and I wanted to be there, so I bought a flight ticket and made my first trip home for nearly three years. Spending ten days at home, catching up with friends and family was great and my friend Gareth got me a ticket. It was the best £60 ever spent.

Our opponents that day were Barnsley another underdog team. They had a great run to the semis beating Liverpool and Chelsea. It was such a great day and everything I hoped for … the atmosphere was electric and the Stella Artois was going down well. I took my seat at Wembley Stadium and my whole body buzzed with excitement. I sat with the same old friends that I had sat with at Ninian Park before I started to travel the world.

The game was a tight affair with not many chances and local hero Joe Ledley ended up scoring the winning goal for Cardiff in the eighth minute. That is still one of my favourite ever Cardiff goals. He used a great technique to hook a shot from the edge of the area, the ball flew past the keeper, and we erupted with joy. What a feeling it was to see your team score the first goal at Wembley for nearly eighty years. The game went on, Barnsley missed a great chance to level the game, their forward was one on one with our keeper, and he put the ball into the side netting. When the final whistle blew, we celebrated wildly, Cardiff was somehow in the FA Cup final.

Straight after the final whistle, my friends started to tease me about coming back again for the final a month later. It was the only thought in my mind as I flew back across the Atlantic Ocean.

After arriving safely back on Útila I quickly ar-ranged with Kate to take five days off to go back for the FA Cup final. She saw what it meant to me and Mr. Mastercard was very helpful in letting me book another set of flights in a few weeks.

Tickets for the game were like gold dust and none of my friends could get me a ticket as they were all going. Things started to get desperate, so I contacted the national newspaper of Wales for help. They ran a story about how I travelled 20,000 miles to watch a couple of matches in quick succession and within a few days of the article, Cardiff City contacted me and told me they had a ticket for me.

The club chairman Peter Ridsdale was quoted as saying, "We are delighted to help out the lad with a ticket ... to travel so far really shows what great support we have."

I ARRIVED BACK in London on the Friday evening before the match and crashed at Martin's place, ready for the big game. The next morning came around so fast and there was no time for tiredness or jetlag. Our opponents were Portsmouth, a Premier League team, that had beaten Man Utd in the quarter-final and West Brom in the semi-final. They were the clear favourites to win the cup.

We had a few beers in London before the game. The atmosphere was building up nicely in the walk up to Wembley Stadium, nearly 90,000 fans would be in the stadium, and the match would be watched worldwide by millions of people. After walking up the steps I had my first view of the pitch and my legs turned to jelly. I sat in my seat, the emotion of the national anthems ripped through me, and the roar of the fans got louder and louder. Flags were waved in a frenzy and the pitch was cleared of all the pomp and bluster. The referee tossed the coin, and soon, the whistle was in his mouth, ready to go.

The game was another tight affair and I'm sure, apart from Cardiff and Portsmouth fans, that the 2008 FA Cup final didn't linger long in the memory. Cardiff were a match for Portsmouth on the day but lost to a soft goal from Kanu following a mistake from the Cardiff goalkeeper. Once the final whistle blew, I just remember standing there feeling really numb. No tears came to my eyes, which was strange as it was such a big day. It was disappointing we couldn't take our chance to win the cup, but on the other hand, my bucket list had got a little shorter as I had watched Cardiff play an FA Cup final at Wembley Stadium. It would be extraordinary if Cardiff got there again in my lifetime.

On the Sunday, I managed to go and meet up with Lizzie and Sasha near Highbury. It was supposed to be a quick couple of drink, but of course it got out of hand. The tequila came out and I passed out at their place. My flight back to Honduras was lunchtime on Monday, but my bags and passport were still at Martin's home. With a stinking hangover kicking in I didn't fancy using the Tube to get back to Ilford, so I grabbed a cab. It took nearly an hour to get to his place, the driver waited for me to grab my bags, and I headed straight for Heathrow.

The M25 was totally blocked with traffic, the minutes ticked by, and the meter got higher and higher. I was very close to missing my flight, but we got to the terminal with ten minutes to spare. The ride cost me a £140, which was more expensive than the cup final ticket.

Puffing and panting I slapped my passport on the check-in desk and said, "You would not believe what kind of weekend it has been."

The tequila residue made me sleep the whole way back to Honduras and the entire weekend seemed like a surreal experience.

It was great to get back and start diving again. Great news from my boss greeted my arrival, as he wanted me to work at his dive resort. This meant getting a pay rise and leading groups of divers ... mostly from the States. The majority of American divers are exceptionally generous with tips at the end of the week, so things took another turn for the better.

The resort was about ten minutes' bike ride from home. It was always a nice ride in the morning, and with Daft Punk blasting on my headphones, it put me in an excellent mood for the day. You could still see some casualties from the shenanigans the night before looking worse for wear on the way home some mornings.

The resort was separated from town by a dark chocolate coloured lagoon with mangroves making a protective home for many juvenile fish species. It was a couple of minutes' boat ride across to the beautiful resort, where cosy cabins faced the lagoon with back porches and hammocks to relax in after diving. The vast swimming pool had a whale shark mosaic crafted into the tiles. The small beach faced the east wind, so the breeze took the sting out of the sun, and palm trees created a haven to hang hammocks with the added danger of your life ending from a stray coconut. The dock looked great at night with lights attracting eagle rays and large tarpon and from above, it looked a picture-perfect exotic dive resort.

No See Ums

THE ONLY ISSUE here were the sand flies. My God these things were everywhere and were a major problem for the guests. These tiny terrors or 'no see ums' lived in their own paradise with plenty of juicy white bodies to feast on. They were on an all-inclusive package and on their eighth plate already.

Guests were attacked so badly, their legs and arms got covered in welts, some of which got infected. Conventional bug spray was no match for these guys, they just laughed at you for even trying something so weak. The best solution was to cover yourself in baby oil, because they would land in the oil slick and drown before they took a nibble on you.

Most of the resort staff were already my friends. The dive shop was managed by seven-foot Angie, who could have beaten the shit out of me anytime, but was always fun to work with. Her fella was Brookes a part owner of the Tranquila Bar.

Once at the resort we loaded the boat with tanks. This was a great workout each morning, because we loaded up to forty tanks, which were stored about a hundred feet away from the boat. After a couple of months, I felt in great shape and my breasts had dropped down from a D to a C cup.

THE RESORT HAD great local captains and the oldest and most grumpy of them, was Waggy. It took time for you to gain his respect, but once you had it, he was good as gold.

The best times were working with Captain Kerry aka Sweet Sweet. He was born and bred on the Cays so he was different to the Utilians. He reminded me of a soft and cuddly Care Bear and he made the guests feel welcome, nobody had a bad word to say about him. During our surface time we often stopped at his mum's place on the Cay, she baked some fantastic cakes and cinnamon rolls that were devoured very quickly by the guests.

Susan's Fish Burgers was an institution on the Cay. It was a good hang out for your surface interval and you could get a fish burger and fries for a couple of bucks. It was always interesting to visit the Cays, because you would watch the salty fishermen bringing in the day's catch, their hands torn up by years of using hand lines. There was a pretty hefty population for a tiny island that you could walk around in five minutes and there were quaint churches and a small school. It really was a unique place, with the majority of residents being of Europe-an descent. It was great listening to the locals chatting, and their dialect was somewhere between Jar Jar Binks from Star Wars and Captain Hook.

Working at the resort meant I had less time to spend drinking myself to death with those young backpacker scoundrels. With groups we did three-day dives each day, plus two-night dives during the week, so it was pretty full-on. The dives racked up quickly and at the end of the week, it was nice to have a day out of the water to let your ears dry out. After a hard day's exercise of loading the tanks and diving three or four times, the last thing you needed was a belly full of rum, and being tucked up in bed early felt really weird but refreshing.

Most of the guests were American, apart from a couple of knob jockeys and it was nice spending time with them. America has always fascinated me, and I got the chance to learn about the different states and make friendships that would last many years. It was fun learning how to pick out accents from Texas and the southern states. One guy Larry told me the reason they called a toothbrush a 'tooth brush' was that red necks only had one tooth to clean! The brash Yankees would come down from New York and give it the big one, and then we would have some far-out people from California, who were so laid-back they could fall over.

There was a lot of diversity, so it was fascinating to meet people from different walks of life. There was one Chinese lady that stayed with us and I did a course for her. While having lunch we got talking about the cuisine in China. She informed me with a straight face, "The only thing with wings a Chinese person won't eat is an aeroplane, and the only thing with legs they won't eat is a table."

After work, we would jump on the speedboat to cross back to town. On one occasion, the driver had the engine in full throttle and he was messing around and not really paying attention. There were always sailboats anchored in the lagoon as it was calm and he was messing around jabbering in Spanish, and getting closer to a sailboat. He waited until the last second before swerving to miss the boat. As he went around the boat, he did not realise that another boat was anchored very close behind it. Everything from there went into slow motion; the guy didn't have a chance to slow down as it was directly in front of us.

Just before the impact, resort manager, Matias, and the driver jumped into the lagoon. I didn't fancy jumping into the lagoon, because it was always stinking and full of massive stingrays. Just before we crashed into the sailboat, I jumped to the floor and curled up into a ball. The speedboat crunched into the side of the sailboat at full speed, and splinters of fibreglass flew through the air. After the initial impact, I was happy not to have been hurt and I put the boat into neutral. Looking behind me, I saw that they were waist high in the shitty lagoon water with their phones still in their pockets totally ruined.

As the shock and adrenaline rush stopped, I start-ed to piss myself laughing. The speedboat bow was smashed to pieces and the guys swam over and climbed back on board the boat. We looked over to the sailboat and there was a very pissed off guy from Argentina wearing Speedos, screaming and yelling in Spanish. We had a closer look at the damage. Some of the metal railings on the side had snapped off and there was damage to the cables that held up the mast. The repairs would cost the driver over $1,000; with his low salary he might still be paying it off today.

It had been pure comedy watching those guys jump off the boat in slow motion into the brown abyss – it was like something from a James Bond movie with speedboats chasing each other before they crashed into a ball of flames. Some people might think the boat owner deserved it for wearing Speedos, but not me. After that incident there was no more show boating and nobody went over two knots across the lagoon again.

AFTER WORKING AT the resort for a few months, I had enough money saved to explore Central America. It was nearly Christmas time and my folks were spending the holidays in Mexico, so we planned to meet up. They invited me to stay at a posh resort for a week, which was a perfect Christmas present. They never fancied coming over to Honduras after watch-ing a documentary about San Pedro Sula being the murder capital of the world. Útila was not really the place to bring them, even though it would have been nice for them to see where I worked, but watching all the loony backpackers running around coked up and rummed up would be too much for them.

MY FLIGHT TICKET from San Pedro Sula to Belize City was in my pocket and once on the road, bad things happened to me, and it was mostly my fault.

The night before my departure, my mate held a party in the middle of the bush. My grand plan was not to get too wrecked as I was on the first boat the next day. It was really going off at the party, fluro backdrops, lasers, a wicked DJ, and everyone was having a blast. My discipline faded after about five minutes and my cut-off time of 2 am got pushed back to 4 am. After finally managing to stop dancing and chatting shit to strangers, I bounced through the jungle to get my bag and head to the ferry.

I made it on time, my wide eyes shielded behind my sunglasses. I got onto the bus in La Ceiba … no problems so far. I got to the airport, hoping for no trouble from immigration and questions about being in the country for so long. I went straight through no worries, it was going great. I made it to the gate and sat down on the chair, and then the night before caught up with me and I started to feel sleepy and passed out. I must have dreamt they were boarding the plane, because I jumped up, saw an aircraft on the tarmac, and without really thinking, opened the glass doors, and walked out towards the plane.

Within seconds, a security guard jumped on my back. He spoke in broken English, "Where are you going, senor?"

"I'm going to Belize City," I replied.

He looked at me as if I was crazy. "Sir this plane is going to San Jose. I need you to go back inside the terminal. Your plane will not depart for another hour." He frogmarched me back into the terminal. "Please sit down and don't move."

I sat down still dazed, and the guy eyeballed me until the call came to board.

The Blue Hole

DIVING THE BLUE Hole was the reason I wanted to visit Belize. Belize City was an ugly place, a bit like Newport but with nicer weather.

It would have been rude not to sample a couple of shots of One Barrel rum while waiting for my boat to Caye Caulker. This paradise is a couple of hours away from Belize City and it is unique, as the island was split into two during a hurricane in 1961. One side of the island is all built up with colourful painted buildings, and the other is just sand and trees. It was pleasant spending a couple of days hanging out eating stewed chicken and I got the chance to visit a shallow sandbar that had a bunch of string rays that were like flat puppies. They swarmed around us eating the free food from the guides, and one of them even picked one up and gave it a kiss.

I booked a three-tank trip to the Blue Hole. It's probably the most famous dive in the Caribbean and pretty pricy. The boat left at stupid o'clock in the morning as it was a couple of hours out to Lighthouse Reef. There were about fifteen divers on board, the sea was rough as shit, and after a while the conversations ran dry. People started to change colour as the dive tanks bounced and clunked together in the swells.

After what seemed like a lifetime, we arrived at the Blue Hole. The submarine sinkhole is three hundred metres across and a hundred metres down to the bottom and the aerial image of the Blue Hole is spectacular. As a superstar dive instructor, they put me with the experienced divers that could go down to forty metres. We jumped into and got onto a sandy ledge and from there you could drop into the dark-ness below. As we descended, the blue water started to turn black and our dive computers began to beep as we reached our depth limit. It was so eerie down there and ten sharks circled below us in what looked like crude oil.

My mind wondered if the sharks could smell our narcosis paranoia about being some place we shouldn't be. Another strange thought went through my head, as I wondered how many lead weights and dive lights were at the bottom of the Blue Hole. Probably a shit load was the answer I gave myself. The DM signalled for us to start our ascent, but the fun wasn't over yet. He took us into some tight swim throughs in the side of the hole, which was probably a bit more exciting than being in the hole. We did a nice long safety stop on the sandy area before surfacing. Blue Hole Belize … tick!

After another dive, we had a nice lunch on Half Moon Caye and took the chance to get our hands on a couple of blue boobies, which is always lovely. The reefs were in great shape in Belize and they had a well-protected marine reserve. The corals looked very healthy with sightings of nurse sharks, hawksbill turtles, and green eels during the dives. With the wind on our backs, the sea was a lot calmer on the way back to Caye Caulker thank God. It was an expensive day diving in the Caribbean; would I pay to go again? Absolutely not.

Cave Diving

MEXICO WAS A couple of hours' north, so I took the bus from Belize City to Tulum. With beautiful beaches dotted with Mayan ruins, Tulum had a friendly hippy vibe to it. I wanted to experience a different type of diving and the cenotes looked very interesting. Some of the images were stunning and there were plenty of dive shops dotted around town, so it didn't take long to get hooked up.

"I don't want to wear a wetsuit. I'll be fine just wearing my shorts and rash guard."

My cave diving instructor looked at me as if I was some kind of idiot. "Yesterday the water was only 72 f. You will get freezing down there."

"It's OK, I will be fine. I have an extra couple of inches of blubber that will keep me warm."

We loaded the dive gear onto the back of the truck and headed into the bush. We stopped in the middle of nowhere and there were just a couple of trees and shrubs near us. We got our gear ready and the guy lowered the tanks into a hole in the ground. Looking down, all I could see was the crystal-clear blue water of the Dos Ojos cave system. The ladder was pretty slippery, but we got down to the water and jumped in. I understood why my instructor gave me weird looks about not wearing a wetsuit, because as my balls touched the water, they immediately decided they wanted to be someplace else. The water was freezing cold, just like the man said.

After a couple of cold moments, the beauty of the caves slowly mesmerised me. The visibility was crystal clear and it felt like swimming through glacier water. Natural light arrowed through cracks and holes topside and sunbeams pierced the water. Looking around at the formations of limestone, some of it looked like giant dinosaur teeth. There was a line that went through the cave, so we stayed close to that. There were a couple of danger signs saying: 'Don't go this way' and it looked dark and dangerous in those areas. I didn't fancy making the Yucatan Daily with the headline *Fat Welshman found dead in Dos Ojos wearing only a rash guard and shorts.*

As we got back to the entrance, my lips had turned Cardiff City blue. We got into the sunshine and I quickly warmed up and my mind was swimming with images from inside the cave. It was like an experience from another planet.

While on the lookout for lunch after the busy morning, for some strange reason, the local Subway store looked the best bet. It was my first Subway for a few years, so I ordered a foot-long meatball sub. Sitting down at the table the sandwich was looking very lovely, and I took a bite. To my absolute disgust, the young Chico hadn't cooked the meatballs for long enough and they were freezing cold, probably about the same temperature as mine were on the dive earlier.

Giving Chico the crazy eyes, I tried to explain to

him in bad Spanish, "Mi meatballs es frio senor, no necesito make me enfirma."

He gave me a new piping hot sandwich, so made my way to the terminal. It was time to head further north to Playa del Carmen and some drift diving in Cozumel, which was recommended by many for its excellent drift diving.

On arrival in Playa del Carmen, it felt like tourist central, full of cruise ship people with cheap tat on sale everywhere. An hour of walking around looking at tourist junk was enough, so I took the thirty-minute ferry over to Cozumel and found an affordable place to stay.

The diving didn't disappoint, but the sites were really crowded. You couldn't enjoy the peace and tranquillity underwater, as there was a constant buzz of speedboats above you. Some of the deep walls were spectacular, with clear water, beautiful tunnels, and gullies that were easy to explore and there were turtles galore and huge green moray eels. Cozumel's endemic splendid toadfish popped out of the reef a couple of times with its wide mouth and black and white stripes. It felt a bit like driving on a busy motorway sometimes, because every couple of minutes a group of divers would fly past us in the current, and you had to be on your toes to make sure that you didn't go off with the wrong group.

I made one more stop before heading for Christ-mas in Cancun. Isla Mujeres was my favourite place in Mexico. The tiny island is thirteen miles offshore, so it was not overrun with gringos. It felt like an authentic Mexican town with tight streets and colourful houses. This was the end of the migration route for the same whale sharks we saw in Útila, but the weather made the sea too rough for us to go looking. I settled for a few dives in the sheltered shallow reefs, and apart from a couple of eagle ray sightings it was nothing to write home about really.

MY FOLKS WERE staying on the outskirts of Cancun and they didn't know my arrival time. On walking into the resort lobby, the front desk girl looked at me as if I was a homeless man and should not be allowed inside, because my T-shirt and backpack were covered in dust from the past few weeks' travels. After explaining I was human under the filth, and we had a reservation, they said it would be OK to surprise my folks on the beach. After searching for about twenty minutes I found them lying on sunbeds. It is always nice to get a hug from your mum, and it felt extra special on that Mexican beach.

We spent the next week at the resort and it was great to spend Christmas Day together. They bought me some great new T-shirts, so I looked presentable at the resort, and we ate and drank non-stop, because the buffet was endless.

You hear all kinds of bad stuff about Cancun and most of it was about right. It was full of teenagers and spring breakers causing mayhem on the streets. We went out and visited all the tourist traps, and my folks got conned for $40 in Bubba Gump shrimp for some glasses, which they took home. They spent the next ten years in the cupboard never to be used again.

My folks headed home on New Year's Eve and we had an emotional goodbye in the hotel lobby. After waving them off, a feeling of loneliness swept over me after spending a great vacation with them. I checked out of the resort; the urge to steal all the towels and slippers from my room was immense.

The road called me again for NYE and I stayed in old Cancun town and met up with a couple of girls from the UK. We went to a nightclub and got through a couple of bottles of vodka. It was hard to shake off missing my folks terribly, which was strange as homesickness never really bothered me during my travels.

THE JOURNEY SOUTH to Honduras began and I travelled from Cancun to Belize, before jumping over the border into Guatemala.

The Guatemalans don't recognise Belize as a coun-try, as it's been disputed for centuries and there have been many flashpoints with the British military. The Guatemalan troops massed to the border only to be put off invading by the military power of the UK. The UK government was supposed to construct a road from Punta Gorda to the Guatemalan border, but it was never completed, and my God I so wished it had been.

The bus journey was one from hell, the weather was so hot, and there was no breeze or air condition-ing. The road had so many potholes my head smashed into the bus roof every few seconds. Aside from the potholes, there were yellow speed bumps every couple of hundred metres – there was no need for the speed bumps as the potholes slowed everybody down. The crossing into Guatemala was easy, but I got the typical shitty exchange rate from a blagger at the border. My destination was the small town of Flores, which was close to the famous Mayan ruins of Tikal.

Guatemala

FLORES HAD A relaxed vibe with restaurants dotted along the edge of the lake; it looked perfect as the sun was going down.

"We will pick you up at three tomorrow morning, please be ready in the lobby."

I looked at the agent in disgust on hearing the departure time for Tikal. It was an early night for me despite some backpackers trying to twist my arm into a drinking session. The reason for the early start was to arrive at Tikal to witness the sunrise.

We travelled through the rainforest, my guide gave me a flashlight, and we started walking on these trails. I couldn't see anything and there were weird sounds from the jungle, which were freaking me out. The sky turned that deep navy blue before sunrise, and we made it to the top of the ruins.

The Guatemalan rainforest sprang into action and the morning chorus of monkeys, insects, and birds all came together in fantastic harmony. I had experienced the morning call in the Amazon, but this time it was different. The noises seemed to be magnified tenfold and they caused an echo that reverberated around the site. Slowly, the sun elevated into the sky and for the first time I saw the ruins sticking out of the rainforest.

I thought it was great because George Lucas had filmed scenes from the Star Wars movies here.

We spent the next few hours exploring the ruins; it was still early so it was relatively peaceful. You couldn't help but be amazed by the quality of construction ... way back in 400 AD there were no cement mixers or forklifts to help the Mayans build it. My guide showed me some chutes where they used to chop off people's heads as human sacrifices.

As the day got hotter, we decided to bug out. It was great to see Tikal and I was even happier to see the place where Han Solo flew the Millennium Falcon over planet Guatemala.

Further south was a place on the Río Cahabón called Semuc Champey. The wooden cabins were situated right on the river and you could grab a couple of beers and float down in a rubber ring. There were some small rapids but nothing too serious. Further down the river were beautiful multilevel turquoise swimming pools and if you climbed up to the hill top; there were perfect views down over the pools. I really loved this place, and as with Útila, people found themselves staying there for months instead of a few days.

Seeing lava was something that had always fasci-nated me and the Pacaya volcano was close to the beautiful city of Antigua. A group of us hiked up the 2,500-metre volcano before reaching the hot stuff. We saw mini eruptions while glowing orange rocks rolled down the mountainside. It felt we were too close to the lava, but our guide reassured us we were okay. You could really feel the heat and he took us to where the lava flowed under our feet. The rocks were really sharp and the bottom of my trainers started to get softer.

As we posed for pictures, a couple of massive rumbles came from inside the volcano. I watched the guide to see if he looked nervous, but he just smiled at us. We started to hike back down the mountain and were happy to get down without Pierce Brosnan coming to rescue us!

Antigua was a lovely town, and in addition to its incredible old Spanish architecture and churches, it had a McDonald's. It was great sitting down having a quarter pounder with cheese and admiring all of the spectacular architecture. There was one more treat in store as an original member of the Buena Vista social club was still alive and kicking in Antigua. Ignacio Perez Borrell played for a few hours once a week in a compact bar with low ceilings and a couple of us managed to get into the VIP area and listened to some great music. Not understanding all of the lyrics didn't matter as it felt like we were listening to something historical. He played on the bongo drums with his Panama hat and huge smile, while romantic older couples danced away in front of us. It was another memorable experience.

AFTER ALL OF the exciting travels, it was time to go back to work. Lizzie had decided to leave Útila and it was a sad time, because we had had such a blast together and it was another blow to see a good mate head off. We have stayed in touch and we have seen each other all over the world since.

I had to leave Fred and Betty's house, which was

sad, as they wanted to do some renovations. Fred was an old school diver; his BCD was just a bit of plastic with a tank attached. He took me diving to secret banks around Útila and he let me try spearfishing for the first time. He was an excellent shot and never missed his target. He shot three queen triggers in succession, but sadly couldn't hit a cow's arse with a banjo, and I missed by miles. It was funny because he had a thick island accent and I could never really understand what he said. Most of the time, if he talked to me, so would just nod and agree with him.

On one occasion, the boss sent us on his big cargo ship to put mooring lines on new seamounts a few miles off the Cays. We used a subsea jackhammer to drill a hole in the reef. It was great doing something different and a strange experience using a jackhammer underwater. Once the hole was deep enough, we inserted a large pin and then brought PVC tubes filled with marine concrete and filled the hole around the new pin. We let the concrete set for a week then we returned to attach the mooring line and buoy. Once completed, we had a new dive site. Fred gave me the honour of naming the dive site. As it was a seamount, I called it Kris's Hill.

THERE WAS A new legend on the island and we became good friends as we liked the same stuff. Chris aka Midget was from Norwich but was a bit different to Alan Partridge. He worked as an instructor for a couple of different shops and he asked me to get a place with him … red flags were flying in my mind at the thought of two liabilities living together.

We found a house right on the waterfront near Alton's Dive Centre. It was a house on stilts with two bedrooms, the perfect lad's pad with a balcony right on the water. Even though it was right on the water, it never had much fresh water, so we didn't wash very often. We never really had much food in the fridge either, but there was always a good supply of rum and other goodies.

Midget was a mad fucker, it was great having a new partner in crime, and he loved to get on the gin and tonic. He got smashed one night and made the mistake of trying to ride his motorbike home. They were doing roadworks and had dug some pretty big holes – health and safety was slack in Honduras, so the holes were not covered. On his way home he managed to ditch the bike into one of the holes. It was a couple of feet deep, so he couldn't get out of it, and he had to wait for some locals to help him the next day.

It was great to get back to the resort and had one of my favourite ever dives with a group from Cleve-land. There was a lady called Erin in this group, and we have remained friends for over ten years now. We were at Spotted Bay, on the west end of the island, we dropped down to the edge of the wall, and suddenly this huge manta ray glided right past us.

This was the first time we had seen a manta while diving in Útila, and I screamed into my regulator and banged my tank like a madman. We all just hovered in the water watching one of the most graceful creatures you will ever see in your life. We then followed it for a while. It was a good three metres wide, its wings moved in slow motion, and it watched us as we bust through our air trying to keep up with it. After all the excitement, everybody was low on air and we were back on the boat after seventeen minutes. It was the shortest but most incredible dive so far.

During another dive at Don Quickset something spectacular happened. About halfway through the dive, dolphin sounds filled the water, their high-pitched squeaks and clicking were very loud so they must have been close. After a few minutes seven bottlenose dolphins swam just above us. We watched in amazement as they swam together, their flukes powering them through the water at great speed. They swam to the edge of the wall before dropping down to the depths.

There were also great sightings on the north side of the island, with hammerheads and devil rays seen a few times. We watched a sailfish chase a school of mackerel; everybody watched its colours flash as the sun reflected off its body. Never had a fish moved so elegantly and it changed direction so quickly.

Thoughts raced through my mind about the possi-bility of it jumping out of the water and spearing me with its sharp bill, its body thrashing around as it was impaled in my chest, my blood spurting all over the dive deck, and Captain Kerry getting pissed off with all the mess, but secretly hoping to take it home to sell on the Cay. I then stopped thinking about this weird stuff and told myself not to stay in the sun too long as it makes you crazy.

Macro Life

EVEN THOUGH IT'S great swimming with whale sharks, dolphins, and bigger sea life creatures, as you develop into a dive pro, you enjoy looking for the smaller critters. The guests judge you on the marine life you find and your knowledge of their behaviour. It's easy finding crowd pleasers like turtles, but it's not enough to satisfy the more experienced divers. You have to look for the weird and wonderful to impress them, and if you found something rare or a most-wanted photo subject it could make you serious extra money for excited photographers.

Útila had lots of neat macro life and my favourite sites were Little Bight and Big Rock. The first time you find a sea horse is a great moment; the sandy bottom had pinecone algae that made the perfect habitat for them to cling onto. You can fall in love with these little guys so easily. There were different coloured seahors-es – orange, black, and yellow, and the fact the males carry the eggs makes them a bit more special. The sand was full of weird and wonderful creatures including the short-nosed batfish. These are straight from the pond next to Homer Simpson's nuclear power plant. They look like small plucked chickens that crawl along the seafloor, and they have this upside-down smile and pointy noses. They are, without a doubt, one of the freakiest fish you will ever see. These guys were pretty rare to find, and we saw them on just a few occasions only.

There were some excellent blennies to be found and one of the most common ones was the secretary blennies. These little guys lived in small holes on the reef, were about an inch long, and had beautiful big yellow and black eyes that seemed too big for their bodies. I could never understand their name as I couldn't imagine them working in an office. My favourite was the sailfin blenny. These feisty guys lived in small rocks, if you had two blennies in a small space they got very territorial. They would flap their sail fins frantically and it looked like they were screaming at each other as their mouths opened and closed fast. Often, they would bite each other in their battle for supremacy.

Frogfish were another top find because they were hard to spot due to their great camouflage. An orange one lived on top of the jagged Pinnacle at Silver Garden, and he stayed there for a good couple of years before getting irritated by all the smelly backpackers gawping at him all day. They became the Holy Grail of finds for dive pros and sometimes you wouldn't tell other guides where you found the good ones, because you wanted to show as many guests as possible. Over the years in other destinations I have heard stories about guides collecting the rarer marine life in plastic bags and moving them to different locations.

You could find common octopus on night dives. During the day, they usually hid in burrows along the reef. On one dive, we found one that had his head stuck outside. On approach, it went further back into its hole, and its arms were all curled up as he observed us from the safety of his home.

Octopus can be playful, so I unclipped my tank banger and left it on the edge. After a while, one of his arms unravelled, the suction cups gripped the metal object and dragged it inside the hole. The shiny object was now owned by the octopus. I didn't really think he would pick it up and he looked at me as if to say come and get it. I didn't want to lose my favourite tank banger, nor did I want to hurt the octopus, so I just waited for about five minutes outside the hole. We looked at each other, then he finally pushed my tank banger back out into the position where he had found it. He had had enough fun playing with me, so gave the toy back.

Earthquake

I HAD BEEN diving with Kim, Banon, Lisa, and Jim, I stopped at the bar with Chris after work. One drink turned into seven or eight, so stumbled home and passed out in my bed. My housemate nearly kicked my door through at around 2 am.

"Kris, Kris get the fuck out of the house there is an earthquake."

I opened one eye. I was still drowsy from the earli-er rums. Chris looked a little worse for wear. He had stayed out later than me and had been eating dough-nuts because he had white powder around his nose.

"Come on ... get out of the house now."

I could hear this massive rumbling, the windows in my bedroom were shaking, and my wardrobe looked like it was going to topple over at any second. I jumped out of my bedroom and ran into the living room. I will never forget seeing my refrigerator bouncing along the floor of the kitchen. The glassware on the shelves smashed all around me, and the TV fell onto the floor – we would never get to watch Sabado Gigante on that TV ever again as the screen was smashed. I got out of the house and onto the road. Little did I know we had just experienced a 7.3 magnitude earthquake, which had lasted a full minute.

A lot of the locals were out on the street and my hands were shaking. It was the first time I had felt the real force of Mother Nature. The next thing cracked me up. Chris came running up to me; his eyes were bulging out of his head. He had the remote control for the TV in his hand, which was missing one battery.

"Kris, we have got to get the fuck out of here. Let's get up to higher ground in case there is a tsunami."

"Let's just hang on for a minute mate. Let's wait for the official word on the situation." Chris looked at me with fear in his wide-awake eyes. "Sorry mate I have to go now." He jumped on a bicycle with the TV remote still in his hand and headed for the hills. A short while after, a message was passed around that all tsunami warnings had been lifted. I looked at the mess in my house and thought sod it, I'm going back to bed we can fix it tomorrow.

Chris never did make it back that night. He passed out in someone's hammock on higher ground. He saved the TV remote but was gutted as the TV was toast.

The earthquake had had a devastating effect on Honduras, with seven people killed in total and many roads and buildings were destroyed. Our house on stilts had sunk three feet down into the sand and we moved out soon after, as the landlady wanted to fix the place up.

The next day, I went to find my friends at the re-sort. Lisa had suffered the worst effect of all of us, as a vase had fallen and smashed her head. She had a nasty lump and had to skip diving. The rest of us headed off and while underwater there was a large aftershock of around 4.0. It looked like the whole reef was shaking, so we decided to get out of the water to be safe.

On the next dive we saw huge chunks of reef had broken off and had rolled down onto the sea floor. It was a totally surreal experience and times like that made you realise we were nothing but tiny ants in this world and we could be wiped out at any time by Mother Nature.

Coup

EVEN THOUGH WE lived in an island bubble, life was always interesting in Honduras. You could find out mainland news from the national newspapers, such as La Prensa, which was the largest, and there were copies in the restaurants.

There was no such thing as censorship, they showed pictures of gang members riddled with bullet holes, unfortunate people killed in road accidents, and politicians slain for corruption. Each day there would be about ten pictures of dead people. It was gory but fascinating at the same time.

While munching down on chicken nuggets at the Seven Seas restaurant one day, Martha told me trouble was brewing for the President of Honduras. He wanted to change the constitution and stay in power for longer. Some other locals told me he wanted to become like Hugo Chavez from Venezuela, there were bad feelings on the island, and it didn't take long for everything to kick off.

On the 28th of June 2009, the supreme court of Honduras ordered the military to oust President Manuel Zelaya from his position. They stormed his home in the early hours of the morning and flew him to Costa Rican exile. He tried to hold an illegal vote to change the constitution, so they kicked him out of the country. There were massive protests in the main cities and a few people were killed. The streets were full of tanks, and military aircraft were patrolling the skies. All the Internet and communications were down for a while until things calmed down again. Marines arrived at the main dock and immediately put the island on a 6 pm curfew and we quickly realised our rum consumption would be cut short in these troubled times!

The majority of the locals seemed happy that the president had been kicked out. The curfew lasted a few days, but life went on as usual. On the mainland, there were more demonstrations and the ex-president made attempts to get back into the country. He tried to land in a private jet but had to abort the landing due to a threat from the Honduran air force.

After a time, the country finally let Zelaya back into the country, and he took refuge in the Brazilian embassy. Most countries around the world con-demned the coup and said it was illegal and the United States cut over $15 million in aid to Honduras as a consequence.

Colombian Airlines

ANOTHER EXTRAORDINARY EVENT that occurred was the crashing of a plane, which had been full of cocaine. It happened around 2 am in the morning and you could hear planes circling the island over and over again.

As far as drug trafficking is concerned, Útila is one of the stops between South America and the States. With a small runway and no security, it is the perfect place for the drug cartels. There were rumours that when a plane was due to land, the road to the airport would be closed and guarded by people with guns. People would light up the runway with torches so the pilot could land safely at night. Once the plane was unloaded, the cocaine was loaded onto speedboats and taken to the next destination.

The island was full of news about the crashed plane. It was a British Aerospace Jetstream 32, the Colombian pilot had been killed, but two survivors were being treated for injuries and ended up in jail. The plane was being followed by the US coast guard and was being forced to land. The aircraft ran out of fuel and crashed into the bottom of Pumpkin Hill. Its cargo consisted of 1.7 tons of pure cocaine worth an estimated $7 million.

What happened next made me chuckle. The local TV station filmed and interviewed the police while they disposed of the enormous amount of cocaine. The problem was that from the video, it was apparent that all they were burning were empty bags. I didn't see one brick of coke go on that massive fire. People were pretty sure all the cocaine had ended up at its final destination and as a poor country it was to be expected.

New Training

AFTER ALL THE coke planes, earthquakes, and political coups, I decided it was better to keep my head underwater.

The dive business become a Scuba Schools International store (SSI). SSI was an up-and-coming agency looking to take a bigger slice of the dive market. Toby and Christine arrived at the resort to run the place. Toby was from Germany and was an Instructor Trainer for SSI. He was brought in to cross over our instructors. We were actually the first set of instructors to be crossed over in Latin America, so it was nice to have that honour. We spent a few days learning the difference in skills for the courses. Most things were very similar, so you didn't really need to change the way you taught your students. We received our instructor's cards very quickly as we printed them in the shop.

After a few months at the resort, Christine and Toby decided to get married. They wanted to do it at sunset on my favourite boat Another Time. They asked if I would do the service for them, as I had a big mouth and someone had given me the idea that you can become ordained by applying online. It was a quick process and within a few days I was officially

Reverend Kristian Mears.

The evening for the wedding was perfect. We decorated the boat with flowers, loaded up with plenty of beverages, and luckily found one collared shirt that hadn't be worn for years. Around twenty of us jumped on the boat and we headed towards the dropping sun. It was a picturesque scene with the setting sun turning the sky a marmalade orange and the east wind was just right and provided a cooling breeze. We tied up on one of the dive sites, and the service began.

Just as we started, my phone rang in my pocket. What kind of Reverend doesn't put his phone on silent during a service? After that little blip, the rest went well and it was really lovely to be part of Toby and Christine's special day.

MY DUTIES AS a man of the cloth didn't end after one ceremony. Two of my best friends from Wales – Claudine and Tim – asked me to marry them on Koh Samui in Thailand. It was a really proud moment for me to do this for them. Many of our good friends came out for a week and it was brilliant to see everyone together.

In 2017, I had to get the dog collar on again as Rob got married to Anna in the Gili Islands, Indonesia. This was another beautiful occasion as it had been nearly ten years since many of us had been on Útila. We had a great reunion, seeing Morna, Dick Williams, Abe and Kelly among others was great. We proved we could still party like the animals we used to be.

ONE OF THE most prestigious jobs on Útila was working on the only liveaboard boat in Honduras. We watched the ship come into dock every Friday, the crew wearing crisp white shirts with epaulettes, looking the part and getting paid handsomely. Over time, I got to know the captain and first mate. They had years and years of experience and my dream was one day to get the chance to work with the guys.

The Big Boat

ONE DAY THE chance came. My boss was taking some guests to La Ceiba, and I needed a fast-food binge in La Ceiba so I hitched a ride with them. He called me over for a chat, I thought I was in trouble for a while, but he said he was impressed with my performance at the resort and had heard good things from the guests. He thought it was time for me to work on the livea-board.

With this great news, I couldn't stop smiling and was bursting with pride. Once the boat dropped us off, I walked around the corner and started jumping up and down shouting, "Yes, yes, yes." People at the dock were giving me weird looks, but I didn't give a toss. After being on the island for two years and having done nearly 2,000 dives, I was about to work for the biggest liveaboard company in the world.

It was so exciting to get my white shirt and uni-form and the captain trained me on the standard operating procedures. Everything changed; it was a million miles away from working on the resort day boats and at the dive shop. There was a lot to learn, and I quickly felt out of my depth. The crew worked six weeks on and two off, the days were long, starting at 6 am and finishing around 9 pm. The boat did five dives a day, so we each did 3-4 dives a day. If you want to rack up your diving experience, then get a job on a liveaboard.

Even though the days were long, the food was good. We ate the same food as the guests, and sometimes the chef made local dishes like red rice and arroz con pollo. The crew quarters had four bunks beds and a shared bathroom, so you got to know your crewmates very quickly. It wasn't the place to leave your underwear on the floor otherwise you got a slap from the stewardess.

It was an exciting feeling leaving the dock for the first time and being on the water for a week. The good thing was you couldn't spend any money, so it was an excellent chance to save quickly. Drinking was not allowed during the charters, so it was a good time to give my liver a well-earned vacation from Flor de Caña.

We put away the ropes and fenders then steamed towards the north side of the island. We were a crew of six onboard so we had to become a 'jack of all trades. One minute we were serving the guests lunch, then the next we were down in the boiling hot engine room helping the engineer fix a broken compressor.

The day began at six, some helped serve the break-fast, others prepared the dive deck, making sure all tanks were full and analysed if they were nitrox. You had to be a good artist as we drew the dive site maps to assist with dive briefings. A lot of work went into these and we added fish diagrams and coloured them with pencils. The guests were amazed that we could do it all by memory.

If we didn't dive, we had deck duty. We helped

the guests into the water, and then kept an eye on the surface to see if anybody popped up. Then we prepared the hot towels and washed down the deck. Once the dive was done, we filled the tanks, logged everyone's dive profile, and then it was time for hot breakfast. After the second dive it was lunch and we helped clear the plates. After lunch there was a chance for a quick thirty-minute snooze if we were lucky. There were two more dives in the afternoon at around 2 pm and 4 pm and then there was dinner, which we helped serve before the night dive. There was hot chocolate and a final deck clean down. We then stayed up with the guests for a while until it was time for bed at around 9 pm.

We worked long hours and had to give the guests the best customer service possible. We had to learn fast to gain the captain's trust and respect and it was essential to work hard and take everything on board that they told us. That included getting a bucket of steam from the engine room. Mistakes are made when you start any new job, and made a total balls up on many occasions, but that was part of the learning curve.

The first thing challenging job was securing the vessel to the mooring lines. On the smaller resort boats it was pretty easy, as the mooring buoys were on the surface. As the liveaboard was so large, it wasn't possible to be so close to shore; otherwise, we'd hit the reef if we swung in the wind. Most of our moorings were below the surface and some were pretty deep. We would balance on the bow of the boat with a mask and fins on and the captain used a GPS mark to get us close to the submerged line. Once we saw the float below the surface, we jumped off with a two-inch rope in our hands. It was about a ten-foot drop to the water so we hit the surface with some force, and then free dived down and threaded the rope through a thimble. We had to be careful as the rope would have plenty of sharp barnacles and crinoids, which could tear our hands to shreds. Once the line was through the thimble it floated back to the surface. The guys picked up the line with a grappling hook and secured the vessel.

I was a shitty free diver. My first time balancing on the bow looking down into the water didn't feel good. The float came into view; the captain put the boat into neutral, and my legs starting to shake like a shitting dog. With the heavy thick rope in one hand and the other holding my mask, I jumped into the water. The force of me hitting the surface knocked my mask clear off my face, so there I was flapping around on the surface looking for my mask before it sunk down to the depths of the Caribbean Sea. I could hear sniggers of laughter coming from the boat and one of the crew jumped in and finished the job. There were no bonus points for this greenhorn and it took me a while to get it right.

Another problem was being terrible at tying knots. There was a seamount way out west. It was tricky as there was no mooring line, just a pin which was fixed to the reef, and we would use a scuba tank as it's impossible to do while freediving.

On one occasion, after a few minutes of frantically searching, I found the pin, threaded the line through, and tied what I thought was a perfect bowline knot. We also tied a big fender to the line to take off some pressure. Happy with my work, I went onto the dive deck. After a few minutes, the first mate came up to me.

"So, did you tie a good knot on the line?"
"Yep, I thought it was good."

He gestured to me to look over the side of the boat. The fender floated on the surface about two hundred feet away. My knot had come loose and the ship was drifting away from the seamount. Thoughts of me getting fired went through my mind if this carried on. The captain started up the boat, and the first mate showed me how it was done.

We didn't get much luck on that dive site. We had planned on spending the night there. It was about 8 pm and all of a sudden, a storm quickly came in and we had to leave fast. The waves were big and guess who had to untie the line? Standing on the bow of the boat with my scuba tank and dive light, the water looked pitch black and there were some nasty swells to contend with. After hitting the water, I went down to the line. This was my first time underwater at night alone in deplorable conditions. It was hard to untie the knot and the line was tight as big waves tossed the ship around on the surface. It took about ten minutes to get it undone. On my way back to the surface the swells were huge, and one smashed me into the ladder. I held on for dear life and didn't even bother taking my fins off before crawling onto the back deck. Out of breath and bruised, I wondered what the hell I was getting into. Jumping off a boat at night in a storm is something that a navy seal, James Bond diver should be doing, not some fat kid from Wales.

AFTER A FEW uneasy charters the work became really enjoyable. The majority of the crew were from Roatán including the captain and first mate, and there were a couple of expats working as dive instructors on board. We had a loony chef from Sweden, who burned people with cigarettes in his spare time. I will always remember him trying to cook dinner while vomiting into a bucket before getting his sea legs. There were two lovely sisters Morna and Candy who also took care of the kitchen and cabins and a great guy called John Glen who was proper Utilian. He made me laugh so hard when he said that if you ate too much barracuda it was possible to get hickory poisoning. I looked at him perplexed never having heard of hickory poisoning. After a short while it clicked that he meant to say mercury poisoning!

MOST OF THE guests were Americans, mixed in with a small number of people from other countries. It wasn't cheap to be on board, so most guests had a decent lifestyle. Most were fine to get along with, but sometimes there were tricky ones that you couldn't wait to get off the ship.

Tough Customer

ON ONE TRIP, we had a couple from Arkansas. The fella was a grain distributor and seemed to love himself and his wife was a quiet lady who wouldn't say boo to a goose.

One night it was noticeable that he had had a cou-ple of drinks. After dinner, we finished our duties before heading to our cabin. I fell asleep for a while but could hear someone knocking on the cabin door opposite us. The cabin was occupied by a lesbian couple so I wondered who would disturb them. I listened for a while and you could hear the southern drawl of the grain guy.

He knocked on the door again and said, "Hey ladies, please let me in I really want to spend some time with you both."

After hearing this, I quickly got dressed and went into the corridor. The guy was still knocking on the door trying to get in, so I put my arm around him and tried to get him upstairs to the saloon. The guy was totally wasted and could hardly walk, but I managed to get him upstairs before waking the captain for help. He became out of control and the captain had to restrain him as he kept trying to go downstairs. Fearing the ladies were getting freaked out, I went to apologise, but luckily, they saw the funny side of it. The guy's wife was distraught and told me he had drunk a whole bottle of rum. She asked me to keep him away until he sobered up.

On returning back upstairs to help the captain, the guy was becoming increasingly abusive and would not sit down. We sat either side of him to keep him under control and tried to sober him up with coffee. We took a lot of abuse from him and it took all of my strength not to chin him.

"Let me go you motherfucking cocksucker. I'm going to beat the shit out of you," was one of his classic lines!

It was 2 am before he finally started to calm down. He tried going to the cabin a few times, but we stopped him. I couldn't tell him his wife didn't want to see him in that state so I stayed with him until 5 am. He started to come around and got really apologetic and thinking he was going to be okay, I gave him permission to go topside for some fresh air. He went outside and I gave him a minute before following him. I couldn't believe it when I did, because I heard the sound of a beer can being opened and he sat there drinking it with a smile on his face.

We banned him from diving for 24 hours and he finally made it back to the cabin and slept all day; not showing up until dinner with a sheepish look on his face. He was awfully quiet the rest of the trip and the only silver lining was he left a $1,000 tip for us. It was my first time pulling an all-nighter in Útila while being totally sober.

APART FROM A couple of bad apples, many people were genuinely inspiring.

For example, there was one lady from Germany who had lost both legs above the knee in an accident. When she first came on board, she wore prosthetic limbs. She was a lovely lady who was so nice to talk to. When it was time to dive, she took off her prosthet-ic limbs, got her wetsuit on, and using incredible upper body strength, went down the ladder onto the back deck. We helped to get her ready before she did a side roll into the water. She was excellent underwater, and with the use of just her arms, she explored the reefs the same as everyone else. Despite her disability, she was a tough, independent lady who led a normal life. I will always cherish our charter together and recently saw a magazine article that mentioned she was still diving, nearly ten years after we had first met.

There was also a gentleman from London who was 78 years old. He was no spring chicken, so he had brought a nurse with him for assistance. He was great underwater, but for the wrong reasons and he remains a scar on my memory. We were filling the tanks after a dive and he was getting changed out of his wetsuit. He was wearing these loose shorts and as he sat down, I looked in the wrong place at the wrong time and got a glimpse of the old man's saggy balls that were resting on top of his locker. It would be amazing to make it to seventy-eight and still be diving, but thanks to this experience, I will make sure I'm wearing a nice pair of Speedos to keep everything under wraps.

My course director told me that the average career length of a dive instructor was one and a half years. I was now into my third year and had the same massive passion for the underwater world as I had on day one and having the ocean as my office was brilliant most of the time.

There are times when things can become compli-cated to handle though and that's when most people can lose interest in being responsible for people underwater. Working in the industry and especially on liveaboards can take a massive toll on your body and you have to be tough if you want to make a career out of it.

If you look at the marketing materials for dive agencies, all you see is smiley happy faces working in calm, clear water and instructors teaching hot bikini babes or six-pack surfer dudes. After paying thou-sands of dollars for courses and getting a job, things change quickly; the enthusiasm can drain from some dive pros at the drop of a hat. After getting past 2,000 or so dives, there were some weeks when my body started screaming at me.

Aches and Pains

WHEN YOU ARE working six weeks straight with no day off while spending on average twenty-five hours a week submerged at pressure, things can turn bad fast.

With a small crew, we still had to dive even when sick. Luck has been on my side with my ears and I have never had a severe infection, or burst an eardrum... so far. The worst trouble was with sinus infections and reverse blocks.

After some dives, bright orange shit came out of my sinuses; just like the orange chicken sauce from Panda express. Reverse blocks were terrible; it felt like someone had smashed my forehead with an axe on the ascent. At the surface, it sounded like someone had deflated a balloon inside my head. Getting dizzy spells or vertigo was all part of the experience ... I quite enjoyed the dizziness though; it felt like being on a rollercoaster, spinning around, going upside down before getting back to normal.

The first time someone had a bad nosebleed on a dive freaked me out. On our safety stop we saw that this guy's mask had a little water in it and loads of thick blood mixed in. He flooded his mask to get the blood out but couldn't clear it properly, so he went to the surface and took off the mask and blood was everywhere.

It's not just underwater where you get health is-sues; being on deck duty takes its toll after a while. When growing up in Wales, we only saw that bright yellow thing in the sky for a few weeks a year if we were lucky. Now, out in the baking sun for long periods, it didn't take long to get a bit red-faced from the sun and wind. If I had a dollar every time some-one said you are looking a little red-faced, I would be a millionaire. Add deck duty to hours looking for whale sharks, and your body takes a battering. Your feet take a hammering walking on the hot deck; the paint is mixed with sand to make it less slippery and after a while, it feels like you have been walking on a cheese grater.

If you want to work on a dive boat then you will probably end up cleaning people's poo a lot of the time. Guests sometimes forgot they were at sea and flushed sanitary items down the toilet; this blocked the system easily and backed it up caused the rooms to flood many times. The marine toilets could be very temperamental and the first mate blocked up the deck toilet once – he had to scoop out his business and put it in a plastic bag as it wouldn't flush. It was the biggest brown fish he ever saw.

Apart from cleaning up blocked toilets there were some other jobs that could be quite hard. I spent hours scraping the barnacles from the ship's hull; this was a messy job and could make you really itchy from the hydroids and other stuff that lived on the hull. Scrubbing out the engine room was also another job that wasn't my favourite, as it was always boiling hot down there when the engines and generators were running.

After putting in long hours during the week, it was nice getting back on Friday afternoon. Once the fenders and lines were secured, the captain switched the engines off and then you could smell the rum from the bar down the road. You could relax a bit, and if the sea had been rough, it was nice to step on dry land again. It was still busy though, as you had to reload provisions, and refill the fuel and water. There were always bits and pieces to organise.

We held a farewell party for the guests and they were free to have dinner at a restaurant. Unless it was your turn to do the dreaded boat watch shift, you were free to have the evening to yourself and be back early the next morning. I used to hate boat watch so much I would pay the ladies $20 to do it for me.

That taste of the first rum after work was like heaven on your taste buds. After being out you felt you had missed out on the fun. You were eager to play catch up, and sometimes it turned messy. We often took the guests to the best bars on the island. One night most of us went out, making the mistake of wearing our sexy white shirts with epilates. We got the flavour and ended up on a monster session. We were all dancing the night away at Bar in the Bush until God knows what time. The ladies loved our uniforms that's for sure.

The next morning, I went to the captain's cabin. We had to transfer the guests back to the airport and I had to shake the first mate who was snoring and dribbling; he finally woke up looking a right mess. After he showered, he was frantically looking for his white shirt, but he couldn't find it anywhere. Once he came round, he remembered giving it away to some chick at Bar in the Bush as a token of his affection, but it didn't work though, he came home empty-handed and shirtless. The captain just looked at him shaking his head.

It took a while for the first mate to like me, he told me he didn't think I was going to last, but after proving myself; we got on great. We both loved a drink and had a very similar sense of humour. He was a bit of a lovable rogue, but one of the best underwater spotters I had had the pleasure of learning from.

He used to pull pranks on me though. We had a $50 bet on who could find a frogfish first and after one particular night dive he came back on board with his camera, celebrating wildly. He showed me a picture of an orange frogfish that he had 'found' on the dive. I was gutted, but handed over the $50 to him. A few years later he admitted to me he that he had taken a picture of a frogfish out of a diving magazine to trick me. I let him keep the $50 out of pure respect for the perfect blag.

He was the top man for finding stargazers at Ted's Point; these fish were hard to find because they lived under the sand. They are an ambush predator so you can see just the eyes and mouth if you know what to look for. They wait until prey is close to their mouths before grabbing it. A group of us were on Ted's Point reef at about fifteen metres, when something heavy landed on me. Looking up, I saw that the first mate was grinning at me and he had no fins on. He started running across the sand with about twenty pounds of weight in his BCD in the direction of the stargazer hangout. He had a high success rate of finding them much to my annoyance.

The guests loved the first mate and people always wanted to dive with him. He gave me the ultimate compliment after being on board for a while; he told the captain I was the best guide he had worked with and that made me very proud to hear that.

We took turns meeting the guests at San Pedro Sula (SPS) airport. Seeing the beautiful reefs and tiny islands from above was exquisite. The forty-minute flight got into SPS airport early in the morning, so we hung around until the new guests arrived in the afternoon. As a burger enthusiast the saving grace of the airport run was a visit to Wendy's; the Baconator always hit the spot, especially if you were a tad hungover from the night before.

There wasn't much to do in the airport; we wore our little sailor's outfit to meet the guests. One of the pretty immigration girls was always smiling at me in the terminal. She spoke ten words of English, and with my ten words of Spanish, we got on like a house on fire. The devil in me was already planning to use my new friend as an excellent contact to fix any visa issues. She came over to Útila a couple of times to see me, which was nice.

AFTER NEARLY A year, I had gained valuable experi-ence on the boat and this was down to the captain, who helped with everything. It wasn't just about working on the ship; it was how to be a good person as well. He was a straight shooter, never drank or partied, was very holy and a dedicated family guy. I felt I had gained his trust, which really meant a lot as he had been a captain for many years and was one of the most respected in the worldwide fleet.

He now trusted me to navigate the boat. After diving around Útila, we used to cross the thirty-one miles to Roatán. He trained me on how to use the GPS, and we would take turns to handle the crossings. When the east wind was blowing hard, the sea became so rough that the waves would be seven to eight metres high and would crash over the top of the boat. A couple of times the whole galley got turned upside down (and one time, the coffee machine ended up on the floor ripping the screws from the worktop). There would be plates and dishes all over the place and usually a few seasick guests.

After being on Útila for a few years, it was great spending time in Roatán each week. Some of the dive sites were amazing and different from Útila. My favourite was Mary's Place, located on the south coast. The topography is spectacular, with many narrow channels and swim throughs to explore. It was like diving through a maze system; there were some beautiful fans and sponges as we guided our divers single file through the channels. On top of the channel lived a beautiful orange seahorse that hung around for a couple of months.

One day, the guests were on the back deck, wait-ing for the captain's okay to jump, and one lady shouted, "Shit, I just dropped my mask."

It sank too quickly for us to try and grab it. The water looked very deep where it dropped and we gave her another mask so she could dive. Once the divers were in, I asked the captain if it was okay to try and retrieve the mask.

"Kris, it's in about two hundred feet of water you will never find it."

Grabbing my tank, I jumped into the water near the spot where it had dropped, the captain was right it was too deep, I got down to a hundred and twenty feet and there was no sign of it. Giving up hope, I started to ascend the reef wall slowly, and there it was, sitting on a tiny ledge at about a hundred and ten feet, inches away from the abyss. I grabbed it and went back up to the surface. The captain could see my bubbles and was waiting for me on the back deck.

"Told you that you wouldn't find it," he shouted at me.

"Yeah you were right it was too deep down there." I waited a few seconds and then I lifted my hand out of the water, holding the mask with a big smile on my face. The guest was delighted when I returned the mask for her; she thought it had gone for good.

Shark Dive

THE MOST FAMOUS dive on Roatán is the shark dive. There is a reef a couple of miles offshore that has a population of Caribbean Reef sharks. For many years some Italian guys had fed the sharks, so the popula-tion was good with around ten to twenty reef sharks. They charged a hundred bucks per diver so it was a licence to print money. Sometimes they had up to thirty divers a day so it was a cash cow.

The problem was the Italian guys thought they owned the reef, which didn't go down well with local people. When we took our guests, they came on board for the dive briefing. One guy was really nice and respectful, but the same couldn't be said for his partner, who was a dickhead of the highest propor-tion. He was about six feet tall with a greasy mop of curly hair and he always did the dive brief in a threatening manner which irritated everyone.

After the terrible briefings, we would jump into the water and you could see the grease coming off the guy's hair that made an oil slick on the surface before he disappeared below the waves. The divers followed the line to a sandy area at twenty metres; the guy placed a bucket of fish heads on the bottom then the sharks would start to circle waiting to be fed. The sharks were, on average, two to three metres in size, so we expected the divers to feel a little nervous if it was the first time that they had ever seen sharks. But these sharks were used to divers so made close passes around everyone. The sharks looked in good health, but there was always a couple who had fish hooks stuck in their mouths.

The divers stayed behind a line and were not al-lowed to swim with the sharks. If they did, the Italian stallion would abort the dive. If you sneezed or farted, he would also abort the dive. After fifteen minutes, the guy would pull the string and the bucket lid would come flying off. Pandemonium would ensue as the sharks made a beeline for the bucket. With fins pointing down they flew towards it hoping to get a free snack. You could always feel the true power of the sharks as they zipped through the water; it felt like a royal rumble in the shark world.

Sometimes, a couple of large groupers and moray eels tried to get in on the action as well and on occasions sharks got their heads stuck in the bucket, which was quite comical to watch. Once the show was over the sharks disappeared back to the deep, and the divers would look for dislodged shark teeth that had fallen out in the battle of the fish heads.

One day, the captain heard a story which made us stop diving with them.
The Italians hated divers going to the reef without paying them and they did things to disrupt them if they did so. If they saw a non-paying dive boat, they would rush out and jump in away from the other people. The sharks would then follow the smell of the fish heads leaving the divers with nothing to see.

The shit hit the fan on one occasion, when the Italian stallion disrupted some divers and a fight happened underwater with a female diver. He turned off a lady's air supply at twenty metres, which was seen as attempted murder and the story made the headlines in the diving world. A few weeks later the Italian guy was reported missing, and then a few weeks after that, they found his body. He would not have the chance to turn off anybody else's air under-water again.

The west end of Roatán has a couple of really nice wall dives and one day, our group was admiring the fantastic drop-off and beautiful barrel sponges on the wall. Schools of blue tangs passed us by and there was a big lobster that looked nervous under a ledge. As I looked over my shoulder something blew my mind; a yellow submarine was making its way up from the deep. There were a couple of people inside the submarine as it passed us on the way back to the surface. It was just another day in the office; nothing could surprise me anymore.

Attack of the Groupers

THE WRECK OF El Aguila was always exciting; it had broken up in a hurricane so there were different areas to explore. It was famous for large groupers and a friendly green eel that had no fear of divers. One time the eel got his head stuck up my board shorts and there were a few seconds where my dream of having a family was in serious jeopardy.

We used to feed them for the weekly guest video, but disrupting natural behaviour didn't sit well with me. The first mate usually handled the feeding, but he was off one day, so the captain asked me to do it. Another reason for being uncomfortable was there was a renegade dog snapper ... a colossal powerful beast that was lightning fast when there was food in the water. The first mate had his finger split a few weeks before, so it already had a taste for human blood. After pleading with the captain, he looked me square in the eyes and told me to stop being a pussy and get on with it.

We used an empty Clorox bottle with the top split open so that we could store the fish pieces inside. During feeding, you would put your hand into the bottle and throw a piece to the waiting groupers and moray eel. Once submerged, I scanned the wreck for the murderous snapper, but he was nowhere in sight. Settling themselves on the wreck the guests waited in anticipation for the feeding. Looking down at the Clorox bottle I noticed that small pieces of fish had escaped from the side, because I didn't hold the top tight enough. Within seconds it meant serious trouble. The groupers saw tiny pieces of fish escaping and an inexperienced young man in charge. In the blink of an eye, they decided to attack me.

Around ten large groupers pounced, some three to four feet in size, and smashed into me to get the fish. You could hear their powerful muscles snap as they headed towards me. One smacked the bottle right out of my hand and the fish went everywhere. It caused a massive feeding frenzy and the groupers showed me who was boss underwater, one bit into my hand near my thumb and then I felt the jaws of another bite into my ankle. There were fish everywhere and I felt like a chicken carcass that was being mauled by a school of piranhas.

With all the fish pieces consumed, I glanced at the guests and my crewmate who had managed to get everything on video. Masks were filling with water from laughing so hard. Green blood spurted out of the grouper teeth shaped wounds on my hands and legs and I had to get back to the surface, hoping no sharks in the area could smell my blood.

I got back to the ship and put my blooded hand on the deck and the captain looked at me. "What happened to you man?"

"The groupers got me, captain." As I climbed out of the water, the captain saw my ankle was bleeding too. I handed him the empty Clorox bottle, "I think it's better if you use somebody else next time."

I cleaned my wounds and patched myself up. The guests were finishing the dive; everybody showed some concern about the attack, but then a few seconds later burst out laughing again. Guest satisfaction was our foremost priority, so I'm happy they enjoyed my misfortune. Some nights I wake in cold sweats about the attack of the groupers. Thank God the wicked snapper was not around to finish me off.

Attack of the Lion Fish

IT WASN'T MY only aquatic injury during my time on board the boat.

Lionfish are an invasive species from the Indo-Pacific Ocean that somehow got into the Caribbean Sea and the Atlantic Ocean. There were theories about how this happened, maybe somebody had an aquarium and released them by accident, or they might have escaped during a hurricane. Other people said they might have come over in the ballast of a ship.

However, they got there, they were causing mas-sive problems in the Caribbean, with no predators and an enormous appetite; marine biologists were concerned they could have a significant impact on reef fish populations. The solution from the marine parks was to use Hawaiian slings, a type of spear to try and control them. Most of the dive pros were able to buy the spears and after a short training session you were a certified lionfish exterminator.

We visited the West End Marine Park office and they gave us four spears for our ship … we were armed to the teeth and ready for war. The guy told us locals were getting four or five fish on the spear at the same time. That target was in my mind as we left the office. The first lionfish we found was at Blackish Point. It was tiny at just about two inches long and it looked a beautiful little fish. My ruthless side got the better of me so I aimed my weapon of mass destruc-tion. I took the shot and the tiny fish was stuck in-between the three points of the spear looking slightly bemused. I got it the second time and took it back to the boat. We were one of the first people to kill a lionfish in Útila.

With thirteen needle-sharp spines and potent tox-ins, experts say a lionfish sting could kill a human. Once speared, they were handled with care and we took sea snips to remove the spines underwater. The marine park asked us to bring dead lionfish to the office so they could check the stomach contents. Lionfish could eat thirty times a day and released over 100,000 eggs each time. It was a worrying period for the islands as most commercial fishing stocks were at critical levels. One lionfish we killed was about eight inches long and when we opened his mouth, we found four small shrimps and a juvenile fairy basslet, which weren't even digested yet. If this was just one meal, then imagine what all the rest were eating as well.

WE HADN'T BEEN able to visit Coco's Seamount for a few months because of bad weather. This dive site was spectacular, with massive schools of fish, sightings of silky sharks, and some of the most pristine corals in the Caribbean. Hardly any divers went there due to its remote location near Cayos Cochinos.

On one particular dive, as we descended, dozens and dozens of massive lionfish greeted us. They had taken over large areas of the reef so we started to clear them out. It turned into a real turkey shoot with three lionfish on my spear in no time. It was exhilarating as we had never seen so many, and looking into the reef I saw another biggie. I pulled back the elastic and felt a sharp pain on my left hand. Looking down a lionfish spine was sticking into my hand. It felt like my hand was on fire; my arm was getting numb and the numbness was spreading up to my shoulder. Still down at twelve metres, my mind started to race, holy fuck I'm about to die underwater, there will be a thread about me on scuba board for sure. My breath-ing started to get heavier, and now I had no feeling in my shoulder.

I ascended and got to the back deck, where I tossed up my spear with four lionfish still attached. The captain looked at me.

"I just got stung by a lionfish."

He helped me out of my dive gear and got some hot water to start some treatment. A bit of panic set in, would the toxins travel to my brain? Luckily, Sara and Randy's group had some doctors on board and they dosed me up on medication. They told me to lie down and monitor any potential bad reaction to the toxins. I silently said my goodbyes to family and friends and went to lie down in my bunk. The drugs started to work and knocked me out for twelve hours.

When I came around it was pitch black and silent in our cabin. I wondered if I had died already, but as it turned out, they were changing generators, and the lights came back on shortly after.

The feeling in my arm came back, but had pain in my hand for nearly three months after the incident. Surviving yet another brush with death, I wondered if I had got stung on my neck would I still be alive.

The lionfish are still a massive problem; they have stretched to the East Coast of the US and down to Brazil. However, they have become a new food source with many restaurants serving lionfish inspired dishes.

THERE WAS ONE more run-in with marine life; this one didn't hurt but gave the guests a chuckle. At Jack Neal Point, the first mate found an electric stingray; we were excited because these guys were semi-rare, but they could give a shock of up to 200 volts. The guests circled the ray, which was half-buried under the sand and the first mate gestured at me, seeing if we could get him out of the sand. There was a broken twig and I slowly started to dig under the ray with it. Suddenly, the ray flew out of the sand and smashed me full in the face. I had no idea if it shocked me, as it happened so fast, but looking around at the guests and the first mate, I saw they were absolutely pissing themselves underwater.

WE ALWAYS MADE funny crew videos for the weekly presentation. On one occasion, the first mate had the video camera in his hand and he said, "Let's make a video of you face planting into the water?"

Always eager to impress, "Sure no worries." I got to the edge of the dive deck before doing a straight face plant into the water. On hitting the surface, the glass in the mask shattered into tiny pieces. I was lucky not to damage my eyes.

The first mate had a massive cheesy grin on his face. "Don't worry, I got it on camera."

EVEN THOUGH THE whale shark migration route was nearer Útila than Roatán, we spent time looking for large pelagics and one day, we saw something massive on the surface. It was black, sleek looking, and around fifteen metres long. As we approached it, a jet of water gushed up, the spray making an instant rainbow. We had found a couple of sperm whales, the largest toothed whale species in the world. They didn't mind us at all as they frolicked on the surface enjoying the beautiful sunshine. Ohs and ahs came from the guests and crew alike, as we watched the giants of the deep clear their blowholes. After a while, the whales decided to move on and we had a final look at their impressive tails as they duck-dived to the depths of the Caribbean Sea. It felt like they had used their tails to wave goodbye to us on the big white boat.

THAT EXPERIENCE WAS eclipsed by an even bigger surprise a few months later and we couldn't quite believe our eyes when it happened.

We had been out for a few hours with no success. Then out of nowhere, we saw the movement of large mammals. We thought we had found a pod of pilot whales at first and we were excited for our guests as we hadn't seen anything significant so far. Getting closer we realised they weren't pilot whales, because as they came to the surface we could see white patches under their mouths. Holy shit we had found a pod of orcas and the whole boat erupted with joy.

We counted a total of ten, including a couple of calves that were only two metres long and stayed very close to the adults. Considering there have only been thirteen sightings of orcas in the Western Caribbean we had the luckiest of days. We followed them for a few hours deciding to skip a dive to enjoy the extraordinary experience. We had no idea they would show up in the warm Caribbean Sea, because when you think of orcas you think of them munching on seals in the freezing waters of Alaska or Norway. After a few hours following we decided to give them some peace, we said our goodbyes, and watched as they drifted off towards the horizon. The sun had started to drop which made the scene even prettier.

Underwater Photography

UNDERWATER PHOTOGRAPHY HAD been of interest to me ever since I had bought a disposable camera in Hawaii; the cameras in the blue housing had had no flash and cost about $15. Once certified, I upgraded to some point and shoot cameras, but flooded most of them.

The crew were all pretty good photographers and they passed on their skills to me. We had many pro photographer guests, who also passed on advice on how to improve your images. We were allowed to join in for special underwater photography workshops on board, so my knowledge was growing.

Every week we made a slideshow for the guests as a souvenir. We all took the camera down, and tried to get shots of them with sharks or the groupers on the wreck. After a couple of months of learning to shoot manually I had a pretty good collection of images.

My fellow crewman, Al, really helped a lot with my photography; we used to have a great laugh working together. He had a sharp eye for macro species and a love for nudibranchs. Once, he got stung on the lips by a jellyfish and had an adverse reaction. His face swelled up like a balloon and his lips looked like they had had a Botox overdose. He was not impressed with his nickname of Angelina Jolie for the rest of the trip.

The first mate would make a video presentation for the guests. The sleek black Gates housing was on the camera table and I used to pick it up and pretend to shoot with it when nobody was looking. It was like the Holy Grail and I always wanted to try it out.

Being the videographer was the next level of greatness, as it gave you a chance to earn some extra money if the guests purchased the video.

One day, we were about to go out for an afternoon dive and the first mate handed me the video camera. He said to me, "I want you to take this, see if you can get anything for me."

A massive grin came on my face and he gave me a quick lesson on how to work it. My love affair with underwater videography was just about to begin.

The nerves were terrible on the first dive and I constantly looked inside the housing to see if there was a leak, then, from the corner of my eye something moved on the reef. It was a couple of common octopus mating. Pushing the record button, I had something decent to show him.

Back on the ship, the first mate grabbed the cam-era; it was his baby so he must have been a bit nervous about giving it to me in the first place. He looked happy it wasn't flooded and he downloaded the files and told me it was a great shot of the octopuses. As we watched the video with the guests, it was a proud moment seeing some of my shots in the presentation.

AFTER MY EARLY success, he often tossed me the video

camera and it quickly overtook my interest in underwater photography. The first mate took care of the editing, but was still more than happy to for me to gain experience.

One dive didn't go so well ... afterwards he told me I had accidentally pressed record, and he had a shot of me swimming around for twenty minutes doing nothing.

My chance to shine came as the first mate was off and the captain told me I would be the video pro. He gave me a quick lesson on the editing software, and I was good to go. All of the stock footage was with the first mate, so the video was made from scratch, which made it a bit more challenging. After shooting some pretty good stuff and editing late most nights I managed to get the production finished. After showing it to the guests, a couple bought a copy so it made some extra money.

From that moment on, it became a major passion of mine and I have been shooting video ever since. My most significant honour was to have my video footage open the Beneath the Sea film festival in New York in 2017. To have my video footage shown alongside people like Howard and Michelle Hall, who have grossed $96 million at the box office, was a proud moment for me.

Tough Days at Sea

As my confidence grew, my mind started to think that maybe I could become a boat captain. It's a lot of pressure being captain, as things can turn to shit fast on a boat. You have to make crucial decisions in seconds that could potentially save or cost someone their life. The weather is the hardest thing to deal with; it can turn nasty in the blink of an eye.

There was one situation where a weather system came in suddenly. We ripped out the mooring line and were seconds from running aground on the reef and becoming a headline on Undercurrent. Another time, a storm came in and we were trying to pick up guests in near-zero visibility with waves crashing over us. It felt like the boat was going to crush some of the guests as it bucked in the water and we all breathed a massive sigh of relief once everybody was on board safely.

There were a couple of medical emergencies during my time.

On one occasion, an older gentleman came up from a dive and put his tank back in place, but then he started clutching his chest before collapsing on the floor. We quickly went to work, getting him on oxygen, and making him comfortable. We thought he had had a heart attack or maybe had decompression sickness. We made our way to Roatán. The east wind was howling and it took us over three hours to get him to hospital. We had plenty of oxygen, so his condition had started to improve, but the doctors advised us to get to the chamber. The captain asked me to go with him.

After the doc had examined him, he said there was no sign of decompression sickness and he advised us to stay for the night and come back for another examination. The resort checked us into a twin room. It was impossible to get any sleep as the gentleman used a CPAP machine. I lay in bed, listening to the sound of Darth Vader breathing heavily next to me. During my delusional sleepless moments, I thought I heard, "Luke I am your father!" and at one point, I thought the guy had died on me, because his rasping breath stopped. I was about to jump over and start CPR, but he started to breathe again.

It was the longest night, so I was happy when the first chinks of sunlight came through. We got up and he felt well enough for breakfast. The doctor gave him a clean bill of health but advised him not to dive for a few days. He told him he was probably dehydrated and he had to drink plenty of water. Being on oxygen for three hours had made a huge difference to his condition. It's vitally essential for dive boats to have sufficient O2 on board and it's one of the first things I check before going diving with anybody.

Worst Day

THE SECOND DIVE accident was, without a doubt, one of the hardest days of my life. We had a male guest who turned up a day late for the charter. We were at Duppy Waters, which is probably the most famous dive on the north side. The divers were just starting to come up.

All of a sudden, the captain screamed, "Oh shit look over there."

I looked over the side of the boat and could see the gentleman was floating face down on the surface. Everything happened so fast. The first mate reached him and brought him to the boat. I grabbed the O2 kit and ran to assist them. We pulled the gentleman onto the back deck and turned him over, but taking one look at him I knew he was already dead, because his eyes were wide open and bloodshot. It was tough because he had many friends on board and they were so shocked to see what was happening.

We checked his vital signs; he had no pulse, so we started chest compressions and rescue breaths. After some compressions we managed to get all of the water out of his lungs, so we turned him onto his side to clear everything. We took turns with rescue breathing. We managed to cut off his rash guard, during the rescue breaths, and there was vomit on the inside of the pocket mask. Looking into his eyes during the rescue breaths I was sure we couldn't help him as he was too far-gone, but one of my crewmates Megan started calmly shaving the guy's chest as we prepared to use the defibrillator. We used it a couple of times, but nothing was happening, and it kept saying no pulse detected.

The captain contacted the owner and he came in a speedboat to help us. We transferred the gentleman onto the speedboat with a backboard. Three of us carried on doing CPR, the sea was so rough, and we were heading right into the east wind. It took us over half an hour to get back to Útila, but we didn't give up doing CPR the entire time, even though it was challenging in the big waves. We finally got to the island and Doctor John was waiting for us with a stretcher. We carried on doing CPR until he told us to stop and within seconds, the colour drained from the gentleman. Dr. John said he had passed away. We had tried our best for over an hour to save him, but it wasn't to be.

As Dr. John took the gentleman away I was left on the speedboat with the first mate.

He gave me a bottle of water and said, "You can wash away the taste of vomit from your mouth."

I took the water and turned away from him as tears started to build in my eyes after what just happened.

Things were about to get more difficult. The ship had come back to the dock so our boss gave us a ride in the golf cart. We saw all of his friends waiting anxiously on the dive deck and we had to give them the bad news that he had passed away.

We had no choice but to carry on with the charter, but some close friends didn't dive for the rest of the trip. It was an emotional time on board and the group leader gave a beautiful speech about his lost friend at the farewell party and it had everyone in tears. Even though this happened over ten years ago, it is my worst day working in the industry. I'm very thankful it has never happened to anyone else since that terrible day. Dr. John suspected the gentleman had had a heart attack on his safety stop. He was cremated in Honduras before being sent back to his relatives in the States.

AFTER NEARLY FOUR years of being on a six-mile-long island, my mind started to think about the next challenge in my life. I had done the best part of 4,000 dives in the Bay Islands and had swum around Moon Hole 27,586 times during that time. A lot of friends had already left and worked in many exotic locations all over the world and it was time to move onto the next place.

The monster of all sessions was the beginning of the end of my time on Útila. I worked with a nice girl from Canada for a while, whose dad was from Wales, so we had a little bit in common. She was leaving the island and wanted to party in style. We let rip for two days… I hadn't partied like this for a while. With no sleep for two days, we left the island for San Pedro, getting some strange looks as we drank a neat bottle of Absolut vodka on the ferry. We didn't care as our sunglasses hid the evidence of our current bender. We stayed at the Intercontinental Hotel and the party carried on for the rest of the night. We destroyed the mini bar, ordered strawberries and champagne and room service, which ended up on the floor. It was carnage by the time we had finished, and the room looked like The Flamingo Hotel out of *Fearing and Loathing in Las Vegas*.

After finally passing out for a few hours I was woken by the girl crashing around the room, shouting, "Fuck, I'm going to miss my flight."

I half opened my eyes and looked around the room, it was wrecked, and there were strawberries smashed all over the walls. After stumbling down to the front desk, we had to endure the pain of waiting while they checked the room and the empty minibar. I imagined the housekeepers checking the carnage we had left behind. We had run up a $400 bar tab, so we paid and got a cab to the airport.

Her flight was due to depart in twenty minutes so there was no chance of making it. We arrived, but the check-in was already closed. We must have looked such a mess to the airline staff. She managed to rebook her flight for the next day and we needed somewhere to stay. Thinking we were probably banned from the Intercontinental we checked into another hotel. Our bodies were both destroyed after partying flat out for three days, so we had a quiet night. We made it to the airport on time and I said goodbye to my friend.

AFTER THIS, IT was time for some R&R, so I headed to the capital Tegucigalpa. My buddy Steve had moved there from Útila, so I had a couple of days hanging out with him recovering. There was concern about the gunshots that rang out a couple of times near Steve's place, but he assured me this was normal for this part of the world.

After arriving back to the island, I checked my emails for any job offers. Nothing was happening, so I went back to work on the liveaboard, where we had some surprising news that our captain had left the boat. We were gutted about this, as we had become a close family unit over the past few years. We had a relief captain for a while; he was a great guy from Arkansas who helped me in my search to find a new job.

We did a few more charters, and then the boat had some down weeks. Then, an email came through, offering me a position as a boat manager in the Maldives. The offer was great with a decent salary and some excellent benefits such as a paid flight ticket home once a year and it took me about thirty seconds to accept it.

Goodbye Útila

THE BOAT MANAGER sent me a video of some spectacu-lar manta ray action from a place called Hanifaru Bay and that video got me really excited about the new challenge. They wanted me to start within two weeks if possible. My boss was okay when I told him about the new job and he thanked me for my work over the years.

It was really sad not saying goodbye to the crew as they were on Roatán. My housemate Chris helped get my dive gear from the boat and I left a farewell note for the guys on the table. I'm sure there would be many tears from them, some tears of joy as they wouldn't have to put up with my snoring and farting anymore.

It was really tough saying goodbye to the old girl for the final time and the ship also left Útila a few months after me. It ended up in the Louisiana swamp for a while before being refitted and finding a new home in the Bahamas. A new ship was under con-struction and after a lot of delays it arrived a couple of months after I had left the island.

My possessions all managed to fit into one back-pack, including my dive gear, underwater camera housing, and some bits and pieces. There was a final night out with my pals left on the island, which was pretty tame by my standards. The Flamingo Hotel room scene from the mainland still scarred my mind. I said my goodbyes to Chris and Annie and walked down to the ferry.

There were no regrets. I had a bunch of new great friends and we would meet again in different parts of the world over time. My new journey would give me the chance to explore much more of Asia, which was an exciting thought. Looking out of the ferry, Útila and Pumpkin Hill got smaller and smaller in the distance. There was time to reflect on the bus ride to the airport. After meeting so many people and enjoying some spectacular underwater escapades, there was one memory that kept sticking in my mind. I couldn't shake the memory of top local character Webb shouting out in his husky voice at Tranquila Bar, "Man I could do with a line of cocaine from here to Baltimore. I'd do it with a two-inch pipe."

The Maldives

AFTER ALREADY ACCEPTING the job I finally researched the Maldives and my jaw dropped on reading the restricted items not allowed in the country. No pork, no porn, no alcohol, no bibles, and no blow-up dolls. The list of not bringing anything fun was endless. The cold sweats came over me. How on earth was I going to smuggle my blow-up sheep into the country!

When you think of the Maldives, you imagine beautiful small islands, coconuts, and crystal-clear water, a great place to have a wedding or honeymoon. As we started to descend from 36,000 feet, my face was pressed against the window waiting for paradise. Sadly, thick grey clouds and heavy rain greeted me during a very turbulent landing.

Immigration was a breeze, but there was no hot officer to help me if there was any visa trouble. Sadly, the ladies looked very serious in their smart uniforms and didn't even give me a welcoming smile while stamping my passport. The rain poured down while I waited to be collected. After a while, this boat pulled up, and I recognised the logoed crew T-shirts. They grabbed my bag, and we took the twenty-minute boat ride to the mother ship.

During the first trip to the harbour you could see

how tiny the airport island was. If the pilot made the smallest mistake he would end up in the sea. The capital island of Male was a further ten minutes away. It looked quite surreal with a New York type skyline on a tiny island, there is no other place like it.

We arrived in Hulu Male Harbor, and there were liveaboards as far as the eye could see. Some were pretty impressive, and others would be better as shipwrecks. As we zigzagged through all the anchor lines, my new home came into view. The pictures didn't really do her any justice and she looked a million times better in real life. This beautiful hun-dred-foot motor sailor was probably the best-looking boat in the Maldives at the time.

The boat was owned by an Italian consortium, and I was welcomed on board by a tall guy with pure white hair, who was very well spoken and likable. He made me feel at home and was proud to show me around the boat. It was much more luxurious than the last gig and the yacht seemed double the size. The cabins were big and spacious with shiny wooden floors and the heads were nearly the same size as the cabins. There were many places on board for the guests to relax and it looked like the perfect working environment.

THERE WERE TWO weeks of training under the depart-ing manager. She was a boat captain and tough as old boots. She couldn't wait to get off the boat and spending a day with her was like working with a menstrual dragon. She introduced me to the crew the next day and there was a feeling that a dark mist was about to be lifted. Having been used to working with five or six crew, I would now manage fifteen staff. The majority were Maldivian with a couple from Sri Lanka and Bangladesh.

Once the training had been completed, I would be the token white man on board. It didn't take long to work out the crew was shit scared of the iron lady and I saw them tense up when they talked to her. Immedi-ately, I told myself I would make the workplace more enjoyable, because the guests could feel the tension in the air, and it shouldn't be that way.

The local captain shook my hand warmly. We would be roommates in his quarters. He was shorter than I was with a greying goatee beard and he reminded me of Wicket one of the Ewoks from Star Wars. He was a nice enough guy but wasn't comforta-ble dealing with the guests. He was very proud of his thirteen kids with three wives.

Our first meeting took a long time as everything was translated from English to Dhivehi. The kitchen guys from Sri Lanka understood English pretty well though. Once the meeting was over, I went to Male to get some things ready for my first charter.

Male is a unique place and the weirdest capital city in the world. It looks imposing as you approach by boat. The majority of the country's 300,000 population lives here and you can walk around the whole city in about an hour. As space is at a premium, everything is built upwards. I wondered how much more weight you could put on a small island before it collapsed into the Indian Ocean. Another problem in the Maldives is rising sea levels, which are forecasted to reclaim many islands over the coming decades.

We jumped off the ferry and my predecessor gave me a quick tour. Hundreds of scooters and motorbikes buzzed around the narrow streets and it was weird having a bike when you could walk anywhere on the island in a short time. The first call to prayer blared out from the speakers at the mosques and local gentlemen locked up shop doors before making a fast walk to the nearest mosque. It was the first time I had seen businesses dominated by religion. The shop owners would close for around thirty minutes four times a day to go and pray. It was crazy seeing the streets empty very quickly and everything went silent for a while.

Male was fascinating, but I wondered what people did for entertainment. You could be thrown in jail if you were caught with a beer and there were no nightclubs to reach for the lasers. The national sports stadium looked like a league two, football ground in the UK. While wandering the streets, my mind was thinking about what to do in my time off. After swapping the marching powder of Honduras for the curry powder of the Maldives life was going to be very different.

We picked up our guests from the airport and headed back. After seeing what Male had to offer, my attention switched to the spectacular marine life around the thousand plus islands of the Maldives. There were two local dive pros in addition to me, and we had to handle twenty guests between us. The ratio was a bit low for my liking, but we managed the best we could.

The diving variety and conditions were a different class from the Caribbean. Gone were the days of no currents and just plodding along. I was introduced to channel diving with the use of reef hooks, and boy was I about to be blown away by everything.

We pulled up the anchor and departed at sunrise the next day. The dive staff were switched on and had everyone kitted out ready to hit the water. We did the dive briefing on the mother ship before embarking the dive boat which is locally known as a dhoni. These boats were about twelve-metres long with a crew of three to assist the divers. The main compressor was on the mother ship and there were extra-long fill whips that stretched across when it was time to refill the tanks. It was a different way of doing things but worked well.

It was my first dive in the Indian Ocean for nearly six years, and it was spectacular. There was a magni-tude of soft corals and schools of reef fish on Hans Haas wall and there were ten times the colours and abundant marine life that you could see in the Caribbean. A honeycomb eel was sharing a hole with another brown moray, taking ebony and ivory to the next level. The eel seemed like a friendly puppy and didn't mind me being up close. It must have been close to a metre long and its mouth opened and closed as a cleaner wrasse went to work on its teeth.

The first thirty minutes of the dive was like a bub-ble-induced dream, my eyes darted everywhere; there was so much to see. We drifted along the wall when the current picked up suddenly, and the dive guides turned us back around to safety. One guest got into the wrong position and the current pinned him up against the wall. If he had been wearing a Spiderman wetsuit, he would have looked the part. The guide swam over to assist him and the guest ended up with some cuts on his hands from hitting the sharp corals. We cleaned him up when we got back on the mother ship.

After my first taste of the Maldivian reefs I quickly realised that the beauty could also spell danger, so I needed to be on my toes when conditions changed suddenly.

We moved the boat to Manta Point at Lankan, which was a brilliant hot spot for manta ray action. The iron lady took me on the dive. The reef looked terrible and there were no corals and not many fish. We swam along some bare boulders and the guides gestured for us to get low on the reef. We sat around the rocks waiting patiently, but all we had for company was an agitated squirrelfish that was mad because we had invaded his space.

After ten minutes, the guests were looking at each other wondering what was up, then suddenly a tank was being banged and the metallic chimes drifted around. From the deep blue came this beautiful manta ray, about seven-feet wide with a chunk bitten out from his back by a shark. He glided in towards the cleaning station, making small circles as the wrasse munched down on the parasite sushi. The manta flinched as the wound on his back was nibbled by the clean-up squad.

They were used to divers so they usually got really close to you, the vast shadows crossed over you, blocking out the sunshine. It looked like they were coming straight for your head, but they glided over you at the last moment. We exchanged eye contact with this ray; it felt like it wanted to communicate with us. We watched in awe for ten minutes as he hovered with the most perfect buoyancy and then, the level of excitement rose again as two more came in.

The boat manager looked at me and nodded knowingly as if to say, "I told you it was fucking awesome, didn't I?"

The most mantas we saw at the cleaning station was sixteen and after a couple of visits, it was confirmed that the Maldives is the manta capital of the world.

Expensive Internet

JUST BEFORE THE old manager left, she handed me a pocket WIFI dongle.

"It has unlimited data so you can use it as you please," she told me.

I browsed the web and downloaded a few songs, thinking nothing of it. After we returned from a charter one day, the shore manager called me.

He sounded concerned. "Kris, I need to speak to you urgently about the Internet. Can you please come to Male ASAP?"

I had only been out for a week so it couldn't be that bad, I thought.

We met in a small restaurant and ordered a drink. The shore manager was a government official, about five-foot-tall, who reminded me of Penfold out of the cartoon *Danger Mouse*. He pulled out the Internet bill from inside his brown briefcase and looked at me with a worried face.

I started to read and when I reached the bottom of the page, my eyes bulged. The amount owed was $5,187, to be paid before the end of the month! I started getting cold sweats, hardly able to speak. After gathering my thoughts, I explained the iron lady had told me it was unlimited use, but it was not going to wash, the bill had to be paid. After much arguing with the owners I had to pay half the bill, even though it wasn't really my fault, so I was $2,500 down before even getting paid. Life in paradise didn't get off to the best start ... not only was it hard to get a beer, but it also had the world's most expensive Internet.

THINGS WERE A lot different to my last job and there were many challenges to handle. It felt as though I needed an extra pair of eyes in the back of my head, because some crew didn't understand the concept of time or schedules.

In the almost two years I spent in the Maldives, we went through over forty crewmen. People were sent to us with no experience working on boats and some people didn't even last one charter. Once, they sent me a waiter who didn't want to make coffee in the morning. I had to go to his room and wake him up.

"Get up now, the guests are looking for coffee." He was hiding under the bed sheet. "Just give me
more five more minutes, sir, I'm exhausted."

I just replied, "Get off the boat now if you can't do your job."

They sent me some terrible people and the only really reliable guys were the Sri Lankans, because you never had to ask them twice to do anything. The captain was nice enough, but he didn't worry about being on time. It was as if I was his personal alarm clock, because if I didn't wake him, we wouldn't go anywhere.

It was my first job where the language barrier was a problem, while talking with the owner I said I didn't feel comfortable about not understanding everything. He smiled at me and said: "Kris, believe me, you don't want to know what they are sometimes saying about you."

They probably resented me as a foreigner, but slowly gained their trust, and after weeding out some rotten egg's things started to settle.

ANOTHER CHALLENGE WAS getting any decent food to feed the guests. As the Maldives was a tiny island chain, they only grew limited fruit and veg. They had fantastic fish, but everything else was imported from India and Thailand. It was impossible to get decent beef for example and they sent us these massive chunks of beef, which the chef had to boil for a couple of hours to make it tender enough to eat. It was a real challenge for them to make something edible. There were no pork products as you needed a special permit that cost a lot of money and they had this horrendous beef bacon, which was like eating the bottom of a shoe. It was chicken hotdogs every day for breakfast if you were a guest and you could see they were not impressed with the selection on offer.

The crew ate chicken or tuna curry for every meal with either roshi bread or rice … no knives or forks they just ate with their hands. After a while I enjoyed curry for breakfast with them.

The Sri Lankan kitchen guys were two of the friendliest people you could ever meet and they tried their best with what they had to work with. We decided to give the bland menu some new ideas by adding a Mexican lunch and some different Western foods. They did make some fantastic curries though, and most of the guests really enjoyed the Sri Lankan lunch buffet.

On the last night of each charter, we had a Maldiv-ian night with some local dishes and snacks. It was a bit of culture for the guests, the crew would sing some songs for them, and we all wore local sarongs, which made me look like a fat fairy.

Hanifaru Bay

THE MOST CHALLENGING charter I had was a sched-uled trip to Hanifaru Bay. This is the best place in the world in which to see large numbers of manta rays, and on a good day, you can see up to a hundred and fifty mantas in an area the size of a football field. The season only runs for a couple of months of the year so it's a busy period and we would run back-to-back charters for the whole time.

What was difficult was that people believed they would see exactly what was on the promo videos every week. It was never as easy as that, but people had high expectations, and it caused massive prob-lems sometimes.

On one occasion, the weather had been looking rough for the week with high winds and waves and I could see the captain was about to change the plan. On top of this, we had a problem with the boat's throttle cable. We had a temporary fix until new parts could be sent from Italy, but it looked like shit because the cables had to go through the saloon area to get into the engine room. It didn't look ideal but it was all we could do so the charter could run.

The captain asked me to tell the guests that we would not be making the trip north to Hanifaru. It would be too dangerous for the boat to cross the open water between the atolls. Instead, we would go to North and South Ari Atolls, which was the most common route. All twenty guests were in the saloon for the bad news and it didn't go down well. I thought the guests were going to lynch me, even though I apologised to everyone for the inconvenience, using my best customer service skills.

It was a shit show from beginning to end and a couple of Italian guests phoned the boat owners behind my back, demanding that we go to Hanifaru Bay. We had already explained the situation before we spoke to the guests, but there was a poisonous feeling on board. Some guests were shit-stirring with the others, to make our life as difficult as possible, but we carried on the best we could in really bad weather.

It was pissing down and really windy for the en-tire week, the diving sucked, and there was minimal manta ray action at the other places where we usually saw them. Things got heated and guests were frustrated. When we did find some good stuff, one guest chased away the marine life with his camera and I had to split two guys apart who were about to start throwing punches due to this.

We tried our luck looking for whale sharks down at Maamagili on the southern coast of South Ari Atoll, one of the best places to see the whale sharks in the Maldives. After a few hours of looking we saw nothing. We tried one more time, but the sea was rough, and the visibility was really bad. There were schools of fish in the blue, so I turned the camera on and swam out from the reef. The fish all swam away from me quickly and on turning around I saw this eight-metre whale shark was heading right at me. I started to bang my tank, trying to get the guests' attention while filming the shark. Nobody showed up, so it was just the beautiful shark and me for a few minutes before it swam away. The shit week contin-ued with me being the only one on board to see a whale shark.

I always took a lot of pride in my work and I hated to see disappointed guests, especially when they had spent thousands on the trip, but it was simply a bad week all around. The video of the week was also poor due to the diving conditions. I wasn't sure whether to add the whale shark footage as nobody else had seen it, but I added it at the last minute as it was one of the best shots I had ever taken. When the Italian guy, who had phoned my boss to complain, saw it, he blew a gasket.

"You never saw that whale shark this week. That's stock footage from Útila."

Looking at him and trying to keep a straight face was hard. It was sad that the other guests hadn't see it, but after all his shit-stirring during the charter, I was secretly delighted he never saw the shark. Afterwards, the guy went to the top of the company trying to get a full refund for everyone. The investigation went on for about two months and he accused us of lying to the guests about the mechanical issues on the boat. He said that the problem with the throttle cable was the real reason we didn't go to Hanifaru, which was untrue.

THERE WERE MORE chances to see the magic of

Hanifaru Bay over the coming months. After learning quickly how things worked, I always explained to guests that we weren't guaranteed to see hundreds of mantas every week. The stars needed to align with the correct currents, tide times, wind direction, and plankton blooms to see all the mantas at the same time. For the magic to happen the high tide had to bring in plankton blooms and as it went to low tide the plankton was trapped inside. Once this happened the mantas came to feed. It was a privilege to see them but not a right, and when the stars aligned, it was a fantastic and truly memorable spectacle.

It was the last year that you could use scuba tanks in Hanifaru so I was lucky in that respect. Marine biologists thought the bubbles disturbed the mantas during feeding, so it was only open to snorkellers in years to come.

On my favourite day in the bay we jumped into the water to find that the visibility was cloudy due to the plankton. In fact, the water was so thick with plankton that at first, we didn't even see a whale shark that was ten feet away from me. It was feeding in a vertical position; gulping down bucketful's in quick time. It didn't move a muscle as we observed him for a while. We then watched around forty mantas flying in formation like sleek Stealth bombers, mouths wide open with wing tips curved up so they nearly touched each other. They came in a straight line as if on a bombing run, one by one they passed you with a whoosh, and there was nothing you could do but hover there with bright eyes and bewilderment. You were not invited to the plankton party, so often wingtips slapped you as they went by. It was a situation where you needed ten pairs of eyes not to miss anything.

One ray was about ten feet in front of me doing barrel rolls and after he had spun around ten times I wondered if they got dizzy feeding this way. I looked to the other side where another five were at the cleaning station getting spruced up before dinner. It was hard to keep track but there must have been a hundred during the hour we were there.

It was one of the greatest underwater shows on earth. They were so agile and graceful, you could have spent all day watching them, but shortly after all the food was gone, they disappeared into thin air, and there was nothing left in the bay.

We got back on the boat with a massive grin on our faces. On this particular day we had done everything that the promo video said we would.

THE MANTA RESEARCH guys were based at a resort close by and they spent every day checking for manta action. They identified over a thousand mantas in a couple of years but estimated the population to be around five thousand in the Maldives. They would identify the mantas from the unique markings on each individual's underside. The protection of the manta rays is essential as they bring in an estimated $8 million each year.

ON ANOTHER TRIP to Hanifaru, we had a group from an EMMY awarding-winning TV show. They had charted the whole boat and wanted to film an episode on Hanifaru Bay.

At the airport, I couldn't locate the final female guest and the leader told me he didn't know the person as she had signed up at the last minute. On rechecking the restaurant area, I saw a lady sitting down motionless wearing dark glasses. I approached her and asked if she was okay. She looked like a rabbit caught in some headlights, but finally she came around and confirmed her name to me. We walked over to the boat and she looked severely medicated, hardly walking straight, and slurring her words. I guessed she had taken too many sedatives on the long flight.

We got to the yacht and she stumbled on board, asking to go straight to her cabin. I tried to wake her for the briefing, but she was out cold and finally came out of the cabin twenty-four hours later. She started to dive and seemed okay underwater once we got her weights figured out.

The following day one of the channel dives disa-greed with her and she came back in a terrible mood, grabbed a bottle of rum, and poured a quadruple. Bottoms up … it was gone in a flash. She went back to her cabin, and we didn't see her again until breakfast. The group leader wasn't really sure how to handle her but we did our best to make her feel welcome. It was apparent that she was having a really tough time in her life and the next day we found the cause of the anguish.

We had been to Hanifaru for a few days and there was no sign of the mantas so far. The guys from the TV show were getting antsy and were becoming more challenging to deal with. They really wanted to get the footage needed for the show, so the dive team suggested we go further north to a shark cleaning station for a while until we got word the mantas were back around Hanifaru. They agreed and were treated to some excellent shark action at the cleaning station. About fifty sharks swam in front of us, including big chunky reef sharks. There were blacktips, whitetips, and some nurse sharks and they put on an excellent show for the guests, which took their minds off the absent mantas for a while.

The guests liked it so much they wanted to go again, so after the surface interval, we returned. The sharks were still around, and everybody was glued to the action. I kept an eye on the lady to make sure she was okay, and I saw her pull out a small plastic pot and open it up. She started to shake the container, and white powder came out into the water column. The dust made the water cloudy around the majority of the guests and the cynic in me thought she had just kicked her drug habit and was throwing away the last of the stash. After a while, the powder drifted away in the current. She got some strange looks from the divers and some of them brushed off remnants of powder from their dive gear.

Once back on-board curiosity got the better of me so I asked what was in the container. I was dumb-founded with her answer. She told me it was her husband. He had died recently and had been cremat-ed. She explained they had been married for many years and had dived all over the world together. She had loved seeing the sharks, so wanted to leave her husband's ashes with them as he would have really loved the place. It was now clear she was still suffering from the loss of her husband, and it goes to show you never know what is going on in people's life so you shouldn't be too quick to judge. After that dive, she came out of her shell as if a weight had been lifted from her shoulders. She was a real pleasure to be with and bonded with the crew for the last few days of the charter.

The trip turned out well in the end, because after the shark dive we had news that the mantas were back in the bay. The TV crew had some excellent footage of the mantas feeding and after what were some worrying days, they were able to make their show.

Pranks

IT HAS BEEN nice meeting many skilled photographers and videographers during my diving career and I have had some great advice from some of the best, for which I'm grateful.

On one occasion, we had a Spanish photographer on board and he was very proud of the books he had published. He was telling me he had been everywhere in the world and we couldn't show him anything he hadn't seen before. He thought he was king of the underwater photography world, so I started to plot a way of showing him something he had never seen before that would deflate his ego just a tiny bit.

We did a wreck dive close to a resort in South Ari Atoll. It was a decent wreck with some leaf scorpion-fish and schools of batfish. Next to the wreck were extensive staghorn coral gardens that looked amazing. There were plenty of nudibranch species on the ship's deck and these gave me a cracking idea to stitch up my new Spanish friend. The guy was cradling his camera setup like a new-born baby.
"Have you ever seen a nudibranch cleaning sta-tion?"

He looked at me as if I was from a different planet. "What is a nudibranch cleaning station? I have never heard about this kind of thing before."

I could feel the bait was in his mouth already, "Really? Wow, I'm surprised that you don't know about this, it's very famous here in the Maldives." The key was trying to keep a straight face now the trap was prepared.

We got on the boat, "Stay close to me, as soon as I find the cleaning station, I'll call you over so you can get great shots for your next book."

We descended onto the wreck and the guy started taking images. I headed off to the wreck's bow and there were three nudibranchs quite close together, which was perfect and just what I needed. I banged on my tank – I had written on my slate nudibranch cleaning station. The guy looked excited to be seeing something new. I got close to the nudibranchs and gestured for him to get his camera ready for the shot. As he prepared himself, I took out a toothbrush from my BCD pocket and pretended to clean the three nudibranchs. He looked up from his viewfinder with a look of disgust in his eyes, tried to keep a straight face, but in the end, he just burst out laughing. The guy swam away from me, shaking his head in disbelief that he had fallen for the nudibranch cleaning station.

Once we got back on board, he had a few com-ments: "Ah yes, you are a comedian from Wales."

There were always some great pranks played while working on the dive boats. One classic was when a group leader poured a bottle of green food colouring inside one of his diver's booties. The diver put his boot on and went diving. When he got back and took it off, his whole foot right up to the ankle was a lovely dark green colour. It was impossible to wash it off, so the diver walked around with a green foot all week.

The shampoo trick was also a good one. The showers were on the lower back deck so as people showered it was easy to squeeze extra shampoo on their head without knowing it. They would be rinsing for ages wondering why it wasn't washing off and we would just hide the shampoo bottle when they looked around wondering what was going on.

I pranked a friend once and couldn't believe he fell for it. We were on the dive deck and there was a tub of silicone grease on the camera table.

"This is the best stuff if you really want to clean your mask well," I said and walked off to set up my camera for the dive.

We jumped onto the skiff and headed to the site and my friend was furiously trying to clean his mask.

"What's happening mate, what's wrong with the mask?"

He looked at me puzzled, "I used the stuff on the table to clean my mask, and now I can't get it out."

The mask had a thick layer of silicone grease all over it and we spent the next 15 minutes trying to scrape the grease out before we could go diving.

IT WAS NICE to visit some of the tiny islands on our charters around the Maldives. You can walk around the islands in just a few minutes, and you always wondered what life was like for the locals, because their houses were very basic and most were made out of concrete blocks with a grass roof.

Even the smallest islands had their own mosques

and the people were always friendly when we visited them. They sold little trinkets made of shells and other things that had washed up on the beach. We were sailing one day and got close to an island and the captain turned to me.

"Kris, this island is not a very good place to visit for you."

I looked at him "Why's that then cap?"

He looked at me for a few seconds not sure if he wanted to share this info with me. "Well, some of the guys there, they are like Al Qaeda and they think differently from the rest of us."

I looked at him. "Well that's fine, but we really should be making a move as we will be late for the next dive." I went to hide in the wheelhouse expecting an RPG to come flying at the boat at any second.

ON MOST CHARTERS we took the guests onto a small island for sunset drinks and dinner and the crew made a whale shark sculpture in the sand, which looked great, they also sang some local songs and even the captain joined in sometimes. I asked him about the lyrics of one of the songs that was really catchy. He looked a bit sheepish but then told me the song was about women's breasts some of which were soft or hard. The next time the crew sang the song to the guests the captain winked at me, because now I knew what the song meant.

Ari Atoll

THERE WERE SOME amazing locations in North and South Ari atoll. One particular place was mind-blowing for night dives.

Maaya Thila was such a popular night dive, that sometimes twenty boats were all tied together for the dive. The reef was very shallow but turned into an energetic circus of activity at night. As dive lights darted around, they illuminated reef fish that hid amongst the corals and from the shadows, white tip sharks zipped around feeling the electric pulses from the terrified fish. The marbled rays didn't care you were there as they looked for dinner and moray eels brushed your legs as they swam freely over the plateau. The giant trevally fish used the light beams to see their targets as they chomped on red-toothed triggerfish, but the hawksbill turtles looked totally annoyed as the lights interrupted their sleep patterns.

Another exciting Thila dive was at Fish Head. It got its name from the fishermen dropping fish heads into the water, which attracted a lot of sharks.

On one particular dive, we saw some guitar sharks on the bottom, which were pretty rare and there was some amazing action between two giant moray eels. Everybody else had gone back to the boat and I was just about to start my safety stop, when I noticed the moray eels were very close to each other. After a few seconds they swam into midwater and started to fight. They were big eels, easily around six feet each and they were biting each other and slamming into the reef. This was all on camera and it lasted a couple of minutes. I got too close at one stage and the eels crashed into the camera. After a while, the defeated eel swam off and I had some of the best moray footage I could ever have hoped for.

Maamigili was the best chance to see whale sharks in the Maldives and sometimes we had great luck in seeing many on the same day. There was no control as there had been on Útila, and sometimes hundreds of people all chased the same shark, which was mental to watch. A couple of times we saw huge schools of devil rays as well.

On one dive, I was low on the reef when I spotted the school coming directly towards me, the camera was already rolling; and I held my breath as they came closer. They were now just a couple of feet away from me and as I exhaled, the school of around thirty rays all swam upwards together making an incredible piece of footage and one of my favourites in the Maldives.

There was one more special place not far from Maamigili. Dhigurah Island had a seamount that was one of the most beautiful seamounts I have ever seen. There were three sections of large reef covered in great sea fans, schools of blue-lined snapper covered the reef, and my favourite part was an area of about fifty square metres that was covered in carpet anemones. I had never seen so many in my life. Most of them were an orange or purple colour, some were fully closed up into a ball, and others were open fully with tentacles flowing in the current. If you are a fan of Finding Nemo, you could spend the whole dive admiring the thousands of anemone fish that lived here.

Hammerheads

RASDHOO WAS A small atoll but a favourite place for our guests, because there was a chance of seeing scalloped hammerhead sharks. It was a blue dive down to about forty metres with no visual reference apart from your fellow divers.

We always aimed to be in the water just as the sun came up … it was still fairly dark as the sun wasn't high yet. Some dives nothing happened and you would count the blue bioluminescent plankton in the water to pass the time. On other occasions, it worked out pretty well. The most we ever saw was six hammerheads.

It was a surreal feeling being so deep. You are surrounded by dark blue water and it's like floating around in purgatory. Then suddenly, you see movement, your eyes take a moment to focus in the poor light, then you see the impressive glossy body of a shark. Its hammer-shaped head confirming your wildest dreams. The sharks were very timid and if you made the slightest sound they would disappear very quickly back into the deep. As the dive is so deep, you don't get much time, but if the sharks showed up even for a few minutes, then it was mission accomplished.

The diving was excellent at Rasdhoo, as the topography was insane ... a narrow slither of reef was covered in healthy black corals, schools of red-toothed triggers filled the water, and many sharks hung out in the blue. There was a colossal Napoleon wrasse in all its turquoise brilliance, and behind the reef was a huge sand patch, where eagle rays fed likes pigs in a trough. Other stingrays and whitetips lazed around on the sand as if on vacation. Many manta rays fed on the incoming tide in the mouth of the channel so it was a great all-round atoll for diving.

IT WAS CHRISTMAS time in the Maldives and the nearest thing we got to turkey was the shitty chicken hotdogs we served for breakfast. Having worked on boats and resorts for the last five years, I had got used to working the holidays and it just felt like another day. One of my best mates was over for the New Year, which was great. I luckily had the week off, so we decided to visit Sri Lanka for a few days after the New Year.

It was the first time Martin had been diving since Honduras three years ago and it took him a couple of dives to get back into it. His buoyancy improved and he regained a lot of confidence. He had never seen any sharks in Útila, so this was all about to change.

We were diving on a seamount in South Ari Atoll, a pinnacle that came up from the ocean floor and was famous for sharks, rays, massive moray eels, and really impressive schools of fish. We were engulfed by jacks and scad mackerel and Martin was loving it. Apart from some small whitetips, we didn't see any bigger sharks for a while. Then, a chunky grey reef shark came from behind Martin. This shark was pretty big for a grey reef; it had a solid muscular body and was around six feet long.

If you have never seen a shark before, this was one that could strike the fear of God into you. The chance was there to make Martin shit his Speedos, so I swam up to him and pretended to be scared and jabbed my finger towards the shark. It was only about fifteen metres away from him. While pointing to the shark, I grabbed Martin and pushed him towards it. I then sped off swimming away in the other direction. I watched him jump out of his skin as the shark passed by. He hurriedly swam over to me and there was a look of fear in his eyes ... and potentially a change of wetsuit was needed for the next dive.

Booze Cruise

BUYING ALCOHOL IN the Maldives was the biggest ball ache and wasted plenty of my free time. Being a strict Muslim country, there were tight rules in place to control its distribution. It felt like Chicago during prohibition ... think of Fort Knox or Guantanamo Bay for security.

There were guard dogs everywhere, barbed wire fences, and CCTV cameras. We had to collect the champagne for the New Year's Eve party on the boat. After starting the paperwork, it took about four hours to receive it, and a couple of cases of beer and wine. Once they deliver the booze, you have to go directly back to the mother ship and store the alcohol under lock and key. The police could come and inspect your stock at any time, and you had to be accountable for every single drop; otherwise, you could end up in prison.

New Year's Eve came, the bottles of champers were on ice, and Martin and I looked forward to the celebrations. However, we had hardcore divers on board, they didn't want a hangover the next morning, and every single guest was in bed by eight o' clock. The night was turning into a damp squib and I glanced at the frosty bottles of champagne thinking what a total waste it was.

My drunk, party boy devil popped up on my shoulder. He hadn't been seen since Útila and he whispered in my ear convincingly: "Why don't you just drink the champagne and enjoy the night with the guys?"

I turned to him and said, "It has been a while hasn't it?"

A few of us demolished every single bottle of champagne and had a really nice evening. The captain, who was very religious, slept through the whole thing, but we had a great time ringing in the New Year.

AFTER THE CHARTER finished, Martin and I headed to Sri Lanka for five nights. Our flight wasn't until midnight, so we had the whole day to ourselves. We did what we did best and got absolutely smashed from about ten in the morning until it was time to fly. We were hanging out at the Hule Hotel pool bar, which is the only place for a drink near the airport. It's a strange place, because if you are a Maldivian, they won't allow you inside, all the bar staff were Sri Lankan as they didn't want any locals serving alcohol.

We weren't in good shape to fly. It was only a one-hour flight to Colombo thank God, but Martin was a mess and got some funny looks from immigration as he told them our destination was Colombia. Once we got to the gate, we did another stupid thing and bought a bottle of champagne for the flight. On top of the all-day beers this was the straw that broke the camel's back.

We arrived at Colombo airport at 2 am. We hadn't booked anywhere to stay and Martin was worse for wear and stumbling around. We got to the immigra-tion line and went to two different officers. I smiled at my officer trying to act sober, but Martin stumbled into the desk next to me. I silently prayed he would be a good boy, but he couldn't hold it together.

The officer asked, "Where are you going sir?" Martin was looking at the guy trying to hold his focus. "I'm going to Colombia."

The officer looked confused. "Pardon sir? Colom-bia?"

Martin's eyes narrowed, "Yes, I want to go to Co-lombia, now stamp my fucking passport."

Oh shit, that's it I thought ... we are about to get kicked out of Sri Lanka before getting past immigra-tion.

My passport was stamped, so I went over to say sorry for any offence my friend had caused. Luckily, the officer stamped Martin's fucking passport, and our journey continued.

Lesbian Dwarf

WE MET THIS travel agent at the airport and we made a deal with him for our trip. We checked into a hotel in the town of Negombo and things got even worse as I was woken up by Martin walking around the hotel grounds in his underpants at about five in the morning wondering where he was.

The other trip highlight was when Martin had his phone stolen by a lesbian dwarf in a bar we went to. He also got charged around twenty bucks for a packet of cigarettes.

EVEN THOUGH MY first visit to Sri Lanka was a short one, I visited a few more times after that. Apartments in Male were expensive, so it was easier and cheaper to go to Sri Lanka and stay on a nice beach and do some exploring.

The boat chef, Chandana, invited me to visit his family on one occasion. They lived a few hours away from Colombia, sorry Colombo. It was great to see his home and he prepared a lovely meal for me and his family.

The trains in Sri Lanka were fun to ride, very cheap, and they looked the same as they did a hundred years ago. The locals were so friendly and the children were interested to learn your name and find out where you came from.

IT WAS HEART-BREAKING visiting the south of Sri Lanka. It had been really hit hard by the terrible tsunami in 2004, and there was a small museum there, which had many images of the damage done to the area. A whole train had been destroyed, killing around a thousand people, which must have been shattering to the local area. There was still a lot of damage to housing which was really sad to see.

Mystery Lady

ON ONE VISIT, I had to interview some Sri Lankan marine engineers for a vacant position on the boat. I had no idea why they sent me as I have trouble working a screwdriver. We had had some issues with our original fella. He was a really nice guy, prayed five times a day, but had a habit of leaving the water maker on and then going off the boat without telling anyone. Then in the morning, the engine room would be flooded, and the captain fuming.

I walked into the galley once and noticed the oven was on. I looked inside and saw one of the pumps from the engine room inside it. I got the captain and asked politely, "Cap, why is there a pump in the oven?"

"We use this to cook the food for the guests so it needs to be kept clean." Cap looked at me sheepishly and said, "Kris, it's the same story. Last night the bloody bastard went back to Male and left the water maker on again."

So, the brainy engineer had decided to try and dry the pump in the oven. This kind of thing would happen on a nearly weekly basis. It was a tough assignment in paradise.

ANYWAY, BACK TO Sri Lanka, the interview with these engineers took place in a shopping mall. The key was trying to act knowledgeable about everything and ask the right questions … and to look smart, I made plenty of notes on each applicant.

A local girl walked past our table a few times and we smiled at each other every time she went past. Once I finished with the interviews, we met up with each other. It turned out she was with her sister, and we went to a hotel right on the waterfront. The girls were really nice to talk to and they were dressed in jeans and T-shirts. After the drinks, we went for a walk on the beach. After a while, the smiling girl took her younger sister home as it was getting late. The smiles told me she wanted to see me again, so I gave her my hotel address.

"Come and visit me later if you have nothing bet-ter to do, I'll take you out for dinner." She smiled again. "Yes, that would be nice."

Back at the hotel a while later there was a knock on the door. I stood wide-mouthed, because the lady had shown up wearing a full-on burqa with just a little slit for the eyes. It was strange because she had worn jeans and a T-shirt a few hours earlier. I was a little bit flummoxed. "Please come in."

She came into the room and sat down. After a while, the truth came out. She wasn't really religious or even a Muslim, but was in disguise in case her husband saw her out late with some strange white guy.

ON ONE TRIP, I made a visit to a turtle sanctuary that

had been run by the same guy for ten years. He did some great work rehabilitating injured turtles. Sadly, there was a blind one that kept bumping his head and another one could only swim around in circles. He paid locals to find turtle eggs on the beaches and he looked after them and gave them a chance in the world.

It was a pleasure to release some hatchlings into the wild. Watching them crawl along the sand to the water's edge was great and as they went into the water you could see their tiny little heads bobbing up and down on the surface. It was my hope they would make it in the big bad world.

There was another place in Sri Lanka that I visited, that wasn't so nice. Manta rays were heavily protected in the Maldives, but it was the opposite there. They butchered them to harvest the gill rakers and the rest of the manta was just wasted. The stupid idea was to dry them out and crush them up and then use them as Chinese medicine to filter the body. It was the biggest load of bullshit I had ever heard.

Channel Diving

WHEN I RETURNED to the Maldives, the monsoon had changed our diving plan and we switched to channel diving. These adrenaline dives were not for everybody and some preferred longer, easier dives around the pinnacles. The channel dives were deep and there could be a strong current, which meant that some-times dives were over in fifteen minutes.

We had to wait for the tide to come in. Diving on the outgoing tide was never as good because the water was murkier, and the action wasn't as good. The boat would manoeuvre to the outside of the channel mouth. We emptied our BCDs of air and did a negative entry, swimming down as quickly as possible to the mouth of the channel. If you descended slowly, you might not get into the correct position and be blown inside the channel. Some people who didn't quite make it down fast enough ended up crawling along the bottom, trying to get back into position. Others were thrown off course and had no chance of getting into the right area.

It was messy and sometimes we aborted the dive and tried again. If the descent was good and everyone was accounted for, we would use reef hooks to stay in position while watching the show unfold before our eyes.

The water from the new tide flooded in from the Indian Ocean, and once hooked into the channel mouth you could see the amazing drop-off down to thousands of metres. The show was mind blowing with sometimes thirty to forty eagle rays with their white spots and long tails cruising by. Huge Napoleon wrasse mixed in with a tornado of jacks and giant trevally in this fantastic mix of large reef fish. Grey reef sharks and white tip sharks swam around, looking to strike any fish that looked vulnerable, and big hawksbill turtles would amble across our line of sight.

If the current allowed, we would cross to the other side of the channel. I once saw three different species of moray that looked deep in conversation as their mouths opened and closed in tandem. Big marble stingrays rested on ledges perched on the edge of the universe and we had occasional treats like passing pods of dolphins and a few marlins. With air and deco time dwindling it was soon time to unhook and explore the channel walls before getting back to the surface.

Kandooma Thila was a channel dive with a sea-mount in the middle. It was not for the faint-hearted and there were many complaints from guests that it was dangerous, so we pulled it from our dive plan. Even with thousands of dives under my belt, it was challenging for me. There was no doubt that it was a beautiful place and there were a number of grey reef sharks that regularly got cleaned here. They would hover vertically during the process. The problem was the current's strength was immense and some divers just couldn't do it. If there was a dive site that could give you a heart attack this was it. It was really risky, had plenty of red flags, and had gained the nickname Kandooma Death Thila. It was hard to control these types of dives, because all it took was a couple of issues then the whole dive was in danger. We literally prayed everyone got back to the surface in one piece.

Hot Models and Gypsies

ON ONE OCCASION, this stinking rich Russian guy chartered the whole boat and he was joined by two really beautiful models.

It was a relaxing charter for us, the guy was just being a Playboy, and his models pranced around all day wearing high heels and bikinis. It was one of the best assignments we could have wished for ... we took them diving and we had to hold hands with these beautiful ladies because if they didn't, the sharks would eat them! The Russian guy couldn't speak much English, but he was easy to handle.

It looked like it was going to be one of the most perfect charters ever, but then I took a call from the boat owners. Another boat they chartered had engine problems and we had to rescue the fifteen Italian passengers as quickly as possible and they were going to spend the final four days of their vacation on board with us.

"What about the Russian guy?" I asked the owner. "Just tell him we are really sorry, but we have no other choice."

I spoke to him, but he didn't understand that his peace and quiet was about to be destroyed by a bunch of Italians. I also explained to him that it was still okay for the models to walk around in high heels and bikinis all day.

We pulled up the anchor and went to meet the stricken boat, taking a couple of hours to reach them. It was an old wooden vessel that had not been maintained for years and was the cheapest of the cheap. When they saw our shiny boat in all its glory, you would have thought they had just won the lottery, because there were plenty of ohs and ahs as these Italians gypsies climbed on board. We half expected to see a horse and cart, and one lady had a bandana on ... I was just waiting for her to put down a tablecloth and get out her crystal ball.

Out of the corner of my eye, I glanced over at the Russian. He was not impressed with his new ship-mates at all and his bikini-clad models stood with their long legs reaching to the sky, hands-on-hips wondering why their private party was being crashed.

The rest of the week was wild, the Italians did a great job of taking over the boat, and it was like a wild party for them. They must have felt the same euphoria as Jack Dawson on the Titanic just after he saw Rose's impressive bosoms. One lady was a fiery ginger who smoked about sixty fags a day. She didn't speak any English but managed to shag half of the crew in a couple of days. It was carnage on board and these guys drank everything ... not my typical charter of quiet Americans by any stretch of the imagination.

We tried to give the Russian guy as much space as possible, but understandably his trip was ruined and after the charter he demanded a full refund from the owners, which never came.

We are on Fire

OUR NEXT CHARTER gave me my worst scare in the Maldives. We were crossing between the atolls, and I was taking a rest in the wheelhouse. The sails on the boat were up and we were making good time en route to North Ari Atoll. Suddenly, my cabin door burst open.

One of the crew shouted, "We have a fire on board. Quick we need to get everyone off the boat."

I jumped up and was downstairs in seconds. Thick black smoke was pouring out of the engine room vents and already there were some guests in the muster station waiting for instructions with a look of fear in their eyes. The fire alarm had sounded, and people came out of the saloon, because it was starting to fill with black smoke. We started to move the guests onto the dive dhoni and provided lifejackets and I went inside to double-check that all the cabins and toilets were empty.

By the time everyone was safely on the dhoni, the smoke had started to subside. The engineer had been down in the engine room and found out the problem. Some plastic bags had blocked the water intake on the hull and made the generators overheat, which caused the thick black smoke in the engine room. Once he and the captain were satisfied the emergency was over, we brought the guests back.

We ate our meals outside for the rest of the trip, because it was hard to get rid of the acrid smoke smell in the saloon. That was the fastest that my heart had pounded in my chest for a long time.

Just a month later we heard mayday calls for an-other liveaboard that had caught fire and had sunk within minutes. That boat was a wooden one, so we were lucky to have a better-quality steel-hulled vessel.

After nearly abandoning the ship we needed something good to happen as the guests were in shock. We returned from one dive and there were plenty of fish jumping on the surface. There was a huge bait ball of sardines and blacktip and silky sharks broke the surface to feed on them. I grabbed the camera and jumped into the water, hoping to get some good footage. Looking down, there were so many sharks; it was hard to count them all. Sadly, the show didn't last very long as the sharks dropped down into the deep, but it made the guests smile again after the fire incident.

ON ANOTHER CHARTER a guest had to leave early due to an emergency and because of our location, the only option was to take a seaplane back to Male. We took him to the seaplane pontoon and waved them off.

Once they were in the air we headed back and I took the wheel of the speedboat. The water was like glass so we followed the marker buoys into the deeper water. Thinking we were clear, I gave the engines some throttle and we skipped across the water, but suddenly, there was a massive crunch and the boat came to a halt. We were stuck on top of a massive coral head. Panic set in and I thought the hull must be cracked open and she might sink. It would be my most expensive mistake since the Internet bill on my first trip. The crewman jumped over the side to check the hull, and luckily for me there were only some scratches on it, so we both lifted the boat free from the reef. I was happy to see that the reef had no corals growing on top so no damage was done there either. I paid him $50 not to tell the captain what had happened and let him drive the boat to the mothership.

THERE WAS ANOTHER charter that coincided with Ramadan and the captain said the crew wouldn't be a 100% strong for the next month as they fasted during the day. The dive team didn't fast because they needed to keep hydrated and have energy for the dives and they agreed to do their Ramadan another time. There was resentment towards the dive team as they didn't partake.

It must be difficult to observe Ramadan while the guests ate all day and it took a lot of determination to do it, so I respected them for that. With me being a greedy bugger, it meant having an extra meal a day as they always invited me to break the fast with them at sunset. After that, it would be time to have dinner with the guests in the evening.

You had to be careful during Ramadan in Male, because it was very hard to get any food during fasting and you could not be seen eating in the streets as it was disrespectful.

One lunchtime, I found that all of the local places

were closed and on walking up to one of my favourite restaurants, I saw that the curtains were shut. I was about to walk away when one of the staff opened the door. Looking left and right, he whispered, "We are open sir, we just have to be quiet about it during Ramadan."

After going inside there were ten other white peo-ple eating in the restaurant and they looked up at me with a guilty glance as if they were doing something very naughty.

AFTER BEING ON the boat for nearly two years, my mind started to think about moving on. Even though mantas and channel dives were spectacular, life in the Maldives was starting to get on top of me. We didn't have a rotating crew so if we had guests we were working and after doing seventeen weeks straight with no day off, my energy levels started to drop and there was a feeling of being burnt out.

The fact there was no place to call home apart from the boat was also niggling me. It was nice to travel a lot during my time off and I had been to Thailand, Malaysia, Sri Lanka, and Singapore, but it was an expensive way to live.

Because of various maintenance issues, there were complaints every week in some shape or form and the food situation wasn't great; we tried all kinds of ways to improve it, but it still sucked. When I spoke to a guest about his experience, he told me it was the first time he had lost weight on a dive trip. Then, there was trouble brewing with the boat ownership as the only trustworthy guy had been thrown out of the company.

The Witch

BEFORE MY ARRIVAL, another Italian guy had been part of the management team. He was tall with long greasy hair and a pointed nose and he reminded me of a male version of a witch minus the broomstick. We met a couple of times and like the rest of the crew, I took an instant dislike to him.

He had been kicked off the boat due to some shocking behaviour towards the guests and crew. With the change in boat ownership, he had wormed his way back into the picture, but he still wasn't allowed on charters. He did however, come to check on things regularly. The tension started to build, and we had some pretty strong arguments.

A few months earlier, the managers of another liveaboard in a beautiful location had come on board for a couple of weeks and had told me if I wanted another job, I could contact them. The job offer was sounding better by the day as the greaseball was becoming unbearable. After another massive row I decided it was time to leave, so I resigned and told the owners I'd work a period of notice to ensure a smooth handover to my successor. Preparations for the new job started right away and the dates worked out well, as I would spend Christmas in the UK with my family before travelling to the next destination.

Things started to get complicated soon after that. The powers at the top of the company didn't want me to leave as I was the only sensible and good-looking person on board! The grease monkey was licking his lips, thinking he would come back full time once I was gone. However, there was a promising local dive instructor that did a good job and I planned to train him for a few weeks so he could cover while they looked for another manager.

My flights back to the UK, and the next destination were booked, the paperwork for a work permit was in motion, and everything was lining up nicely. It was my final few weeks of work and there was massive excitement about the next chapter of my dive career. The local instructor was keen to learn, so he took care of everything and it was like being on holiday.

One day, I had a phone call from my new boss who sounded angry on the phone. "I thought you were coming here in the first week of January? I have just had a call saying that you won't be coming until the end of March."

I was stunned and said, "No my plans haven't changed, my tickets are booked, and we are on schedule."

There was silence for a few seconds before she said, "Well you better sort it out with them because they are telling me a different story."

What the hell had happened? I sat there flum-moxed and wracked my brains. There had been an email from the company asking me if I had a new job and I had told them the destination, not really giving it much thought. They had gone behind my back and contacted my new boss telling them I wasn't coming until three months after my agreed date. It took a few phone calls to get everything sorted out, but finally, they understood that my time with them was at an end.

The final week came and it was time to say good-bye to my favourite manta rays and dive sites. The boat purchased my Canon G10 and housing, and they paid me my remaining salary. It was sad saying goodbye to the captain and crew and they were all dreading working with the witch again.

I took my Maldivian SIM card and tossed it in the bin … no one could contact me anymore, and then I splashed out on a night at the Hule Hotel thinking I might have a few beers on my last night, but I ended up crashing out early.

Sweet dreams of chicken and mushroom pies filled my mind. The weather was amazing as my flight took off, there was a final view of the boat, and I got my wish to see the beautiful atolls from the sky. I enjoyed my last glimpses of paradise without pork or porn and headed to Heathrow.

Memories

MANY THOUGHTS FLASHED through my mind on the flight home, particularly about the many unforgettable experiences with manta rays. Even though Hanifaru Bay had been spectacular, another manta memory was still my favourite.

There was another channel with a cleaning station and on one particular dive the current had been raging as we got down to twenty-five metres. There weren't many places to hold onto as it was mostly sand, and the current was pushing me inside. I found a rock and I wrapped my legs around it. The top of the rock was flat so it was the perfect place to rest my camera, my back was facing the current, and you hear could the furious whooshing of the water as it surged by. My leg muscles started to burn as they struggled to keep me in position, but my reward came a few seconds later. Four mantas came within a few feet of me, also struggling in the current as their wings flapped hard to keep them in position to be cleaned.

My camera caught some stunning images of these mantas and we watched each other for around ten minutes. They must have wondered what the hell this guy was doing there holding on for dear life with this shiny black box pointing at them the entire time. It was a stunning moment in challenging conditions and that summed up diving in the Republic of the Maldives.

MY LIFE HAD changed so much. The job had turned into a massive challenge and had pushed me to the limits of my patience and it was easy to see why managers didn't stay long on board. The two before me lasted just four and six months respectively, but it was sheer determination that had kept me there for longer.

Working in a strictly religious country wasn't so easy. The majority of people were very nice, but the lifestyle wasn't for me. Usually, when you stay somewhere for a while, things grow on you, but the thing that grew on me the most was a taste for breakfast curry.

There are no memories of any local music that stuck in my mind, in a cultural sense, nothing much was learned either. It almost felt like the locals preferred to keep everything to themselves, which is fine.

When I had left Honduras, it felt like the culture had really left a mark on me and plenty of music stuck in my mind, and things like the carnival and Inde-pendence Day were great occasions. I didn't have that warm fuzzy feeling of being part of something with the Maldives.

On the plus side, leading a sheltered life for a few years did wonders for my bank balance and the health of my liver.

Reach for the Lasers

ON ARRIVING BACK in London, the plan was to go home straight away. However, that changed at the last minute and I met up with Martin for a few quiet beers. Feeling knackered after the flight I knew it wasn't going to be a big night.

We met up in Victoria Station and I stuffed my luggage in the corner as we had a couple of Stella's and a good chinwag.

I was thinking about getting the last train back to Wales when we got chatting to this lady.

"Are you guys going to see David Guetta to-night?"

My ears pricked up on hearing this and I looked at Martin. "Let's go."

He took a little bit of convincing, but it didn't take long.

The problem was my luggage and the $15,000 in my pocket that I didn't want to carry around Brixton, which doesn't have the best reputation in the world. Luckily, there was a luggage storage place at Victoria, so I stuffed my money deep into my bag and prayed to God that the staff was honest.

We headed to Brixton Academy and got a couple of tickets to see the most famous DJ in the world at that time. We got off our nut and danced like dogs until the show finished. It was an amazing show with some of the best lights and lasers I had ever seen.

We got back to Martin's place at around five in the morning, passed out for a few hours and then decided to get a massive English breakfast at a proper cockney cafe. After that, it was a quick drink in an Irish pub near his house. That soon turned into ten pints and some shots. What a mess ... it was like all of my frustrations from being sober in the Maldives all came out over a cracking weekend.

I went back to Victoria on Monday morning to get my bags that had been locked away for two nights; I looked inside, and was so happy when the money was still there.

I then made my way home to Wales, and it was nice to get a hug from my mum even though I was two days late arriving.

WE HAD A lovely family Christmas together and it was nice to see my family for a few drinks. I showed them some videos of diving with the big sharks, and they thought it was mental. New Year's Eve was spent with my friends in Chepstow. Nothing much had changed with my pals, although there were some kids popping out here and there. Even though it was always good to see my old friends, it was hard to explain to them what it was like working in the scuba world.

ONCE CHRISTMAS HAD passed and only the shit Quality Street sweets were left in the tin, it was time to pack again. My nice new Gates housing and video camera arrived just in time.

I flew into the Philippines and had a one-night layover in Manila. There had been no fish in my life for a few weeks, so I booked myself a hotel with an aquarium in the room. After the long flight, exploring Manila was the last thing on my mind and after seeing the state of the airport I'm sure it would have been pure carnage.

It was another three-hour flight to my final desti-nation and as I walked into the terminal building a huge poster of a grey reef shark welcomed me to the world's first shark sanctuary. It was the middle of the night so I saw nothing on the ride from the airport. The cheapest hotel was a $100 hundred bucks a night and it looked like it hadn't been cleaned since 1985.

Micronesia

PALAU WAS VERY attractive for a number of reasons. First of all, the aerial images of the Rock Islands instantly made you want to visit, the second reason was the Jellyfish Lake, where you could swim with millions of harmless jellyfish – this only happened in a few places in the world – and the third reason was the history of the Second World War and the subsequent battle on Peleliu Island. The thought of diving German Channel and Blue Corner was also exciting as these were rated as some of the world's best dives.

On waking up, the hotel room looked even worse than on arrival, dated furniture and some unidentified stains on the carpet hastened my need to get some fresh air. The main street had about twenty small shops and a couple of large supermarkets. My watch showed midday, so I listened out for the Muslim call to prayer, but there was silence.

I ordered a teriyaki burger for lunch, which was a delight as the beef melted in my mouth. As I sat at the table outside enjoying my burger I looked down and there were massive blood splats on the floor. Holy shit, someone must have been stabbed here last night I thought to myself, and as I looked again at the half-eaten juicy burger my hunger waned somewhat.

As it turned out, nobody had been stabbed outside the burger bar. It was the juice of the betel nut. I chatted with the nice lady who prepared my burger, and she told me about the tradition of locals chewing these nuts and spitting the remains on the floor. She said it acted like a stimulant and gave people a mild buzz, a bit like a nut version of Red Bull, but it could destroy your teeth and mouth. It had been a cause of mouth cancer in some people and the government was trying to stop people from doing it. After a while, I began to notice signs everywhere, saying *No Spitting*.

While I was people watching in the street, I no-ticed some pretty big guys and girls. The Pacific islanders are a big bunch, but they seemed very welcoming. Some people were chewing betel nuts as they walked around and you could tell this as their mouths were red and often some of their teeth had been destroyed.

After the Second World War, the islands came under the administrative control of the US after the Japanese were defeated. The country became a republic in 1994, after voting against joining the Federal States of Micronesia and it was under a compact of free association from the US. It used the US$ as its currency and the US postal service to send packages. The population could serve in the US military and could travel to the States without a visa, so the people of Palau had a pretty sweet deal with Uncle Sam watching over them and giving them over $200 million a year in funding.

The biggest supermarket was like Walmart with so many US products for sale, but glancing at the prices, it made me feel happy to be out at sea most of the time. Everything was imported, so the prices were pretty high. It was Cheetos galore and they had every chip ever invented on the shelf. The produce section was so highly priced you wondered how people managed to afford to buy any. There were also plenty of foodstuffs from Japan and Korea on sale too.

The boat was in the Malakal Harbour, so I went to meet my new crewmates. My new captain seemed like a good guy and we got the paperwork and contract signed. It was a massive pay cut from being in the Maldives, but worth it for a different quality of life.

The crew usually numbered seven or eight for eighteen guests and we all chipped in with every job on board, from filling tanks to washing dishes. They were a mix of Filipino, Palauan's, and a bunch of white guys from the UK and the States. The photo guy John had visited the Maldives, so it was good to have a friendly face on board.

We trained to work on two boats and often switched between them. The boats were very similar and they had a hydraulic lift on the stern to pick up the diving skiff. They were old looking and needed some work, but most people were so excited to be diving in Palau they didn't care too much.

One of our diving skiffs was called Sherman after the tanks in the war and it looked like it had been around since 1945. It was the worst boneshaker I had ever been on and you would have thought it had been used as a landing craft for the Marines to storm Peleliu. It was amazing it even floated and every journey shook our bones as we hit the waves.

First Charter

WE WERE ALL set for my first charter in Palau. We picked up the guests from nearby hotels, did the briefings, and went to bed.

We left the dock early and it was amazing seeing the Rock Islands for the first time. They were mush-room-shaped with the Pacific Ocean eroding the bases and from just above the waterline, foliage covered the rest of the rock. Shallow reefs were visible from the surface with schools of small reef fish darting around. My new surroundings were perfect, and it was a different type of scenery to any I had ever seen before.

THE HISTORY OF the Second World War has always been of interest to me and finding out that there were so many Japanese shipwrecks in Palau was exciting. There was a great book on board that told the story of all the wrecks in Palau and it fascinated me. It had every detail that you could imagine on each wreck, where and when it was built, the number of crew on board, which planes sank the boat, and how many people had died. It was one of the most interesting books I've read, and made my wreck dives even more special.

Our weeks mostly started off with a couple of wreck dives. My favourite was the Depth Charge or Helmet Wreck. The details on the history were sketchy, and it was thought that the Japanese Navy had stolen the boat from someone … but no one was sure from whom. The wreck was an easy one at eighteen metres deep and there were so many artefacts onboard it was incredible.

My vivid imagination went into overdrive, when I explored the wreck for the first time. I tried to imagine what it was like for the crew on board to be bombed and strafed by the US Navy planes. It must have been terrifying. I looked at the massive holes and twisted metal on the bow and thought about the bombs' impact and the noise they must have made. Swim-ming towards the wheelhouse, I saw a gas mask and a machine gun lying there. There was live ammunition on the deck and a shoe from a sailor. The most startling area was the cargo hold with around thirty depth charges all stacked together. They were all corroded, and a toxic green haze was coming off the barrel-shaped bombs. There was a crocodile fish sitting on top of one of them, its flat body looking like it had been run over by a steamroller.

After exiting the cargo hold and the green haze, I wondered whether people should really be allowed to dive there with so many depth charges. The next cargo hold had an engine of a Zero fighter, and there were bottles of sake on the deck next to another machine gun and a rifle. It was so interesting to see so many artefacts and I always looked forward to exploring the wrecks each week.

My favourite wreck was the Iro Maru. This tanker

was 142 metres long and weighed 14,000 tons. It was pretty hard to see the whole wreck in one dive due to its massive size. The visibility was usually not great, but she was still mind blowing. We followed the line to reach the wreck, and on the bow was an intact seven-inch deck gun encrusted with hard corals. This wreck had been damaged by a torpedo in an earlier attack while travelling to Palau from the Philippines.

I would go to the bow and swim down. There was a massive hole that you could swim through and again, there was twisted metal, so you had to be careful not to cut yourself or get tangled up. The wreck was covered in many beautiful hard corals and gorgonian sea fans and you could find the longnose hawk fish hiding amongst the branches.

The main deck area was twenty-five metres deep, and big school of jacks would circle above our heads. On one occasion, whilst looking inside one of the cargo holds, I nearly swam into this menacing looking great barracuda. He was a beast, at over a metre long and he looked at me with a sinister eye while grinding his pointy teeth.

The Power of the Barracuda

THE BARRACUDA'S REAL power was put on show a few weeks later. We had a Thai group that had a famous photographer with them. He got a big money shot of the barracuda taking out one of the jacks and it was one of the best videos we had ever seen.

The jacks were all swimming close to the deck and the barracuda was hiding just out of sight. As the school started to swim upwards, the barracuda picked his victim, then, in a split second bolted from his cover and bit the jack clean in half. These jacks were not small, but it was destroyed in seconds. The rest of the school left the area sharpish.

The guy filmed the remains of the jack twitching with green blood, leaving a trail. The barracuda came around again and took another bite leaving just the head. Before the head hit the deck, he came around once more to finish his lunch. It showed the power of the barra. If he could take down a foot and a half jack in one bite, then I'm pretty sure he could cut through an arm or leg as well with those razor-sharp teeth.

THE JAKE SEAPLANE was another dive that was always enjoyable; it was an easy dive in fifteen metres of water. The plane was intact, but the propeller was damaged when it crash-landed.

It was amazing looking into the cockpit and my imagination always ran wild thinking about the Japanese pilot sitting there flying the plane before crashing into the ocean. The history books didn't know how the plane had crashed, so Palau still had mysteries to be solved.

There have been other plane wrecks located around Palau, but most are kept secret. The latest was a Japanese long-distance recon plane that was found in a river in 2017.

LIFE ON THE boat was going well. It was great getting to know my new crewmates and there was plenty of banter going on. The crew quarters were good and the beds were a nice size, which is unusual for a livea-board. The chefs cooked fantastic food and there was no tuna curry for breakfast anymore … it was bacon and decent sausages all the way. Considering the location of Palau compared to the Maldives, the quality of the food was so much better. The guests were not going to go hungry on board here, and neither were the crew.

THE CHARTERS WERE simple, because the boat didn't have to travel far. The longest navigation was just a few hours. We had four different moorings on the surface, so securing the boat was simple. The areas were protected from the weather, so it wasn't that challenging for the captain to keep the ship safe.

The majority of the time was spent close to Ger-man Channel. The boat had jet engines so we could navigate through the shallow man-made channel, which had been made by the Germans as the name suggests. They mined a lot of phosphate before the First World War, and being the most efficient people in the world they wanted to cut down on travel time from Angar to Koror.

German Channel

GERMAN CHANNEL WAS only ten minutes away from some of the best dive sites in the world. It was good for manta rays, and although was nowhere near as busy as Hanifaru Bay, it was not too shabby.

The mantas exhibited the same behaviour as their cousins in the Maldives. The best time to interact was on an incoming tide when the moon was new or full. It brought in plankton from the Pacific, which got trapped in German Channel making it easy for the mantas to feed. The population was healthy with over 300 identified mantas. We saw sixteen in the same spot once … which was terrific. Even if there was no food, the mantas still came to the cleaning stations and we would just rest on the sand waiting for them to come in. Sometimes the sharks and mantas would fight it out for cleaning station space.

On one-night dive, we were looking for shrimps and nudibranchs when out of the darkness a colossal manta nearly swam right into me. My face felt the full force and swish in the water as it changed direction at the last second to miss me.

There was plenty of other action in the Channel and on one occasion, a great hammerhead shark swam in front of us. Its magnificent narrow dorsal fin confirmed the species and it was the most impressive we had ever seen at around five metres long. There were always plenty of grey reef sharks and whitetips hanging around and they would feed on large schools of scad mackerel. Other predators included giant groupers and trevally. We watched many attacks on the scad; the shimmering school of fish would become tighter as other fish darted in for the kill. You would find feathertail stingrays buried in the sand, once their cover was blown, they swam out with their tails fluttering in the water column sending the sand that covered them cascading back to the seabed.

Some crazy things happened in German Channel, one of which was the oceanic phenomenon of an upwelling.

On one dive, our group was in the mouth of the Channel and suddenly the water temperature dropped quickly. Looking at my computer, I saw it had fallen by eight degrees in a couple of minutes. We glanced out into the deeper water and saw a vast cloud of dirty turbid water coming rushing towards us. Within seconds it engulfed the whole group and visibility dropped to nearly zero. It was staggering how the conditions had changed so quickly. We had no option but to abort the dive and met everybody back on the surface. It was a new experience for everyone on board and the only time I ever saw it happen.

The inside of German Channel was very shallow and was mostly sand with some sea grass beds. We saw a dugong swimming around there one day. Tiger sharks were often seen in the area, but we weren't lucky enough to see them. We went inside the

Channel when the weather was rough and sometimes the crew would do a spot of fishing.

One night, Andy and Jim pulled in a huge giant trevally. This fish had finally run out of lives – there was a broken rusted spear stuck in its side that looked like it had been there for years.

The Blue Towel Incident

MISTAKES ARE ALWAYS made in a new job and my usual brain fart happened in my first week.

There was no room in my luggage for a towel, so I bought one from the department store. The towels were right next to the fake Quiksilver T-shirts they were flogging for $50. When you live on a tiny island with 20,000 people, they can get away with that sort of daylight robbery.

My new towel was blue, just like my beloved Car-diff City. After showering the next morning the blue dye from the towel was all over my body, so because I looked like a fat Smurf I got back in to rinse off again. Later, while on deck duty I asked Agnes the steward-ess if I could use the washing machine to get all the blue dye out of the towel.

She pointed in the direction of the guest cabins where there was a small room with the washing machine. "You know how to use this, right?"

"Yeah, of course, no problem." I was thinking it can't be that hard to wash a towel. The towel and some powder went in the machine and I closed the door. There was plenty of time before the divers' return. DJ Tiesto was playing extra loud in the saloon and chef cam was bouncing away in the galley preparing some pesto.

After twenty minutes I went downstairs and opened the door and the colour drained from my face, because there was a massive flood all down the hallway. The washing machine was still spinning, but the water was gushing out and leaking into the first two guest cabins. It was everywhere.

After running upstairs Linford Christie style, I pleaded with Agnes to help me.

She came down. "Hay nako Kris, what have you done?"

We got the shop vac and started to suck up the mess and luckily none of the guests' belongings had got wet. The divers were just getting back to the boat and the captain saw me furiously sucking the carpet. He looked the same way Captain Eddy had looked at me when the groupers attacked me in Roatán. The look that says I can't be angry with you; because you're so stupid kind of thing.

It took nearly three hours to suck up the water and the jokes about the blue towel went on for the rest of the week. The village idiot had arrived and was doing well.

THE FIRST MONTH went by quick as a flash and it was my turn to be off for a week. Two lovely ladies Lee and Johanne stayed in Palau for a few days after the charter, and they arranged a private tour of the island and asked me to join them.

We drove around the whole place in a few hours and it was nice to see the greenery of Babeldaob, the northern island of Palau. It was the only volcanic area in Palau and it reminded me a lot of New Zealand's North Island with small volcanic cones covered in grass. We visited traditional houses where the clans would meet to discuss things like the price of coco-nuts. There were stone monoliths that had been there for hundreds of years and nobody had any idea how they ended up on the island. It was quite amazing as they weighed as much as five tons.

We explored some stuffy Japanese bunkers and gun emplacements, which overlooked Malakal Harbour and after lunch, we stopped by the prison. The inmates made woodcarvings called storyboards and the stories came from Palau folklore and legends of the past. The craftsmanship that went into the carvings was excellent; it was almost worth breaking the law to learn this great skill.

We dropped by the government offices, which were like a paper mache fusion of the White House and St Paul's Cathedral. Massive pillars were made with chicken wire and looked like they would probably fall down if the wind was strong enough. With only a small population of people to look after there was probably much thumb-twiddling going on there.

PALAU HAS STRONG ties with the US, but the Big Mac hadn't arrived on the island yet. The restaurants were mostly Japanese and Korean and there was a place which served fruit bat but I didn't fancy it. There was one Thai place which was pretty good. The Taj served authentic Indian curry and was home to some decent late-night parties.

A few of us dropped by for a beer one day and there was a gentleman sitting at the bar drinking a glass of red wine. It turned out he was the President of Palau. He had no security and no motorcade and was just a regular guy letting off some steam at the end of the day.

The bar life was pretty muted, but more interest-ing than in the Maldives and we spent time at the Drop Off Bar near the dock where they served wicked poke, but had terrible Internet. If you could send one email in an hour then it was a pretty good day. We renamed it the Drop Out bar for that very reason.

There were some discos that opened late but they always mixed in the good music with karaoke which never works. It was my first taste of the karaoke scene and if you ask me, the majority of the world should only be allowed to sing in the shower. The only way to cope with karaoke was to drown it out with tequila, headphones, and chicken wings.

Peleliu Island

THE VISITS TO Peleliu Island were always fascinating as it had a bloody history – one battle between the US Marines and the Japanese, cost nearly 14,000 lives in just a couple of months.

The boat ride was a couple of hours from Koror and it was the most southern part of the trip. Even though the diving was rip roaring, the relics were also very interesting.

The guests had the option of a three-hour land tour and the majority wanted to see the relics of war, while others carried on diving.

The excellent tour guides would pick us from the man-made south dock. One of the guides, called Tanji, was a flamboyant chap to say the least, and Godwin who was the Rasta king of Peleliu did a great job talking you through the history. There was so much to see that it had me hooked instantly.

The island has been made famous by Tom Hanks and Steven Spielberg who created the HBO miniseries *The Pacific*, which was a follow up to the spectacular *Band of Brothers* series. Some books written by veterans Eugene Sledge and Robert Leckie were turned into a multi-million-dollar Hollywood blockbuster. The battle of Peleliu was covered in a few episodes of the show and if you have never seen it, I recommend sitting down and watching it for ten hours straight. It's really riveting and shows the real horror of war. It's impossible to believe the kind of horror those heroes went through and after visiting Peleliu, my interest grew and I ended up reading nearly every book on the Pacific theatre during World War Two.

We would board the minibus which took us around the island and after just a couple of minutes, you could see a Zero fighter plane that had crashed on the edge of a swamp. On the mangled, twisted wreckage, you could still see the faint red circle of the Japanese Empire flag on the fuselage. Tanji always did a great job of explaining everything to the group and he had the ability to set the scene with his explana-tions making us feel part of the battle.

We would visit White and Orange Beaches where the Marines landed on September 15th, 1944. It was so hard to comprehend that where we stood the blood of hundreds of young men had been spilt. There were relics everywhere and people still found new things all the time. They had discovered a bunker that been buried for many years, and there were live ammuni-tion rounds on the floor outside.

We drove across the main runway, which was the reason why so many men had died. The US thought the airfield was a threat to its assault on the Philip-pines Islands. The remains of a Jap tank made by Mitsubishi was on the side of the road and it was still in good shape despite being outside for over seventy years. You could see where the anti-tank rounds had gone through the steel to knock it out and it must have been horrendous for the tank crew, as they got annihilated by the shells.

The visit to the cemetery was always a moving experience. There were some rusted American helmets, which had been placed on one of the crosses and there were small American flags and flowers left as a mark of respect. Sometimes, we had ex-servicemen with us and you could see them holding back the tears in the cemetery. The American govern-ment repatriated most of the remains back to Arlington cemetery after the war, but the remains of the 12,000 Japanese dead are still buried on the island to this day. Japanese people also came to the island to pay their respects, they constructed a beautiful garden memorial, and there were often flowers left at the old headquarters building.

We would then move up into Bloody Nose Ridge where there was an American tank – the white star still visible. You could see the great engineering that went into the tanks as some bearings could still spin after being out in the tropics for decades. Mortar tubes and anti-aircraft guns were still embedded in the ground next to the cave entrances. The enemy made a maze of tunnels all through the Umurbrogol Pocket. We would look inside and find a mortar plate on the ground and beer and sake bottles all over the place. There was a memorial to Colonel Kunio Nakagawa who had committed suicide in his cave after realising the battle was lost.

At the top of the ridge was a monument to the Marines and the 81st Wildcat division. Tanji would show the guests pictures of our location during the battle. It was a scene of carnage with destroyed tanks still ablaze and the rock face that was now covered in vegetation was bare after being bombed with napalm to expose the hidden cave entrances that were firing on the American forces.

On one of our trips, we saw a team of guys from Australia clearing all the leftover bombs and ammuni-tion from the battle. The conversations we had with them were fascinating. They had found skeletal remains of a Japanese soldier in a sniper position still holding the rusted remains of his rifle and on the same day, they had found over fifty hand grenades on one of the beaches. After they collected so many muni-tions, they would have a controlled explosion to make everything safe. The hills were covered in small red flags where they had found shells and bombs, which were due to be cleared away.

There was a Sherman tank there that had driven over a landmine. It had blown a massive hole in the bottom, killing the four crew inside and flipping the tank over onto its turret.

We would spend time in the museum, which was full of fascinating relics. The outside walls were full of shell holes and pockmarks from bullets. Inside, were machine guns from both sides, rifles and mess kits, canteens with loads of shrapnel holes, and there were articles on the wall from US newspapers, and uni-forms from each side.

Many of the veterans, including Eugene Sledge, made return visits after the war. It would have been a privilege to have met the heroes of the battle. The memoirs of these heroes are a must-read and give chilling accounts of close combat on the island of Peleliu.

The tour always finished up at the thousand-man

cave entrance. There were massive spiders in there so I didn't venture too far inside … you can put me in the water with sharks, but there is no chance of me being next to a spider.

Peleliu Island had me gripped from my first visit. It had a tiny population of around a 1,000 people, there were a few stores on the island but no bars and restaurants, and it was hard to think about what kept people busy during the day.

It was interesting talking to the locals especially Godwin, he was half Japanese, half Palauan and ran one of the small resorts on the island. His mother told him the Japanese influence on the island was a good one, and they educated the people well. There was a feeling that some people would have been happy if the islands had stayed in Japan's hands. Godwin told me it felt like the island was haunted sometimes with all the people that had died in the battle.

South Dock

THE SOUTH DOCK was where the boat was anchored during our trips to Peleliu. It had been constructed by the naval Seabees during the war and the dock area was quite small; it could be tricky to get the boat secured sometimes. We would drop the bow anchor and attach a stern line to the dock, so the ship didn't move too much. To secure the stern, one of us would jump into the water swim across and tie a bowline to the dock.

We had a chef from Nepal who got really confused at the dock one day. We came in when it was high tide and after a few hours of being inside, the tide had changed, and the water level got pretty low.

The chef came out to have a cigarette and he start-ed to get crazy, "Where has all the water gone? It was very much deeper earlier on."

He had no idea how the tides worked so we had to give him a lesson telling him, "Don't worry it will all come back in a few hours."

WE HEARD THERE were saltwater crocodiles in the water, and one day John managed to see one. He took his camera and got a couple of good images.

We started to get concerned about jumping in the water, thinking that the crocs might fancy chowing down on us. The captain always said, "Don't worry about it, the locals have said there has never been a crocodile attack, so it's okay."

I still wasn't convinced and always looked around in the water before tying the line as quickly as possible before flying back onto the boat.

The story took a twist just a few weeks later, while I was on a rest week enjoying some lunchtime beers at Sam's tours. I was admiring the beautiful Rock Islands while demolishing my Stella, when suddenly a boat came towards the dock at breakneck speed. An ambulance pulled up in the parking area, and paramedics headed towards the dock. I watched with interest like a nosey prick when something terrible was happening. The boat came in and they quickly put a guy on a stretcher and wheeled him towards the ambulance. I glanced at him as he went past. It was hard to see him as his head and upper body were covered in bandages. They got him in the ambulance and sped off to the hospital. I asked one of the bar staff what had happened and nearly spat out my beer at her reply.

"This guy from Taiwan was snorkelling in the South Dock down in Peleliu and got attacked by a crocodile."

1944 Coca-Cola

LUCKILY, THE GUY survived the attack, but had severe lacerations to his head and body.

He would have some cool scars to tell his kids about when he got older.

We didn't have to jump into the water any more for a while after that, until, one day; one of our guests dropped a piece of his dive equipment over the side of the boat. Duty called and I went to look for it, down to the bottom. It was just about three metres deep and the visibility was near zero. Using only my hands to feel around the bottom, I felt something hard, which was partly submerged. I dug it out and saw that it was a bottle of some kind, so I put it in my BCD pocket and carried on looking for the lost equipment. Once back on the boat, I pulled out the bottle and gave it a nice clean. It was a Coca-Cola bottle with the date stamped 1944 on the front. I was so excited that after all of my interest in the battle of Peleliu I had my very own souvenir to take home with me. The thought of an exhausted marine that had just been through the agony of battle drinking the coke and then throwing it into the water made the discovery even better.

THE DIVING WAS excellent around the south of Peleliu Island and we used to love watching the archerfish swimming close to the surface. These guys were so cool; they could knock insects from the branches of the mangroves by shooting a jet of water at them, which knocked them off into the water where the fish would eat them. This is an excellent example of Mother Nature at her best and giving us humans something amazing to watch.

The most famous dive site was Peleliu Corner. On a bad day, it could chew you up and spit you out in seconds. In terms of geography, it was the end of the line because there wasn't much land to the south for a very long time. The dive briefings were deadly serious and were designed to make divers aware of the powerful currents. There was a reason for the strong briefing … a couple of years earlier, a group had been lost at sea for nearly eight hours after being swept off the Corner. After that happened, they tried to make the dive as tight as possible, and it worked, as people were shit scared after the briefing.

The dive was a beautiful but intense one. If the tide was incoming you would start on that side and if it was outgoing then the opposite side. You had to be careful because sometimes the current could switch during the dive. If it was possible to, you could swim across to the other side as the majority of fish were where the flow was. Sometimes the current would be ripping and you would do a negative entry from the boat, getting down to around twenty metres as quickly as you could. The current would try and push you across the top of the reef plateau, so you had to swim sideways to keep in position. There were a couple of places which were called 'hook in areas' and once there we would help the guests to get hooked in before watching the performance unfold. The danger of diving on the corners was you could be swept over to the other side of the wall and potentially get stuck in a down current.

There was always decent marine life at Peleliu Corner and the wall was covered in stunning yellow soft corals, which made a beautiful colour contrast against the purple barrel sponges. The hook in area was just bare rock worn down by thousands of divers over the years. Usually, you could see twenty to thirty grey reef sharks hanging in the current. Divers would struggle like hell to hold their position in the water, but the sharks just cruised around and glided through the ripping currents. When you looked over the edge of the wall, it felt like you were looking down to the edge of the universe. The thrill of the hook in dives could be challenging. If you didn't quickly set your reef hook, you could get swept away from the action quickly and sometimes it was not possible to get back.

Once securely hooked though, you felt like you were flying. The rope from your reef hook pivoted you from side to side, and the strong current blasted past your face, causing you to bite down a little harder on your mouthpiece because it felt like it was getting ripped out of your mouth. You could feel your mask shaking. It was an exhilarating experience if you were an avid diver, but if you were new to diving, then you might question your sanity being chucked around in the current. Sometimes reef hooks came out of the reef, so you had to keep an eye on everyone closely as the dive unfolded.

The Corner was a good place to watch the sea bream aggregation. This was a great time of year and you would watch thousands of blue-lined sea bream come up from the deeper water to release their eggs. Bull sharks were visitors to the Corner and my eyes were always looking out for them as they were near the top of my most-wanted list.

One day, my luck finally changed and I caught a glimpse of a bull shark. We were on our ascent and my safety sausage was up as a diver was low on air. As the current pushed us across the plateau, we looked down and saw this chunky looking shark below us. Even though it was twenty metres below me I had never seen a shark with such girth. There wasn't enough time to swim down for a closer look, but I had a confirmed sighting of one of the world's most dangerous sharks.

A FEW WEEKS later, we got a lot closer to a bull shark. Our group was on the edge of the wall when Jim got excited and there were muffled screams coming through his regulator. Looking to my right about ten metres away was a four-metre bull shark. Its body was so sleek and muscular and getting my camera ready, I got a fifteen-second shot of the massive beast. My mother would have had kittens if she had seen me swimming after one of the most dangerous sharks in the world. Once it swam off it took me a while to calm down and get my breath back. The adrenaline was flowing freely through me … my word what a buzz.

Rogue Turtle

THE ATTACK OF the sea turtle happened on a night dive at West Wall close to Peleliu Corner.

Our group had been exploring the site and we had already seen a couple of whitetips. We were looking for porcelain crabs in anemones that cascaded down the wall like a bubbly waterfall. Lee was a few metres ahead using her light to explore the ledges, and her light was fixed on something inside. Suddenly this giant 200 lb green turtle came flying out of the reef. It turned at the last second exposing its white underside and smashed Lee in the head. Never had we seen a turtle move so fast and you could hear the sickening crunch as they collided. The turtle was a good size and after the collision, it swam off into deeper water.

My rescue training kicked in and I got to Lee quickly as she looked dazed and was trying to fix her mask. It was night, so it was hard to see the damage without blinding her with my dive light. We made a very slow ascent to the surface; there was a cut and lump already forming on the forehead. The mask frame had been cracked so would not seal anymore, but luckily the glass didn't shatter.

We got back onto the boat, and Lee was shaken up. We thought she might have a concussion injury, so we put some ice on the lump. Luckily, she didn't sustain any long-term damage. If the turtle had been a few inches lower, the injuries would have been a lot worse. We figured the turtle had been dazzled by the light and got confused before swimming directly towards it. The moral of the story is never shine your light in a turtle's eye ... not all ninja turtles live in the New York sewers!

ONE DAY A typhoon hit Peleliu very hard. It was unusual to have storms this close to the equator and we couldn't dive there for a few weeks. There was sustained damage to the island's homes, and trees were knocked down, but luckily nobody was killed or injured. It was gut-wrenching to see all the soft yellow corals had been ripped off the wall in the storm surge. It looked like a totally different dive site. There were hardly any fish or sharks to be seen and the corals were covered in sand, which can kill them quickly. It was as if an underwater apocalypse had happened.

We got down to Peleliu Corner and looked at the reef and there were massive holes blown out of it. We concluded that the storm surge had dragged some bombs and shells up before they had exploded on the plateau. It was surreal to look inside the holes. You could see fossils of old coral and crustaceans layered in the reef and I reckoned that these layers under the reef were hundreds maybe even thousands of years old. If you were an archaeologist it was probably the stuff of dreams, for us lowly dive pros it was utter devastation.

Blacktips

ON THE WAY back from Peleliu we would spend a day moored at Turtle Cove, which was an area between Peleliu and German Channel.

We did great night dives there and often found mating pairs of cuttlefish and some scarce macro finds like the ornate ghost pipefish. Once we had moored the boat, we would be circled by many blacktip reef sharks, which would swim around the boat day and night waiting for leftover food from the disposal unit. These sharks were great for the guests to see and we used to chuck them some chicken bones after lunch. It was a great chance to see sharks close up and I would lie on the back deck, holding my camera just below the surface, filming the sharks feeding just in front of my lens. There were usually at least twenty blacktips flying in to get a free snack and I hoped they wouldn't mistake my fat sausage fingers as food. Luckily it never happened, but did get some great close-up shots of the sharks feeding.

Blue Corner

AFTER A FEW months on board, I started working as the video pro and cruise director. The great Captain Ike would take care of the boat so I did most of the briefings and looked after guest issues. Usually, the first words out of a guest's mouth was: "When are we going to Blue Corner?"

It's been voted one of the top five dives in the world and you can read this in every dive publication known to mankind. We would go at least two or three times every charter. Blue Corner was always better when the tide was incoming and the sharks got closer to the guests during these conditions. This was another hook in dive with areas at different depths. It was similar in topography to Peleliu, but a little bit smaller and shallower, it still had strong currents, but wasn't as dangerous.

There were certain times of the year when the action was at its best and most spectacular and one of them was when the Moorish idols and the orange spine unicorn fish used to gather. The sharks would go into a frenzy during this time trying to feed on the schools.

Another great time was when the sharks were mating. Man, it was a tough time for the female sharks because they got bitten to shreds by the males. I saw many female sharks with loads of lacerations all over their bodies. The males would bite and hold the female sharks around the gills while mating and these wounds would sometimes take months to heal. There was no chance of any Marvin Gaye music being played while this happened and I was sure some of the females needed some therapy once it was all over. I imagined the female sharks rocking back and forth in the shower, trying to forget the experience ever happened.

BLUE CORNER IS a magical playground, the corals were not that great, but there was so much going on it was out of this world. There are not many places in the world where so many grey reef sharks mixed with big schools of barracuda and jacks. The grey reef sharks were used to divers and would pass right by your face, and sometimes the jack fish swam into the sharks to knock off parasites. A couple of hammerheads and mantas also cruised by the hook in areas a few times. There was never a dull moment at Blue Corner that's for sure.

A very friendly Napoleon wrasse would befriend us on every dive. The guests thought we had some magical powers because the wrasse performed like a circus chimp. Like most things in life you have to pay for a show and our pay was boiled eggs. The wrasse would hang around long enough so we could take images of them and the guests and once the guests' backs were turned; we would reach into our BCD pockets, take out some eggs, and feed them to the wrasse. They were skilled egg eaters, and carefully took the shell off the egg inside their mouths before spitting it out. They were a magnificent fish and would let you hold them for a few seconds as a thank you for feeding them. Big Ben had a great relationship with these fish and I think he must have given them double portions.

The wrasse got smarter and more aggressive though and sometimes, they would bump into you if you were slow giving out the goods. One day I made the mistake of leaving my BCD pocket open and one smaller wrasse snuck up from behind me and stuck his snout in my pocket stealing my egg, the little bugger!

Moray v Octopus

I SHOT ONE of my favourite ever videos at Blue Corner with Alexey and Tanya. It had nothing to with sharks or the schools of fish, but was a battle between an octopus and a yellow margin moray eel. The eel was swimming on top of the reef, when it stopped suddenly and looked into a hole. I swam over wondering what was happening and saw a common octopus in the hole. He was protecting himself with some broken coral, which he was using as a shield. They had a stand-off for a while, then all of a sudden, the three-foot eel made his move, and darting into the hole, he grabbed the octopus and started to pull it out. The octopus held on for dear life, gripping the reef with its suction cups. The eel had a secure grip and started its death roll with its body twisting inside itself and thrashing around. The octopus was now stretch-ing like elastic then finally the strong jaws of the eel won the fight and the octopus was ripped in half. I watched as the eel guzzled his meal; the arms of the octopus were still moving around trying to grip the face of the eel before being devoured. It was one of those 'damn nature you're scary' moments and I said a little prayer for the octopus: "I'm sure there is a place for you in heaven."

Just down the reef were the Blue Holes, which were one of the most spectacular places to dive in the world. There were small holes that entered a large cavern, and if you looked up, you could see the sunrays shooting down into the area. There were caves at the back with some turtle bones, but we never risked going inside with guests because they might not make it out again. Electric clams or disco clams were tucked inside the walls and the blue flashing light through the mantle did something to our divers, turning them into John Travolta and they would begin to bust some moves underwater all in aid of the weekly highlights video.

Even though Blue Corner was the most famous place for sharks in Palau, the largest number of sharks I had ever seen in my life were at a site called Siaes Corner. This site was not as well-known as Blue Corner, so the corals were in great shape and you almost didn't want to hook into the reef as it was so healthy.

There were always big dogtooth tuna, and eagle rays were popular there. On the most fruitful day, we could capture over two hundred grey reef sharks on camera. They would just swim up and down the reef in an endless parade of shark action and were so close together that they made an impenetrable grey wall against the blue backdrop of the Pacific Ocean.

Siaes Tunnel was close to the Corner and this place was spectacular. It was around fifty metres long and big enough for a double-decker bus to fit through. The ceiling was covered in sea fans and sponges, which lit up nicely with the dive light. Down on the floor you could find some rare decorated dart fish. The tunnel opened up into the deep blue at nearly forty metres and schools of jacks sometimes enjoyed the shelter of the tunnel. As you approached the end of the tunnel, brilliant blue light would guide you to the exit back onto the reef wall.

ULONG CHANNEL ALSO had its fair share of sharks and I have never seen a channel like it before in my life. The sharks hung around at the mouth and we would hook either side of the mouth watching the action. Once it was time to unhook, we drifted inside the narrow channel, which was only about twelve-metres across. The corals were pristine on each side of the channel and there were red sea fans and table corals. Towards the end of the channel there were some cabbage corals that were full of squirrelfish and snappers.

This area of Palau was one of the most colourful I have ever seen and we would visit Ulong Island for a couple of hours at a time. It was a picture-postcard island with squeaky white sand and lush green trees. A plane had crashed a long time ago, and one of the wings was still partially buried on the beach. They filmed a TV show there called *Survivor* a few years before my time. There were also other things to enjoy at Ulong such as the fantastic grouper spawning. We would drift down the channel on a dive, and there were literally thousands of groupers in all shapes and sizes. They were waiting for the tide to be just right before they released their eggs and sperm at the same time. The sharks loved this time because it was easy pickings for them.

The spawning of the bumphead parrotfish also occurred in the same area. Seeing these guys in a school was great, you could hear them munching on the corals, and scraping away on the algae. They were a funny looking fish ... like some bucktooth karate kid fish, and they would excrete the limestone, which had been crushed to sand. You can thank this species for their contribution to many of the world's most beautiful beaches and islands.

AFTER SIX YEARS, I was a pretty confident diver, but the only time not feeling comfortable was on a night dive at Ulong. Due to our schedule we didn't do night dives here because we had moved away from the area, but on this occasion, we stayed the night. I had always had a love-hate relationship with night dives, as it was tough getting ready, especially after dinner. However, once we were in the water it was usually pretty good. I didn't fancy doing a night dive at Ulong though, because of the number of sharks in the water. There had been several sightings of bull sharks recently but we had one guest who was mad keen to do a night dive, and of course, it was my turn to go.

We jumped into the water and the only thing on my mind was bull sharks. We started to explore the reef and we were buzzed by whitetips and grey reef sharks. They were in hunting mode so didn't care about us, but my mind was wandering ... what if the next one was a bull shark. It was the most uncomfort-able I had felt underwater and needless to say we called the dive after twenty minutes as the sharks were getting into more of a frenzy, with their fins pointing downwards and aggressively flying around the reef.

We got back to the boat and the guest looked at me and said, "Good call. It was getting kinda hairy down there."

IT WAS STILL lovely to meet many different people each week from all over the planet and on one occasion, I was talking to this giant of a man, who must have been nearly seven-feet tall. I asked what he did for a living.

"I work in insurance."

I looked at him and wondered how the hell he fit his legs under a desk. After talking to him for a while longer he told me he used to play for the Dallas Cowboys American football team and he had won two Super Bowls back in the day. He was such a great guy and at the end of the trip he gave all the crew a Cowboys hat and T-shirt which I still have today. Chef Cam had to wear the shirt as the gentleman wanted to get a group picture of us, but he also wore a fake smile because he was a massive Chargers fan.

Ed the Turtle

THERE WAS AN incident in Palau that needed an international rescue effort to return something very important to one of our guests. Lila is a lovely lady from the Southern US states. Her friend Ed had been around the world with her diving for years. On a dive in Palau sadly Ed and Lila were separated in a very strong current.

While back on the boat we tried our best to console Lila over the loss of her long-term friend. The charter ended and she returned back to the US with a heavy heart. A few weeks later while diving we discovered Ed lying motionless on the ocean floor. We recovered him and bought him back to the mothership. After a few weeks Ed made a full recovery and was nice and dry after his ordeal. While back on the island we managed to contact Lila and asked for her address as we had something that belonged to her. Ed was then shipped first class from Palau to the US to be reunited with her owner. After a few weeks the pair were back together in an emotional affair.

We were delighted to be part of the rescue effort and it was no trouble for us to go above and beyond the call of duty to help our guests. For the record Ed is a soft toy turtle that is about five inches long. The pair have been together since with no other drama's so far.

Crazy Russians

WE HAD A few Russian groups diving with us. They could be very tricky to handle because they mostly didn't give a shit about anything. We were very strict about no drinking and diving, but some of the Russians didn't count beer as alcohol, and thought enjoying a Heineken with their cornflakes was fine.

Before going to Jelly Fish Lake one day, one Rus-sian guy started pouring whiskey into a coke can. I tried to explain that he couldn't drink, but he just looked at it, downed it, and left the empty can on the side.

A couple of charters got out of hand, but it was quite entertaining to watch. My favourite time happened on the last night of one of the charters. They came back from the bar and still wanted to party. I was on boat watch, so was asked to stay up and keep an eye on them and they started dancing in the saloon. One guy was dancing close to another lady and his wife wasn't happy, so she grabbed the glass coffee pot from the machine and smashed it over her husband's head. Blood poured out of his head, and the smashed pot was all over the carpet. He looked bemused the next morning when the captain gave him the bill for a new coffee pot.

With another group, the captain caught some guy smoking marijuana while they partied upstairs. The captain was pissed because if the police found any drugs on board, then he could lose his licence, so he gave the guy a severe warning and told him if it happened again we would go back to the dock. It was quiet for a few days, and then on the penultimate night, it happened again. True to his word, the captain took us back to the dock and the guy was arrested on arrival and kept in a cell overnight in Koror. He came back on board and was very sorry for wrecking the end of the trip.

WE WERE A close-knit crew on board; we all got on well, and worked like a well-oiled machine most of the time. We covered each other backs and it was a great laugh working together.

One bell end tried to ruin the party for a few of us after he was fired from the boat though. He was a chef, who wanted to get out of the galley and try his hand at being a divemaster. After a while, the captain wasn't happy with his performance and he was canned. The twist in the tale was his girlfriend was working on board as a stewardess. She blamed us for getting him fired, which wasn't true in the slightest. He got canned because he was a poor divemaster. The evil stewardess made up a story that three of us had been smoking weed during the charter and tried to get us all fired.

The captain took all four of us into the wheelhouse to figure out the full story. Things got very heated and aggressive in there and the stewardess was pulling out all the stops to get revenge for her boyfriend losing his job. I personally hate smoking and just said to the captain I would go to the hospital right there and then and do a drug test for marijuana. It would put me in the clear and prove that she was lying. The other two guys also pleaded not guilty and the case was sent to the boat managers in Hawaii.

After a few weeks, the owners decided that noth-ing was going to happen to anyone and, in his own words, it was a draw. I was pissed at that and told him it shouldn't be a draw because we had done nothing wrong. We continued to all work together and the atmosphere was not great for a few weeks. I had to laugh when the stewardess told the captain we weren't speaking with her as we had before. No shit, you tried to get us fired so why would we talk to you. Things thawed after a few months, but what she had tried to do was always in the back of my mind.

A FEW WEEKS after that incident, our captain had to stop working due to decompression sickness. The way it happened was so dumb that it could have been avoided.

There were some weights on board that the guys would use to keep in shape mostly during deck duty times. Divers are told not to do any hard exercise during diving activities, but the guy went diving a while later and came back with terrible pain in his shoulders and elbows. He had got bad decompression sickness and was airlifted out to the chamber in Guam. The doctors told him they were unsure how long he would be unable to dive for, so he had to resign his position. Ever since that day, I have made it my goal never to lift a weight or go to the gym.

THERE WAS ONLY one terrible injury in Palau that kept me out of the water for a while. I had a pain in my right buttock, so I showed one of the crew and he found that a massive boil was forming on my butt.

Once we got back to shore, I went to the hospital for a professional opinion. Within minutes my shorts were down and I was lying face down on the bed. Dr Pimple Popper took out a needle and gave me some anaesthetic. She took out the scalpel and sliced into my cute cheek, and then spent what seemed like forever getting all of the infection out of the hole. As I'm a sicko, I asked her to take some pictures of the wound for me. She cleaned me up and gave me antibiotics for a few weeks and I was under strict orders not to dive. It was impossible to sit down or lie on my back. I still had to work on the charters but was on deck duty only and the crew gave me a lot of shit for being a lazy bastard for a few weeks.

There is still a little scar on my buttock to remind me of my time in Palau. To date, it has been the most severe injury I have sustained in my diving career so far, so I am thankful for that.

Jellyfish Lake

OUR CHARTERS FINISHED up with a relaxing final morning of activities. First up was the hike up to the Jellyfish Lake. Ben would be the one to take pictures of the guests there so I didn't go that much. It was a little bit of a tough hike for people who were out of shape such as me. We would be puffing and panting as we got to the platform at the lake entrance.

This lake is one of the most unique things Mother Nature has created and is home to an estimated 13,000,000 jellyfish according to Nat Geo. I'm not sure who counted them, but fair play because that was some task! Over time, the jellyfish had evolved not to sting people. Once the sun came up, millions of jellyfish would come up from the deeper water and bask in the sunshine, and they would follow the sun around the lake before going deeper in the late afternoon.

We would jump into the lake and swim a couple of hundred feet over to the highest concentrations of jellyfish. No scuba diving was allowed, so everybody just wore rash guards, shorts, mask, and fins. Once we had found them in large numbers, we would take pictures of the guests amongst the jellyfish. It was a really lovely souvenir of the trip and a great experience to swim with them, as there are only a couple of places in the world where this happens.

The lake was filled with brackish water and was nearly a hundred feet deep. You couldn't even free dive very deep because the water was highly toxic. I once free dived down to about twenty feet, and the water changed to a weird green and pink haze … it was totally surreal. Swimming through thousands of jellyfish was also surreal. It was like being on another planet and was almost a psychedelic experience. I would imagine eating a load of magic mushrooms and swimming with thousands of jellyfish would be quite a buzz.

There was a whole ecosystem in the lake that had evolved from the ocean. The jellyfish had to be careful not to swim close to the lake's edge, because there were hundreds of white anemones waiting to trap the jellyfish before slowly eating them alive. I'm sure a couple of times I heard jellyfish screaming out in pain. Some species of goby had also evolved, deciding to stay in the lake instead of being out in the ocean.

We humans do a great job of destroying many of the world's most beautiful things, and the same went for this lake. Even though we told everyone to be careful with fin movements, many jellyfish were getting killed every week. One wrong fin swish can chop a jellyfish in half and I hate to say that many got destroyed each time. If you add up the hundreds of visitors each day, then it doesn't take long to have an effect on the population of jellyfish.

I was so sad to hear that most of the jellyfish had died and the lake was closed to the public a few years after I left Palau. I listened to the story about there being a drought which had caused the demise of the jellyfish. I also heard that some tourists were drying out the jellyfish on the side of the lake and even taking them out in zip lock bags. So, there were several different reasons why their numbers had decreased.

Chandelier Cave

THE LAST DIVE was a spectacular ending to the trip. We went into Chandelier Cave, which was only a few minutes boat ride from the dock.

There was a small cave entrance about ten feet underwater, where you swam through into some mind-blowing caverns. The formation of the limestone and the ambient light coming into the system gave it a very eerie feeling. The stalactites looked like huge dinosaur teeth and it felt like we were almost swim-ming inside the mouth of a T-Rex. The system had four chambers to explore and once inside, you could swim up to the surface and admire the impressive formations that had been carved into the cave over thousands of years. There wasn't much life inside the caves apart from some glassy sweepers and squir-relfish. It was all about the scenery.

As you got deeper into the caves it became a lot darker, the chambers became smaller, and the fourth chamber only had room for about six people. It was quite claustrophobic, and you could feel the air draining away after being in there for a few minutes. You could see a few nervous looks on the faces of some of the guests. As dive guides, we were influen-tial in this situation, we had control over life or death, so we took this opportunity to discuss the tipping policy onboard. Tip well, and we will guide you out of the cave safely.

As we exited the last cavern, the guests were men-tally down a few hundred bucks more in their minds. You could faintly see the blue glow of the ambient light that was coming through the entrance of the cave a few hundred feet away. For added effect, we turned off our dive lights and swam slowly out admiring the views one last time.

We finished on the shallow coral reefs outside of the cave entrance. There were some of the most colourful fish in the world there, such as mandarin fish, which were only a couple of inches in size but looked like they had been splashed with rainbow paint. They saved energy during the day, but in the evenings, they became the horniest fish on the planet. They mated at sundown most days of the week. They came out of the corals looking for a partner, flirted for a few moments, and then swam up from the reef releasing the eggs and sperm together. They then headed back into the safety of the corals for a cigarette and an argument.

Rock Island Tour

WE ALWAYS TOOK a final tour of the Rock Islands. They really were one of the world's most beautiful locations and as you sped through the mushroom-shaped islands, the blue water sparkled and the coral reefs fringed the edges. It was a great feeling to be in the middle of nowhere.

We used to stop off at the famous arch for pictures while scoffing some of Andy's famous brownies and joke with the guests that the arch was imported from the Galapagos Islands as it looked similar to Darwin's arch.

There were still plenty of relics from the war to be discovered. We visited the Japanese gas station, which was a large cavern that was filled with oil drums that were used to refuel the boats during the war. You can see bullet holes from where the US fighter planes strafed the area. There were a couple of gun emplace-ments that were protecting the waterways.

We had to dive inside the Rock Islands in the rainy season because of the bad weather and we found a load of fifty calibre shell casings on the seafloor. My mind would wander again into war mode and I thought of the Corsair fighters flying above the islands shooting at Japanese targets. It was the best adventure playground I had ever played in.

Nice Lady

FOR NEARLY EIGHT years, I had been a single guy ploughing most of my love and affection into the ocean. Even though I had met some really nice girls along the way, there had been nobody that could tame the beast. Being out at sea for weeks or months at a time could be a lonely business and even though you met some great people during the week, there was a chance you would not be seeing them anytime again soon.

It was tough seeing some crewmates missing out on their kids growing up or their parents getting older. You could see how hard it was for people to deal with those situations and there were tears from some who simply couldn't handle it after a while and had to get back on dry land.

I MET A really nice girl called Beverly from the Philippines while working in Palau. Things started slowly for us, but over a few months we began to get closer. It was always a good sign that I liked a girl if I shared a cheeseburger with her.

The moment things started to get serious hap-pened during a crew day out at Blue Corner and

German Channel. We had a down week so the captain thought it would be great if we took friends and family for some bonding time. Beverly came with us; she was already a certified diver and had a few dives under her belt.

We planned to dive Blue Corner first, but she had never been before and was slightly worried about the strong current and the sharks. She looked concerned but still got in the water. The current was pretty intense, but we descended without any issues and drifted down towards the Corner. I hooked her into the reef and inflated her BCD a little so she floated. We watched the show … the sharks were on great form and were right on top of us and the Napoleon wrasse were as playful as ever.

I watched Beverly closely to make sure she was okay and not about to bolt to the surface, but she just looked straight ahead with not too much emotion on her face. I took a couple of shots with the video camera, and then we unhooked and drifted over the reef for our safety stop. We got back on the boat safely and so happy with the shark interaction.

"Did you enjoy the dive?" I asked her.

She looked at me with a smile, "Yes I liked it, but I don't like the sharks."

We headed back towards German Channel for the second dive, kitted up, and went down towards the manta cleaning station. We played around on the sand for a while then three mantas came in at the same time to be cleaned. I was so happy and started whooping and cheering underwater. We settled down on the sand and watched the three mantas slowly circle us for around fifteen minutes before they swam away. I watched her again during the manta interaction, and she just had a calm look on her face.

We got back to the boat and as we were taking off our gear I asked, "So did you enjoy the manta rays, that was a pretty impressive show right?"

She looked at me and said, "The manta rays were beautiful, but I'm most happy just to be with you."

With that one line she had got me hooked, and things blossomed from that day onwards.

End of the Liveaboard Road

AFTER BEING IN Palau for just over a year my mind started to think about the future. Even though Blue Corner was one of the best dives in the world, I began to get tired of going there and although it was still fun being on board, the end of working full time at sea was coming. I had been doing it for nearly six years and it had been a great experience, but I secretly started to plan my next move during my down weeks.

An old friend of mine Larry had been working in the Philippines for some time and we began chatting about life in that part of the world. My now girlfriend was also happy to consider moving back to her homeland after working in Palau for a couple of years. I applied for the position of dive shop manager in a well-known dive resort in the Philippines. There were a couple of intense phone interviews, and after a couple of weeks, I was offered the position and happily accepted the new challenge. The captain was great when I told him about the plans to move on and we agreed not to say anything to the crew for my last week on board.

IT WAS MY last charter, so I said my goodbyes to

Peleliu Island and my favourite tour guides. I told Tanji I was leaving Palau and thanked him so much for helping me learn about the history on the island. I waved goodbye to the crocodile that mauled that poor guy from Taiwan and also made a silent thank you to it for not mauling me. I hooked into Blue Corner for the last time and there was a tear in my eye after saying goodbye to the Napoleon wrasse and the sharks.

Floods of Tears

THERE WAS ANOTHER reason for crying during my last week. My Gates housing flooded when something stupid happened. A tiny screw had come loose inside and the zoom handle came off in my hand. I watched in slow motion as water started to get inside my housing, I quickly pushed the zoom handle back into position, but already knew it was curtains for my camera. It had only cost $1,200, so it was not the end of the world.

Over the years, a lot of cameras had flooded on my charters and it was always painful watching the look of helplessness on the photographers' faces. I now felt that pain and anguish and it was not a nice feeling at all.

As we got back to the dock for the last time, I washed my gear really well.

Ben looked at me and said, "Dude, you never clean your gear. What's going on … are you leaving us?"

I tried to keep a straight face and replied, "It's been a long time, so I decided to give it a good clean, that's all."

We had the end of charter cocktail party and it was emotional watching the last slide show of all the crew and the guests. As it was my last charter, I got the boat watch shift and used the time to pack my gear, but this time was truly busted as Ben caught me putting my stuff into my dive bag.

"So, you are leaving us, I knew it."

There was no excuse this time and I finally admit-ted I was moving on.

It was a quiet departure from the boat and I said my goodbyes at the meeting before the next charter. It had been a lot of fun working together, and we had shared a lot of good laughs. Ben and John gave me a lot of pictures from our charters together, which was a great memento. I took my last steps off the ship. It would be my last time working on a liveaboard vessel.

AS I HEADED to the airport for the next chapter in the Philippines, I had an excited feeling in my stomach. After being at sea for many years, it would be nice to go home every night after work. There would be times I would miss being out on the water, as you had many tranquil moments while out at sea. Listening to the water lapping against the boat while watching the sun go down was one of my favourite parts of the day.

A few friends came to wave us off at the airport. It was just a couple of hours flying time to Manila. As I had a final look at the massive shark sanctuary poster on the wall, it was time to digest the end of another chapter of my life. Palau was an enormous highlight with some of the best diving in the world and I would miss chatting with some of the local betel nut guys like Robinson. My only bad feeling about Palau was it was so expensive to live there. Being in the hook in area at Blue Corner was one of the best experiences in the diving world and seeing sharks' inches away from my face while the current pounded into me is something I'll never forget.

All good things must come to an end though and it was time to immerse myself in the culture of the Philippines.

Mabuhay, Philippines

I HAD A few days before starting my new job so wanted to go and meet Beverly's family. They lived on the east coast of Luzon, around five hours from Manila so we hired a van and travelled through the night.

She had told me her family was impoverished, but I was still shocked at the place where she grew up. Her family was big with four sisters and two brothers. We arrived in her village and I felt a bit like Indiana Jones when he saved all those Indian children from working as slaves. People crowded around wanting to have a look at this white guy. We walked over to what I thought was the garden shed.

"This is where I grew up."

I looked inside, there was no flooring, it was just standing on dry mud, there was one double bed that five people slept in, and a small kitchen out the back. There was no cooker because everything was cooked on charcoal. I wondered where the toilet was but didn't bother asking.

They made some space on a wooden bench for me to sit down. After that, I was interrogated by her sisters and mother for a long time. Her older brother was pretty hostile and didn't have much time for me, but the other was a nice guy and seemed pretty friendly.

It was a bit of a struggle seeing how Beverly lived. She showed me around her village and everybody seemed so happy and friendly. There was one small shop which had the only TV in the village and of course the dreaded karaoke machine. We went to the beach for a walk and there were so many children splashing around in the sea.

I thought for a long time about the situation of the locals. Even though they didn't have much, material-wise, they were happy and seemed to enjoy life. I had worked with people from the Philippines in Palau, but compared to people living in the provinces they were like millionaires. It was a great reminder to me that you don't need to have loads of money or materials to be happy where you live. We stayed around for the rest of the day and saw there were a bunch of fishermen and some guys that did hooka diving.

There was no chance of being able to fit in the bed with five people already sleeping in it, so we checked into a local hotel for the night. The next day I departed for Mindoro Island and Beverly would follow me a few weeks later.

I met up with my new boss in Manila, who was also a Brit. From the questions in my phone interview I knew he was a meticulous thinker and paid attention to the smallest details. He was really great to learn from and was probably the smartest guy I ever worked with.

From a diving safety aspect, he had every base covered and I was amazed by the plans he had in place to cover any diving accident or emergency. He was also a great guy with whom to have a couple of beers. He had made a solid dive team of local guys and turned them into some of the best guides on the island.

Puerto Galera

PUERTO GALERA IS a small town on the island of Mindoro, the seventh largest island in the Philippines, and I was looking forward to seeing the true beauty of the place.

It takes around twelve hours to drive around the whole island, so there were plenty of places to explore. There is a mountain range very close to Puerto Galera with the highest point being Mount Halcon. The mountains had beautiful waterfalls and there were some great places to swim in the rivers. The rice that grows on the island of Mindoro is some of the best in the Philippines. They didn't have much farming machinery, so in the vast rice paddies work was done by hand, with the assistance of the famous carabao, which is a species of water buffalo.

The journey to the resort was very scenic, a two-hour ride past volcanoes, coconut plantations, and Starbucks. It was then a one-hour boat ride across the Verde Island Passage. The mountains of Mindoro looked impressive as did the shoreline of my new home.

As we came closer to Sabang beach though, I wasn't impressed. It looked like the town planning had been done by Stevie Wonder and the area looked even worse close up. There were crudely constructed buildings with poor drainage and sewage pipes that were in full view of everyone. We walked past this place called the Big Apple and there was a woman sitting outside laughing at herself. I looked at her hand and noticed she was missing a couple of fingers.

Jewel in the Rough

WE STARTED TO walk along the shoreline and all of a sudden, an oasis opened up in front of my eyes. There was a beautiful restaurant with proper landscaping, a nice bar, and a well-organised dive shop. It was bizarre that something so beautiful could be in a place that was so ugly. I had the same feeling when I visited Swansea in Wales … it felt like an ugly, lovely town.

They gave me a face towel and some paperwork to fill out, as I was crashing at the resort for a while until finding a permanent place to stay, and after putting my stuff away, I had lunch with my boss.

I went over to where he was sitting and we chatted away for a few minutes, before this other guy came shuffling over towards the table. I looked at him; he had a bad look on his face and an aura that didn't feel right to me. He joined us and introduced himself as the owner of the resort. He didn't really say anything to me during lunch, he just sat there looking angry and pissed off.

It was funny as I had heard nothing about this guy during my interviews for the job. I'm a pretty good judge of character and my first impressions of this guy were not great. I was concerned about how things would work out from day one.

I showed up for work bright and early the next morning and looked forward to meeting the team. The resort manager was a tall Scottish fella and was a decent chap. I walked through the dive shop down towards the beach, the sun was just coming up, and the water was flat calm. As I looked out towards Verde Island, my peaceful morning thoughts were shattered by this Western guy who was walking at a fast pace down the beach.

The Ladyboy and the Goat

HE WAS IN a deep and heated conversation with what I first thought was quite a nice-looking lady.

"You owe me one thousand pesos," the lady shouted at the man.

He turned back to her and said, "Nothing hap-pened between us so I don't owe you shit."

As they came closer to the resort, I could see that the lady was actually a ladyboy. "You are a fucking liar," he or she yelled at the guy.

The Westerner started to pick up his walking pace while the hairy ladyboy screamed obscenities.

"Fucking leave me alone you crazy bitch." He now started to jog away.

With that, the ladyboy took things to the next level, took off a shoe, and threw it towards the guy.

I watched them carrying on all the way up the beach and stood there scratching my head and thinking where the hell have, I ended up. Just as things couldn't get any weirder, I looked back on the beach and saw a local guy taking his pet goat for a morning stroll. I hurriedly made my way back into the safety of the restaurant before anything else weird happened.

I DIDN'T REALISE it, but the resort was pretty close to the red-light district in Sabang. The dive team decided to take me out for a few drinks on my first night and it was pretty mental to say the least.

It didn't take long to work out that some people came to Puerto Galera not just for the underwater diving but also the muff diving. The guys gave me the guided tour of the bars, and it was an eye-opener. Every night was like Saturday night and after being at sea for many years, being back on dry land started to feel pretty good.

WHEN I FIRST arrived, the dive team was in excellent shape. They were all local lads, had been trained into becoming great critter spotters, and were well drilled in all aspects of dive emergencies.

It was a busy time at the resort with over fifty divers arriving in my first week. It seemed like quite a daunting task compared to the eighteen arrivals I was used to. I just observed the check-in procedures and was happy to say it ran like a well-oiled machine, this didn't surprise me because the operations guy was all over everything.

It was great to teach more dive courses and as it had been a while since I had taught open water, it felt refreshing to introduce people to the underwater world again. We had families that stayed with us, so did bubble maker courses with the kids, which was always enjoyable.

Side mount diving was gaining in popularity as it had evolved from cave diving into recreational diving, so a few of us did the course with a guy called Rick.

We became side mount instructors and bought all the equipment, but it didn't really take off as people expected it to. It was fun for a while and I did about forty dives, but one tank was enough for me and after a few months, I sold all of my side mount gear.

The local diving was very different to my previous experience and it took a while to get used to it. In the Maldives and Palau, it was all about the big stuff, but now it was all about the macro life and some of the creatures were the size of my thumbnail, so it was a big adjustment to make.

Puerto Galera is part of the Verde Island Passage, which is the biggest channel that runs through the Philippines. The current was tricky on some dive sites, but nothing was too complicated for me to judge. Some places had strong down currents and there were lots of missing diver searches in the area mostly down to tech divers.

THE PHILIPPINES IS in the coral triangle, which has the most marine biodiversity in the world. It has over 2,000 species of reef fish, over 1,000 nudibranchs and over 400 species of coral. There were occasional sightings of whale sharks and we had regular sightings of thresher sharks and some whitetips. Puerto Galera has around forty dive sites very close to the resort areas around Sabang, the diving is outstand-ing if you are into macro life, and the unique subjects are some of the weirdest and wonderful you will see in your life.

Muck Diving

THE FIRST FEW weeks were spent underwater and getting to know the team and it was soon time to learn how to muck dive. We went over to a place called Giant Clams. We back rolled into the water and went down to a plain old sandy bottom.

The guide swam slowly, pondering over every square inch of sand. While not being used to this kind of dive, I started to get agitated. However, he then got excited and started banging his tank, so we went over to look at the subject. It was one of the most beautiful things I have ever seen underwater. It was a flamboy-ant cuttlefish that was only four inches long. I got in really close with my mask just a few inches away and watched in amazement as this tiny creature pulsed its colours right in front of my eyes. It was mesmerising and I felt like it could hypnotise me. It used its front tentacles to steady itself before grabbing a tiny shrimp.

From that second, my whole diving world changed. Muck diving was the dog's bollocks, so I spent as many dives as possible in that area.

The assortment of life on the sand was beyond belief. One day, the guys showed me a mimic octopus, the transformer of the sea, that makes Optimus Prime look like a fairy. It changed shape to look like a flounder and it used its black and white arms to pull it across the bottom. The video audio was full of screams underwater, because I was like a little kid on Christmas morning. Its cousin the wunderpus could also be seen here. This one was more of a brown and white colour and mostly lived under the sand, popping its head up like a periscope to look for food.

On a good dive, you could see the ornate ghost pipefish, hairy frogfish, and poison ocellate octopus. There was an abundance of seahorses curled up on the algae; on one dive we counted twelve in a small area. The tiny pipe horse and Ambon scorpionfish also hung out.

Shooting macro footage helped me evolve as a videographer. It was reasonably easy to shot the wide-angle stuff, but the macro was a different story. You have to purchase diopter lenses and strong lights to show off macro subjects. It was also challenging to shoot, as the zoom was fully out and the slightest movement of the camera ruined the shot. It took a lot of practice to learn this new skill of macro videogra-phy.

Blue-ringed Octopus

THE BLUE-RINGED OCTOPUS was the most-wanted critter on divers' wish lists. They are not ultra-common and there were months when we didn't see any. This octopus grows to a maximum of twenty centimetres and is one of the deadliest creatures on earth. It flashes its dashing blue rings when threat-ened and the toxins which paralyse prey are mixed with saliva and delivered by a bite from its razor-sharp beak.

Apart from the muck, Puerto Galera had a tasty variety of different diving. The soft corals were in premium condition and the shallow reefs full of Zenia coral gardens. They looked like tiny little flowers opening and closing as the current flowed through them. The reef looked so colourful with multicoloured crinoids everywhere and if you looked closely, matching coloured shrimps and squat lobsters lived inside them.

On nearly every dive there were multiple peacock mantis shrimp. This species is unique. They can break glass with their special punch and they use a spear to smash crabs' shell to get into the meat. Their eyes are so mesmerising because they look like tiny spinning cricket balls. Most of us have just three colour receptors, but the mantis shrimp has an impressive twelve and they literally see things in a different light to us. As one of the fastest species in the underwater world, they are a genuinely fascinating critter you never got tired of seeing.

It was great to tick off the pygmy seahorse from my most-wanted list. Thax took me to see a sea fan and he looked around for a few moments, before showing me my first pygmy. It was so small, that if you took your eye off it for a second, it was hard to find it again. They were the masters of disguise and it took me a few months of practise before I could find them myself. It is even harder to get a good video of them because much like Gizmo they don't like bright light. The most we saw on one sea fan was seven seahorses.

It was fun trying to show them to guests, especial-ly the ones with bad eyesight. We would point them out and then after the dive, would say, "Well, did you enjoy seeing the pygmy?"

The guest would look at me for a while and say, "That was a pygmy? I thought you were just showing me a sea fan."

That happened with at least twenty people over the years.

My girlfriend was getting ready to come down and join me, some of the guys helped me to find an apartment. There weren't many places to rent, so we ended up in a little pink house about ten minutes away from the resort. It wasn't much and nowhere near our plush apartment in Palau. The infrastructure of the area was poor and there were power cuts nearly every day. Freshwater was on and off as well unless you had a deep well. The cost of living was much cheaper than living in Palau, but the overall standard was much lower.

With a place to live my girlfriend finally came down. We hadn't seen each other for a couple of months, so it was great to be together again.

THE DIVE TEAM loved to drink a lot and drinking with the guests was encouraged to help build relationships. The drinking got out of hand though and because there were a lot of bars and clubs down the road, we ended up wasted on many nights. The guys could polish off a couple of bottles of brandy in quick time and they drank Redhorse beer that gave you a proper hangover the next day.

If there weren't two or three staff who were highly hungover each day, something was wrong. Some days we were all hungover together and the meeting room would stink of alcohol … it was surprising that no one got decompression sickness due to dehydration.

Red Lights

IT WAS HILARIOUS watching some guests' reactions when they realised we were close to a red-light district. A public pathway went right through the resort, and every evening at six all the working girls made their way to the bars. Some of the male guests couldn't believe what they were seeing and their eyes bulged out of their heads while these young scantily clad ladies walked by. Once they clicked, some guys quit the scuba diving altogether and went on a mission to hang out with these ladies.

On a few occasions, some guys went missing for three or four days in a row and the other group members became concerned about where they were, so we would have to send out search parties to where the girls lived. I'm sure a few marriages have been broken in Sabang over the years ... wives would have to keep their guys on a leash.

The resort didn't mind if guests bought back a 'friend' for the night. It was hilarious the next morning because as guests were having breakfast, somebody from the group would come into the restaurant holding hands with a hooker looking proud as punch with his purchase. There were sniggers from some members of the dive groups, but others were outraged at what was going on.

Sometimes, the local ladyboys would hook up with the guests. I was chatting with the front desk staff late one morning and a ladyboy came skulking through the restaurant with a look of shame on his face. He asked the girls something in Tagalog and when they replied, he then picked up the pace and headed out of the resort. The front desk girls were chuckling to themselves.

I asked them, "So, what did he say to you?"

They looked at me and said, "He was just asking what the time was." They were still laughing.

"So, you told him the time, then what did he say?" They both burst out laughing and couldn't hold it in anymore.

"When we told him, it was 11 am he said shit, I had better get home because you will be able to see my beard soon."

We all burst out laughing together at the thought of the ladyboy with a five o'clock shadow running down the road before he turned into a pumpkin.

Under Pressure

EVERYTHING WAS GOING great for my first six months, we had many happy guests, and it seemed like a great place to work. However, things changed when the owner started spending longer periods at the resort.

Two of the most experienced dive guides resigned in one day after an argument about maintenance work, because we didn't have many divers. I watched the owner arguing with the guys in front of the guests which amazed me, and they both resigned on the spot.

You could feel a massive change in the atmosphere when the owner was around. It felt like a dark cloud was hanging over the place. Everybody was walking on eggshells and many staff were reduced to tears due to his nasty ways. I found out from meetings that he pretty much hated the dive team and wanted me to get them all on final warnings so he could fire them as soon as possible. I tried to explain that these guys were some of the best-trained dive guides in the area and would be hard to replace, but he didn't want to hear it. It was like a battle of the egos and he even didn't like the way some of the team walked around the place. It was as if he couldn't handle the fact they were very popular with our guests.

I started to lose faith when he questioned putting

an extra dive guide with a group because one of the guests ran out of air quickly. He sat me down and told me straight. "Kris, don't think of your team as dive guides, think of them as assets. If you can get them out of diving for them to do maintenance, then that is better for the business."

I tried to keep a straight face while he was telling me this, but deep down I knew I was fighting a losing battle. It was hard to figure out why a dive resort owner would have such a negative opinion of his entire staff.

The bullying of the guys continued and Rusty was one of his favourite targets.

One day, Rusty was sitting in the dive shop wait-ing for his open water student to show up to start a course and the owner was in his usual seat in the restaurant where he would regularly disrupt the guests' peaceful breakfast time by shouting at the staff or talking really loudly into his headset. He was looking down into the dive shop and he called me over.

"Kris come over here. Why is Rusty just sitting in the dive shop doing nothing?"

"He is teaching an open water student this morn-ing, but the guy hasn't shown up yet." He looked like he was about to blow a gasket so I took a step back. "Can you please give him something to do until his student arrives?"

"His student is due anytime now; that's why I didn't assign him another job this morning."

He nodded at me, and I walked off, but a few minutes later, he called me over again. "Rusty has just walked in front of the dive shop doing nothing."

I looked perplexed. "He is waiting for his stu-dent."

He looked at me again with fire in his eyes. "This is horseshit," he yelled at me. "Give him something to do until his student arrives."

I walked down to the dive shop and a few seconds later, the student showed up. I was growing tired of working with this moron already. It was hard to keep a good morale in the team while they were treated with contempt and it was the first time in my life that I had worked with someone who had a hatred for his employees. I couldn't understand why a wealthy guy who had everything he could ever need in life wanted to mistreat people. Every time he spent a few weeks at the resort, we would lose staff and a manager. It was unbelievable.

The dive guys were getting sick of his shit, and one day, things turned bad. I wasn't even at the resort when it happened. I was off work as my parents were coming over to visit me. I had not seen them for nearly three years and was excited to see them and was waiting at terminal one for my folks, when my phone started to ring.

We had a new resort manager by this time, a Dutchman … he was the fourth manager in just over a year. It was the manager on the phone. "Kris, we have a big problem with your dive team. They all left the resort at lunchtime and didn't come back to work this afternoon. They came back at 5 pm, and three of them are drunk and sleeping at the bar."

I didn't really know what to say. "I'm at the air-port today, so I can't really do anything until I get back from vacation."

There was silence on the phone for a few seconds. "The owner wants you to come to the resort tomorrow to discuss what happened."

My folks came out of the terminal. My mother took one look at my face and said, "Oh no, what's happened now?"

I said, "Sorry, I will have to cancel our plans to-morrow as I have to sort out some problems."

There is one day a year in the Philippines when it is okay to get drunk; the fiesta day in each barangay is a big celebration where everybody goes to each other's houses to enjoy some food and drinks. It's a great tradition in the Philippines.

The guys from the team were all working, but there were only five divers at the resort, so the majority were doing general cleaning around the resort. At lunchtime, they wanted to join in the fiesta and went off to friends' houses. They made a mistake and started drinking, one lead to five, and they got drunk. The whole situation could have been avoided if they had just taken half a day off work and enjoyed the fiesta. But, after all the shit they had taken over the last year I guess they'd just had enough and thought sod it let's get drunk. They made the mistake of going back to the resort drunk, and that's when the owner lost it.

I got back to Sabang with my parents and checked them into a hotel. My folks could tell there wasn't any happiness in my work any longer.

Even though it was my vacation, I went in the next day. The manager and owner made it sound like it was the start of World War Three so listened to them go on for half an hour about what a shit team they were blah, blah, blah. I was thinking the team would get a verbal warning for going off to enjoy the fiesta, but I was wrong and the owner was rubbing his hands with joy as he got his wish to put another knife in the team.

One of the most popular guides was fired on the spot because he had had a few infractions on his HR file before. My assistant manager was given a final warning along with another one of the top guides. I had never worked in such a toxic environment and everything was telling me to get out now, but my pride told me not to give this guy the pleasure.

Most weeks he would tell me, "Kris if you don't like the way I work then all you have to do is leave." What a stupid ideology to have.

I left the resort to try and enjoy some time with my family and even though on vacation, the owner kept calling me every couple of hours. It was as if he was trying to ruin my vacation.

He called me the next day and asked me to come back into work again to meet with this guy from Hong Kong. I was getting mad, so in the end I just turned my phone off.

THE MAIN REASON for leaving the UK for the tropics was to get out of the rat race. There was pressure while running the liveaboard boats for sure, but it made me work harder to succeed. At the resort, it was a different type of pressure that sucked the life out of everything. Every single aspect of the team was micromanaged, including productivity reports that were used solely on the dive team. I was accountable for making sure I knew what they were doing down to 15 minutes in each hour. It was total bullshit, and it was making me unproductive, as I spent my time filling out the forms. Half the time, I just made shit up to get them done.

My assistant was in the firing line one day. He had been working on servicing our tank valves in the workshop, the owner came to me and asked how many tank valves he could service in one hour. I didn't know the answer because I had never timed how long it took before. All we wanted to know was that our valves were all clean, and our guests never had to worry about a leaking tank. I guessed it would take between twenty and thirty minutes to do one valve.

I had visions of the owner standing with a stop-watch, much like that Nazi from *Schindler's List* who timed the poor guy who was making door hinges. If Norms didn't complete them on time, the owner would pull out his Luger and shoot him in the back of the head.

The list went on; when he wasn't at the resort it was a great place to work, but when he came in, he would throw a couple of hand grenades in each department and then let his business partner pick up the pieces and deal with the consequences.

The owner would often ask me to take him to dive on the wreck of the Alma Jane. Many of the staff would joke with me, asking if I could cut his hoses on the dive. They told me they were joking, but deep down, I knew they were deadly serious. The guy had serious anger issues and he would get so wound up some days, that he would have to go and take some tranquilisers. After a few hours he would come back all zoned out and trying to apologise for screaming at everyone.

Many of the guests also started to dislike him as they saw first-hand how he treated the staff. One guest left a bad review on the travel forum TripAdvi-sor. He said that his stay had been ruined by this old gringo guy mistreating his staff.

The owner went ballistic about this and pinned me in my chair. He wagged his finger in my face and his eyes turned red, much like an albino rabbit. "Someone in your dive team has put someone up to write this shit about me."

I couldn't believe my ears when he tried to blame the guys for something that he blatantly did every time he was at the resort.

AFTER LIVING IN Sabang for a year, we decided to move to a nicer part of town. My friend Gary had come to stay with us and when he said our place was like living in a Brazilian favela; I knew it was time to move.

We moved to a small barangay called Sinandigan, which was about a thirty minutes' walk away from the resort. We moved into a house that had a good water supply and a generator and there was a lovely garden with some mango trees. It was so peaceful there and we were a few minutes away from beautiful cliff tops with spectacular views over the Verde Island Passage. It was a different world to Sabang and we were so happy in our new location.

Daddy's Girl

OUR DAUGHTER HANNAH was born during our time in Sinandigan and we had to rush to the hospital in Calapan, which was one hour away from our house, because our baby's heart rate was slowing down. They had to do an emergency caesarean.

There was a rumour flying around that if the hos-pital knew the father was a white guy, it was an automatic caesarean … even if you wanted to have a natural birth. The hospital was about a $1,000 better off that way. When a white guy walked in, you could see the dollar signs in the doctors' eyes.

Things are different in the Philippines; the men are not allowed to go into the delivery room when the baby is coming out. That was fine by me as I can't think of anything worse than being covered in afterbirth and umbilical cords. I just sat in the waiting room playing Candy Crush on my phone and feeling surprisingly calm in what I thought would be one of the most stressful times in my life.

After a few hours, the doctor came out and con-gratulated me on becoming a father. Beverly and our baby, Hannah, were doing fine. After a while, they put Hannah in the viewing area, and I nearly melted on seeing her for the first time. I watched her sleeping in her little crib and I felt like smashing down the viewing window to grab hold of her.

I just stood at the window with a massive grin on my face and then called my mum to tell her she was a grandmother which was a great moment. I had travelled the world for the past ten years and my mother thought she wouldn't have grandkids.

Once Beverly had been fixed up with the million-dollar stitches, we moved into our room and I got to hold my daughter for the first time. She was perfect and so tiny.

We stayed in the hospital for another day before heading back to Puerto Galera. We were now a little family and there was a significant change in my thinking straight away. Beverly's mum had come down for a few weeks to help us and she was the perfect mother-in-law in waiting. She didn't speak any English so we could never argue and I highly recom-mend that kind of mother-in-law; it's perfect. Hannah was born at a bad time because her arrival meant me cancelling a trip to Tubbataha Reef with wetsuit Sally, Dick, Chuck, Neil and Erin. They were gutted they missed out on my amazing company on that trip.

MY CAREER TOOK a new turn over the next six months. The owner was happy as many of my diving friends came to the resort so he saw the dollar signs in his eyes, much like the doctor who just brought my daughter into the world. He was not suited to running the operations of the resort, but he was a different animal when it came to selling dive trips.

Even though he would drive me up the wall with

his aggressive behaviour, he started to train me on sales techniques with the aim of me going around the world selling diving packages for him. He gave me some excellent coaching and spent a lot of time with me. With a new baby, I was thinking to the future. It wouldn't be possible to dive forever; one serious ear issue and that it's, this was the next logical step to help me stay in the dive industry. I started to research dive operations in Asia, the UK, and Australia with the aim of making trips each year. We agreed to combine the dive shop job and sales work at the same time with the goal that on leaving my position in the dive shop within a year.

The transition had a few issues as it was hard to sit behind the desk all the time … there was still a massive urge to be in the water.

One day, we had a walk-in guest and sold him a bunch of specialty dive courses. I started the courses with him right away as he only had limited time. After the first dives in the morning, one of the reservation staff came into the dive shop looking sheepish, with a scared look on her face. She told me to go and call the boss right away and he went ballistic at me on the phone, because I had left the desk to teach the courses. I also took another call from the sales manager in the US, who told me not to move from the desk until was told to.

The boss treated me with a bit more respect as I made him money but was still a useless dive shop manager. As a reward he let me join him for a liveaboard trip to Tubbataha Reef, which is the most famous location in the Philippines. Putting aside the thought of being in close quarters with him for a week with nowhere to hide, because the world-class diving was such a lure.

Tubbataha consists of three tiny atolls in the mid-dle of the Sula Sea, only accessible by a liveaboard. It has been a protected marine park for twenty-five years and the rangers spend a few months at a time in a tiny complex built on a sandbar. They are from the coastguard, navy, police, and some are volunteers. Most of the liveaboards dropped by to visit as they sold Tubbataha T-shirts and rash guards.

The boats also often brought leftover food for these dedicated souls and I was always happy they brought the food because as they were in the middle of the sea, it was only a matter of time before they became cannibals. I saw them looking at me with a hunger in their eyes. I was a meal for fifteen no problem.

The reef made world news at one point, when a US Navy minesweeper ran aground, costing the US $7,000,000 in compensation. The ship had to be dismantled on the reef as it was well and truly stuck, the operation took a couple of months to complete. Luckily, the minesweeper didn't hit any of the pristine areas, and some people might say that it was a good deal for the Philippines as it mostly hit barren areas. The captain of the boat blamed bad charts, which were half a mile out of sync. I'm not so sure he will ever be captain of a vessel again, not even a kayak.

We flew down to Puerto Princesa. I had known the boat captain and first mate from my time working on liveaboards, so it was nice to catch up with them. We sailed a hundred nautical miles overnight, it was a smooth crossing, and we woke up in the middle of nowhere to some of the calmest water I had ever seen. Looking over the side of the boat, you could see the reef about sixty feet down. The visibility was perfect so we couldn't wait to jump in the water.

The diving was spectacular and during our first descent I actually felt myself gasp as we dropped over the edge of the sheer wall. The walls were covered in the biggest sea fans and giant stingrays were resting on ledges, before sliding off into the depths as we got closer to them. The corals were in immaculate condition, with so many soft and hard species fighting for room on the packed reef. Tubbataha is the perfect example of a well-run marine protected area and really hope they can keep this level of protection for the future. After seeing a significant decline in most of the reefs I had worked on, Tubbataha gave me hope for the future that we could turn around the destruction of our oceans and reefs.

Despite the Chinese fishermen's best efforts, there were still plenty of sharks in Tubbataha. I have visited four times in recent years and always pleased to see that the shark action is still plentiful.

There was a place called Shark Airport, which usually had many juvenile grey reef sharks. Along the sandy area there were whitetips lying on the sand, as you approached, they would swim away towards the reef ledge before taking off in the blue abyss.

On one of my favourite dives, we watched around ten grey reef sharks circling in the depths and as I looked up two whale sharks passed by. I swam up towards the sharks with the camera and got some great footage. On turning around a school of barracu-da, which must have been a thousand strong, appeared. The current pushed me into the perfect position and watched them grinding their teeth on my approach. Please don't bite my arm off Mr. Barracuda, I come in peace, so got right into the middle of the school, surrounded by silver brilliance loving every second of it.

There were so many turtles around Tubbataha, after a few days you just swam past them without a glance. You could count them in double figures on most dives. On one dive a green turtle was well out in the blue, so swam out towards it and was happy that it didn't bolt away from me. I got really close in with the camera and took a great shot of the turtle swim-ming against the bluest of backdrops. After a while, the turtle looked right into the camera lens, and it winked at me before swimming away. It was my favourite turtle moment ever.

If you really like to be in the wilderness with no phone signal or internet for a week, then Tubbataha is the place for you. The waters are at their calmest during the months of April and May, and are so still that the only ripples are when a flying fish exits the water before landing again. One tiny island has a lighthouse on it and it must be covered in a couple of tons of bird shit. People are not allowed on the island as it's a bird sanctuary, not because the authorities want to protect the birds, but because they don't want people to drown in bird poo.

OVER MY FOUR visits to Tubbataha, only one shark has still evaded me, and it is beginning to haunt me. The elusive tiger shark has yet to make its presence known to me. It is a monkey on my back, and I will not stop going there until it's ticked off my list. On three of the trip's others saw tiger sharks, but, sadly for me was always in the wrong place at the wrong time.

BACK IN PUERTO Galera things were going well in my dual role, but worked (and drank) long hours to stay on top of everything. There was less time spent underwater and more time spent behind a desk, which was okay during the rainy season or when the water was colder in January and February. I would go down and check to see how the guys were … their lips would turn blue once the water temp dipped into the low twenties.

Isla Verde

IT WAS ALWAYS great to visit Verde Island. It is an hour away from Puerto Galera and one of the best sites in Asia. The dive site is a pinnacle called the drop-off and is half a mile off Verde Island. This was another dive where you had to give an intense briefing to divers because of the strong down currents that had caught out and killed divers over the years.

The pinnacle breaks the surface of the water and there are plenty of jagged rocks that make it hazard-ous for passing ships. It's one of the main shipping lanes in the Philippines with many large vessels passing through it. The topography underwater is immense; it's shaped like a volcano with a deep side and a shallow side. There is still volcanic activity as bubbles rise from under the reef – if you are a fish Mother Nature has placed this volcano in the perfect place.

The area is blasted with strong currents and not for the faint-hearted or inexperienced diver. If you were not careful you could get caught in a downdraft and be in serious trouble. When you reached the edge of where the current was moving, and you peeked over the top of the reef, it felt like the current would rip the mask clean off your face. The fish loved it because the current brought in food for them and you watched millions of tiny orange anthias fish being spun in the washing machine-like currents. They swam out to grab some food, then, the current sent them into a spinning somersault before they took refuge behind the corals.

The number of fish on the pinnacle was out of this world. Sometimes the schools of fish seemed so dense that you couldn't even see the reef behind them. It was as if an impenetrable wall of orange anthias fish created a protective force field over the reef. Schools of sweet lips did their best impersonation of a classic Mick Jagger pose, there were scorpionfish everywhere so you had to be careful not to touch them, and nudibranch so big that they looked like they had been taking steroids. Gargantuan tuna sometimes joined in with the show and it was a great feeling hanging onto the edge of the reef with the current pounding past you. If you swam a further couple of feet then you could be dragged down to the abyss and never be seen again. It was one of those situations when you thought to yourself that you shouldn't be doing this; living life on the edge and taking risks for the rush.

MY COUSIN DAI came to visit, he'd been travelling around Australia and Asia with his girlfriend, Zara, and they had become divemaster's in Malaysia along the way. He had secretly planned to propose to her on a dive so suggested we did it over at Verde Island and capture the moment on video.

He took the ring and hid it on the reef and called her over, before using a dive slate to ask if she would marry him. After much deliberation, Zara said yes and bubbles flew everywhere as they embraced underwa-ter. They were married a few years later and are living happily in Wales with their first baby.

THERE WERE A couple of fatalities at Verde Island during my time – mostly inexperienced divers that had severe issues. It used to wind me up that instruc-tors from other shops didn't really care about the experience or training level of their divers. In Puerto Galera, there were often diving accidents with typically a couple of deaths each year. In my time, there were around ten missing diver searches … mostly tech divers that had been blown off from the canyons area. Most of the divers were found over five miles away from the island.

The Canyons

THE CANYONS WAS one of the best dives in Puerto Galera, but the current could be so strong that some days it was perilous, there were some aborted dives due to people being swept away from the reef.

If you stayed with your guide then it really was a beautiful experience. The deep canyons were covered in delicate soft corals and the pinks, oranges, and purples splashed over the reef looked staggering. Schools of jacks, eagle rays, and giant trevally made this a perfect marine adventure park. The experience of seeing hawksbill turtles mating was interesting, because it looked like they were slapping each other in the face for a while before the magic happened.

In the last canyon lay an anchor that is embedded in the reef, nobody knew the exact history of the anchor but it was from a pretty large ship. This is the last stop for a photo opportunity as the current would whip you away into the blue after that. The ascent was a bit of a rollercoaster as you had to deal with both down and up currents, dive computers got confused with all the up and downs and bleeped frantically in the confusion. This was another dive where you would surface a couple of miles away from shore so boatmen needed to be alert for the pick-up.

The operations boss did a great job building a very safe dive operation and when the DAN dive insurance rep came for an inspection, he said the emergency assistance plan was the best he'd ever seen in his career. This was the highest accolade you could wish for.

When people are doing up to five dives each day, you will always get a few decompression incidents each year. The owner made damn sure his team knew what to do in an emergency, and I saw it first-hand on a few occasions when people got bent. If there was an emergency in another dive shop, then they would come running to us for assistance. This was down to us having superior training and keeping all the emergency equipment well maintained and ready for use at all times.

Rescue Day

DURING DOWNTIMES, WE did scenario practise for emergencies and sometimes we arranged a joint exercise with the Philippine air force. On the rescue day we would practise all of the rescue scenarios and swims before the air force came down in a Huey helicopter and practised picking up divers from the sea by a winch.

On one occasion, we finished the training and a few of us were lucky enough to hitch a ride in the helicopter. It was pretty old and I wondered if it had served in the Vietnam War. The pilot was a female, and after my initial concern about women drivers, I thought she did a great job by not crashing into the sea. We took off from Big La Laguna, and I started to hum the tune of the ride of the Valkyries in *Apocalypse Now*.

We went around Puerto Galera Bay; the area looked even more beautiful from the air. We looked down at the giant clam area and saw many of the local children were waving at us. Then we went around to the lighthouse and over towards my house. I called my girlfriend to look out for a helicopter close by but I think she was too busy eating chicken intestines to come outside the house. We made a flyby across

Sabang Bay and we could see the line of hookers looking like ants down below. We made a safe landing and I thanked the lady captain. It was an enjoyable flight and one of my best days in Puerto Galera.

In the Name of Science

ON ONE OCCASION, a group of marine scientists stayed with us for six weeks and set up a laboratory in the restaurant. There were forty people at one time, so it was a challenge logistics wise to please everyone. They had government permits to remove many fish species from the reef in the name of research.

One gentleman was famous for coining the term: *'The centre of marine biodiversity in the world.'* It was a little hard for me seeing buckets of fish being brought into the resort after each dive and there was a beautiful black frogfish in one, which nearly made me blow a gasket. All the dive guides were busy so there was no option but to join the scientists for a few dives and assist them in gathering the fish species.

They used a natural chemical called rotenone, which is a white powdery substance made from the seeds of plants. We chose dive locations away from the main dive sites and they would descend onto the reef and sprinkle handfuls of the white powder all around the corals and then wait for a while. Another five divers were in the water armed with butterfly nets ready to start catching the fish. The rotenone worked by blocking the fishes' gills, so after a while, they swam out of the reef as they couldn't move anymore, the divers then scooped them up with the nets and took them back to the boat. They would get on average a few hundred fish on each dive, it was heart-breaking for me, but it was all in the name of science.

Once back on the boat they quickly sorted the fish into categories and one of the scientists picked up one fish and said, "Once you get to the resort you can check the name of this species. I was the one who discovered it a few years ago."

We got back to the resort and couldn't resist the temptation of looking at the fish book, and sure enough, the fish was named after the guy. Even though the way they did things pulled at my heart-strings, by the end of the expedition they had discovered over a hundred new marine species which was pretty spectacular.

On the Road

MY TIME AS the dive shop manager was coming to an end. I was now being sent to many dive shows all over the world and in just a few months I had been to the UK, Australia, La Vegas, Singapore, Beijing, and Hong Kong. It was nice to be able to travel again, although it was a bit hard missing time with my wife and baby. However, we had to think about our future.

The only place that was tough to visit was Beijing; if you don't speak Mandarin, then you can feel out of your depth. I went out for a walk to try and find some food, but there was nothing that looked appetising ... there was a McDonald's but that was barely edible. I soon realised I was lost. I had brought my room key from my hotel and there was a load of Chinese writing on the card so I assumed the address was there somewhere. I jumped into the cab, the driver spoke no English, and so gave him the room key. He looked at it and started talking to me in Mandarin and then began to drive around for about an hour. It turned out there was no address on the room key just the logo of the hotel. The hotel had fifteen locations around Beijing and after a long time, he finally got me to the correct hotel. I smiled sheepishly at the driver as if to say sorry for being a dumb tourist in his country.

MY NEW ROLE was going well, already building up a good network of people in the industry over the past few years. There was always an ease talking to people, and so promoting the resort was no problem. After doing thousands of dives and capturing video from many places, I had all the tools needed to get people interested in trips.

It was going in the right direction, but the boss was still getting on my tits. Even though I had made him a decent amount of money in a short space of time, he was still never happy and always demanded more and more from me. It felt like he wanted me to work twenty-four hours a day plus overtime and it was dragging me down. Sadly, he was still mistreating a lot of the staff at the resort and we had bust-ups most weeks.

In the end, it was too much and my wife was get-ting worried about me due to the bad moods after our fights. Even though it was a decent company we both knew after nearly three years that the time was up.

THERE WAS A chance to visit Dumaguete in Negros Island for a few days showing some people around the sister resort. The diving was a lot different to Puerto Galera as it was mostly muck diving on black sand. It was still nice, especially seeing twelve frogfish on one dive. Three of them even yawned for me, which always makes a nice video clip.

We went over to Apo Island for a day trip, the hard-coral gardens were out of this world, there were plenty of green turtles, and sea snakes were checking out all the crevices looking for food. We went ashore and purchased some T-shirts from the local vendors and had a walk around the village.

We took the guys on a tour of the hot springs and a visit to the city. Dumaguete seemed like a very nice place to live and had decent facilities for expats. There were some nice restaurants along the seafront as well, so it ticked a lot of boxes for people who wanted to relocate. It was an hour's flight into Manila with flights costing $50 dollars so it was pretty well-connected travel wise.

The boss was making me look a dick and belittling me in front of some of his friends down in Dumaguete. Even though I was diving all day with our guests and editing videos, I still wasn't working hard enough for him. We had another couple of arguments in front of the staff before flying back to Manila.

On our return to Puerto Galera, Dirty Harry and Mike wanted to extend their stay with us for a couple of days. They wanted to visit Verde Island, so we went over. We had the best luck on the dive as a whale shark showed up and hung around with us for a while. It was the perfect end to the trip and we came back with some very happy guests. It turned out they would be my last dives working for the company. The next day the guys departed and we waved them off at the ferry.

The Final Straw

AS WE WALKED back from the ferry, he blew up in my face again over a $140 bill that he wanted in cash instead of a credit card payment. We nearly came to blows in the middle of town. I hadn't punched anyone in the face since school, but came close in that moment. Things had gone far enough, so wrote my letter of resignation and handed it to him. Once done, it felt as if I could breathe again and it was such a massive relief.

Some staff told me later that there were rumours I had left the company over the $140 bill. That is 100% untrue. The reason for leaving was being sick of working for a bully that had mentally abused a lot of people over many years.

After a few days, he asked me to meet him in the restaurant and he said to me, "Kris, I have fired so many people in my life and you are one of the only ones that I felt sorry about."

I paused for a few moments. "You didn't fire me, I resigned." I smiled at him, and could see the fire in his eyes burning once again. It looked like someone had shoved a stick of dynamite up his ass. I walked away from the table with a smile on my face before he could explode again.

I HANDED OVER all of my work to my colleagues, and left as soon as possible. After working nearly three years for this guy, I owed him a lot for the advice he'd given me. However, there was a sour taste in my mouth due to him mistreating staff in Puerto Galera. It had been sickening to watch grown men and ladies crying after he attacked them and it was sad seeing waitresses' hands shaking when they brought him coffee.

During some of my toughest days working for him, I read a book called how to stress less. I read it, but it didn't teach me much and in reality, the stress disappeared as soon as I quit working for him. My advice to anyone is this ... if you hate who you are working for; then leave. Life is too short to work in a poisonous atmosphere and your health and family should always come first. I lost sight of those funda-mental values for three years and won't let it happen again.

I TOOK THE next couple of months off and enjoyed some quality time with my family. After working a lot of hours, it felt like I had been missing out on my daughter's first year. My wife was happy it was over, it seemed like the gloom had lifted, and we could be happy again.

Exploring

THERE WAS THE need to explore parts of the Philip-pines as we were unsure about moving to another country, so took some time to visit Cebu to look at some other resorts for potential future employment.

The Mactan area wasn't really impressive, so headed up to Malapascua. This beautiful little island has charming beaches and a chilled atmosphere. The main draw was the thresher sharks that visited a cleaning station at Monad Shoal. My interest level dropped though on hearing the boats left at 04:30 am so thought it would be tiring waking up so early most days.

The thresher sharks are really interesting though and there is a 70% chance of seeing them at Malapas-cua. It is one of the best places on the planet to see them. The way they feed is unique as they use their long tails to whip schools of fish, knocking them out before eating them. Their large black eyes look similar to the eyes of great white sharks, but luckily their mouths are small so not so ferocious.

You could walk around Malapascua in less than an hour and there were a couple of places to eat and drink. However, there was feeling you would get bored quickly so crossed it off the list of potential new homes.

For a new experience I took the slow boat home from Cebu to Manila. It took a whole day and cost about $25. It was nice to see more of the Philippine coastline, as the boat went past Puerto Galera I considered jumping off and swimming to shore because the 24-hour karaoke singing marathon had got the better of me.

Life in the Philippines

AFTER NEARLY THREE years, we had a good idea of what life was like in the Philippines, we had already got used to the quirks of living on small islands in the Pacific. The brownouts and the water supply prob-lems are some of the worst issues in Puerto Galera. They can drive you mad some days, but that's the way life is. If you don't like it, then find another place that fits your needs.

It's also a challenge to buy furniture, because everything is designed for slight Asian people and not big Western guys. The only place that is comfortable is lying in bed or a hammock.

There are some things that make me chuckle here though. The guys use tarpaulins for every occasion, you get one for every birthday, one for graduation, and you even get one when you die. So, if you reach eighty years old that is a lot of tarpaulins.

The Philippines is one of the best value places to live in the world. If you choose to retire here then you could have a decent life on around $1,000 a month if you're sensible. If you stay close to a tourist town then it can be expensive and as a Westerner, you have to change your mentality.

If you have to do anything official, you need to

give it a couple of extra days as it's never straightfor-ward, you will need a degree in photocopying when applying for visas or business permits. Simple tasks can take forever and it gets frustrating. Not much is automated so they waste a lot of trees with the amount of paperwork. Everything works at about half the speed of the Western world, but if you can handle that then you will love life here.

The charm of the Philippines is terrific, the people are some of the nicest and resilient you will ever meet. As you walk around, locals smile and shout out, "Hey Joe" and it took me a while to figure out that it was a greeting given to American troops in the Philippines around World War Two. Even when the shit is hitting the fan the locals still have a smile on their faces ... they always say what will be will be.

For a country that is battered by super typhoons, earthquakes, political unrest, and terrorism in some areas, they sure know how to fight back. The people in small towns get together and help fix the issues. The infrastructure is miles behind, roads and drainage are poorly designed or non-existent in many places. There is not much thought given to town planning and when the bad weather comes, everything can grind to a halt quite quickly.

There was a video of a couple of Filipino guys who were stuck in a flood. One guy was in a house and the other out on the street. The water was up to their necks and everything in the house was ruined, but in the face of adversity, they still found a way to smile. The guy inside the house poured a couple of shots of brandy and then placed a shot glass inside a large metal dish, which floated on the water. He then pushed it outside to his friend in the street and once it had drifted over to him, he picked up the glass and drank the shot while up to his neck in water. They both cheered even though the situation they were in was terrible. That is why I love the Filipino people.

Natural Disasters

WE WERE IN Manila when Super Typhoon Haiyan smashed into the Philippines. It was the biggest typhoon on record to make landfall, but the track of the storm passed south of Puerto Galera, so we were spared the worst damage.

In total, over 6,000 people lost their lives and most of the fatalities were in Southern Leyte due to the storm surge. A lot of people could have been saved if they had realised just how big the storm surge was going to be. This disaster showed me the resilience of the people once again, and I watched the TV reports in horror. There were interviews of people who had lost everything, but they still smiled through the pain.

We had to wait three days until the storm passed before we could get home. The sea was still rough, so only the big roro ferries were crossing. As we turned into the channel, we thought the ferry was about to capsize as it lurched to the starboard side. Passengers started to scream, but once we got out of the turn, it wasn't too bad. The water had turned a milky brown colour from the river run off, and it was full of broken trees and vegetation. We were hundreds of miles away from the eye of the cat five storm, but it still badly affected our area.

WE WERE LUCKY that we did not have a typhoon as big as Haiyan making a direct hit on Mindoro, but the day after Christmas 2016, a category 1 typhoon hit us and that was bad enough.

We decided to wait it out in our house. My family was safe in the middle room, which had no windows, but I couldn't resist having a look out of the other windows during the storm. I watched in awe as Mother Nature showed me who was boss. The typhoon made landfall on Verde Island, about five miles away from my place and it felt like the windows were about to blow out at any time. The winds were so strong, that roofs come flying down my street before lifting off into the sea. The storm carried on for a couple of hours, we went out the next morning to find trees down everywhere, and people's houses simply flattened.

The Christmas spirit had been destroyed in just a couple of hours. It took over two weeks to get all the power lines fixed, so it was a bad start to 2017 for many people on the island of Mindoro.

The damage to small towns along the highway to Puerto Galera was horrific. There had been massive flooding around Baco, and all of the banana trees had simply been snapped in half. Massive boulders had been washed down river and into people's front gardens and there was thick mud everywhere. It took weeks to clear up, but while driving through the area, I could still see people smiling through the mess.

Best Food in Asia

IF YOU ARE thinking of moving to the Philippines, you must know that the local food may not be to your taste. The fresh ingredients are of an exceptional standard with many delicious fresh fruits and vegetables, but I'm not sure what happened to the local style of cooking though.

With excellent cuisine from countries like Thai-land, Vietnam, and Malaysia not so far away, it's hard to put your finger on why the food is so poor in the Philippines. I guess the Spanish have a lot to answer for, and the American influence has led to hot dogs being added to the menu. I smile to myself when I'm in the supermarket as there are probably over a hundred different varieties of hot dogs in the freezers.

BBQs are massive in the Philippines; if you are a fan of chicken feet, liver, and intestines, then you will love it here. On special occasions, they serve a whole lechon and, if you want to, you can try the delectable soup no 5, which is made with the penis and testicles of a cow. There is also another dish made with pigs' blood that I didn't fancy so much.

The most famous Pinoy treat is balut, which is a duck egg that is twenty days old. When it is ready to be eaten, you break open the shell, and there is a duck foetus with a little beak and feathers starting to form on the body. The locals add some chilli vinegar before munching down on the little ducky. In my eight years in the Philippines, I have been asked by many people to eat balut, and I've managed to avoid it so far. It is supposed to make you strong as a bull. I would rather walk around like a newborn calf than eat that.

Moving Forwards

I'M LOOKING FORWARD to what the future will bring our family in the Philippines. Our son Max was born in March 2018 and we can already tell he has an adventurous side to him.

We moved one hour away from Puerto Galera to the city of Calapan. The ride from Puerto Galera is through windy mountain roads, past gushing waterfalls, and along some magnificent coastline. We live in a beautiful place which is just a few minutes away from the beach and on the other side you can see the mountain ranges and many rice fields. The traffic is a nightmare and you can be stuck for at least ten minutes at rush hour. The real reason why I wanted to move here was to be closer to McDonald's … we live about seven minutes away from a juicy quarter pounder.

THE REASON FOR writing this book is because many people have told me to. When telling my friends the diving stories over the years, they would say to me: "Dude, you should write a book."

I wanted to do this to celebrate working in diving for ten years and also the fact of turning forty in 2018.

Even though my hair is getting grey, and my waistline is not shrinking, there is still plenty to do in the underwater world. In my mind there is a bucket list of places to dive while I'm still healthy.

People always ask me what my favourite place to dive is. Its always a struggle to answer that question because there is deep love for every place differently. I scream through my reg if a manta goes over the top of me just as hard as if there is a blue-ringed octopus. I pump my fist the same way if I get a good shot of a bull shark or a rare nudibranch. I simply love the underwater world and all creatures great and small. It is the same for marine life; I can never choose my favourite because there are so many. I have yet to see a great white shark, so maybe that will get to the top of my list.

My plan for this book is to inspire some people to become scuba divers or maybe instructors one day. On leaving school with nothing, I didn't worry about the future. There was always a confidence there would be a way forward. If you work hard and you really want to succeed, then chances will come your way. On a visit to Washington DC I met Ronald while having a few beers watching football in a sports bar. He was from the Honduran mainland and we got chatting about diving in the Bay Islands. Within a few years he left the US and became a dive instructor in Utila.

If you have never tried diving before please get to your local dive club or shop and sign up to Discover Scuba. Even if you shit yourself and panic during the first stages, pick yourself back up and get it done. If you just stay an open water diver that is fine; the key is to get underwater and see the beautiful world. Don't just sit at home watching David Attenborough on the Blue Planet, get out, and see it with your own eyes. The current rate at which we are destroying our world means that a lot of corals and marine life will not be there in fifty years. Get yourself underwater today, and you can thank me tomorrow. I can't wait to teach my kids to dive when they are old enough. I love to show them videos of the underwater world, and I'm excited when my daughter says to me, "Look, dad, it's Nemo."

While approaching my forties, it was a good time to reflect on what has happened so far. Little things happen in life to send you on your path and some-times a split-second decision can turn your whole life around. I'm not a strongly religious man, but felt that something has guided me on my way, such as meeting certain people like the girl in Honduras, who told me to go to Útila instead of Roatán. That meeting changed the course of my life. Or, meeting the girls in Indone-sia who took us to the orangutans that I didn't even know existed. It is all part of the ride, and it's been a blast.

I'm a father and a husband now so my plans have changed and want to give the best I have to Beverly, Hannah, and Max. Some people seemed surprised that I turned into a family guy, they probably thought I was a rum pig on the road to nowhere.

I'm still working in the dive industry promoting diving in the Philippines and you can see me at many dive shows all over the world. I still love the underwa-ter world so much. Who knows, when I'm sixty I might write the sequel to this book.

I want to thank all the people who enjoyed work-ing with me over the years, many more deserve a mention here but I'm running out of ink and my fingers hurt. My biggest thanks are for the people who have supported me by visiting in different countries over the years. You are in my heart always and hope to see you underwater again soon.

The End, For Now

About the Author

Kris Mears is originally from Wales in the UK and he has been travelling and working overseas since 2003.

His travels have taken in over fifty countries. For the past 12 years he has worked in the scuba diving industry as a divemaster and instructor before moving into corporate sales. He is a keen videographer and marine life enthusiast. Currently he is living in the Philippines with his wife Beverly and children Hannah and Max.

Enjoy the authors underwater videography work at the links below

www.facebook.com/scubasheepproductions
www.youtube.com/user/krstianm
www.pond5.com/artist/krismears

Look out for future publications

'Confessions of a Divemaster 2'
'A year in the Land Down Under'